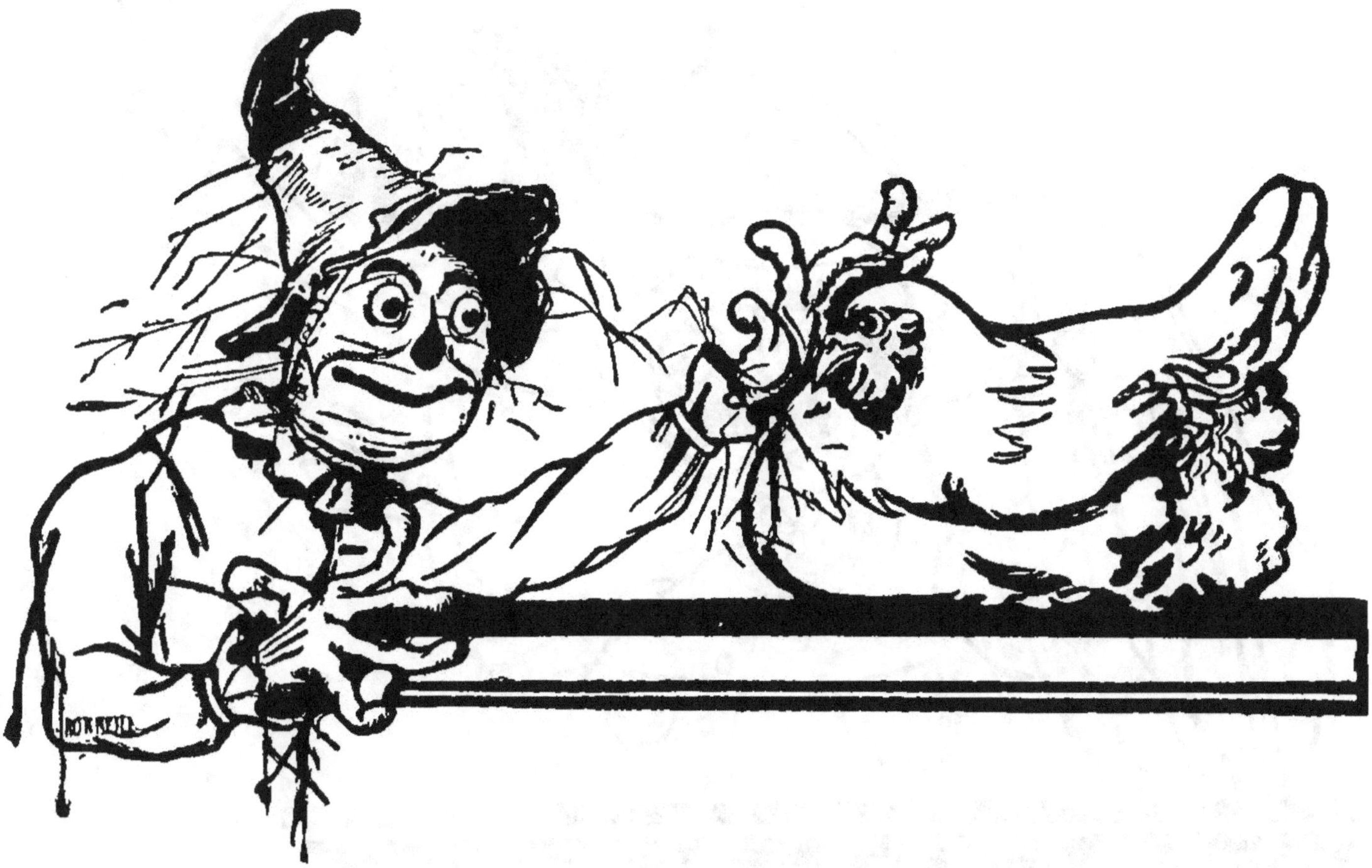

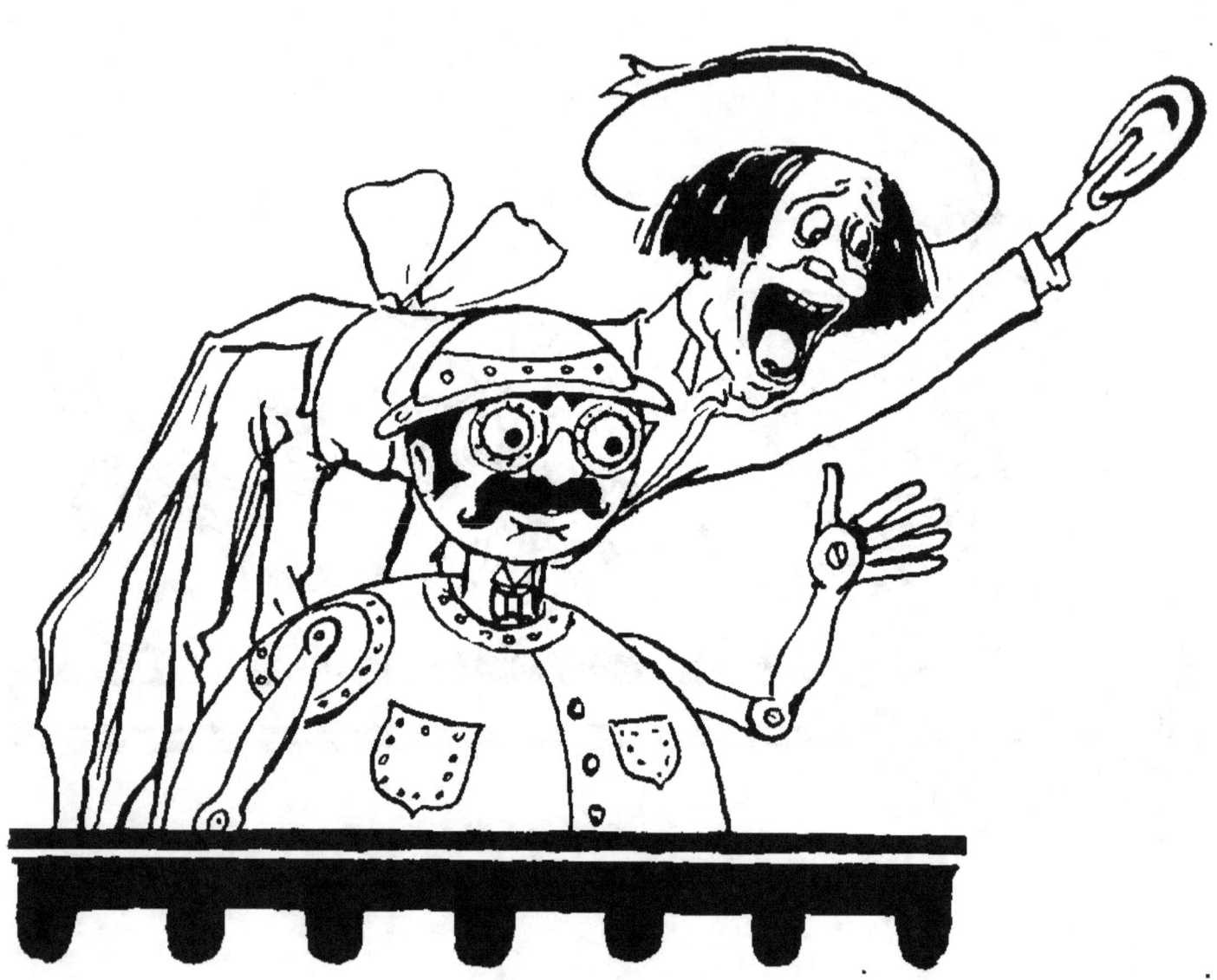

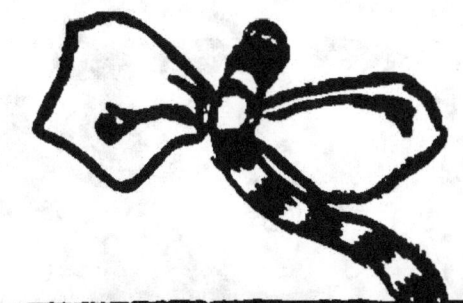

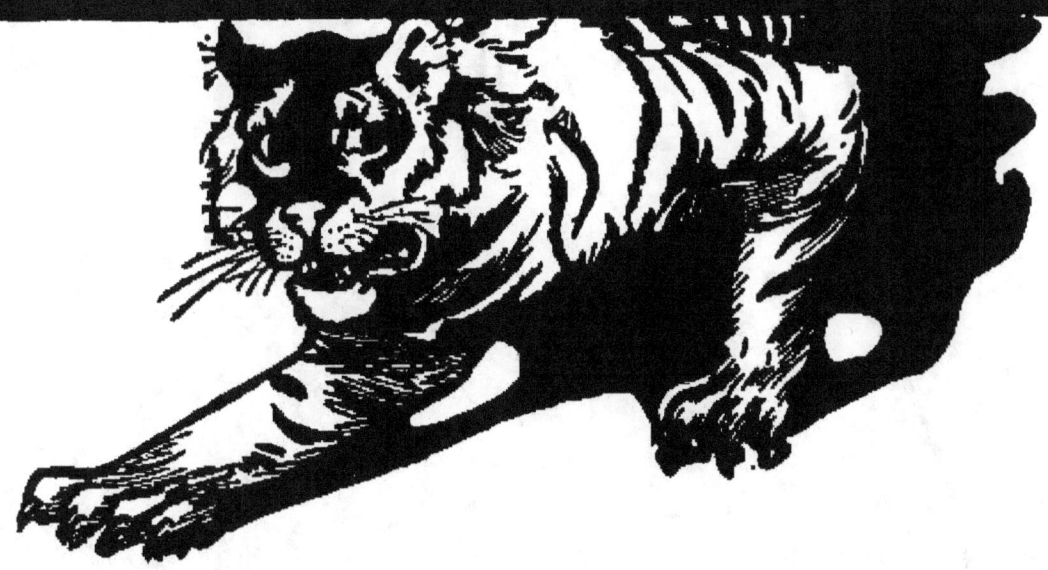

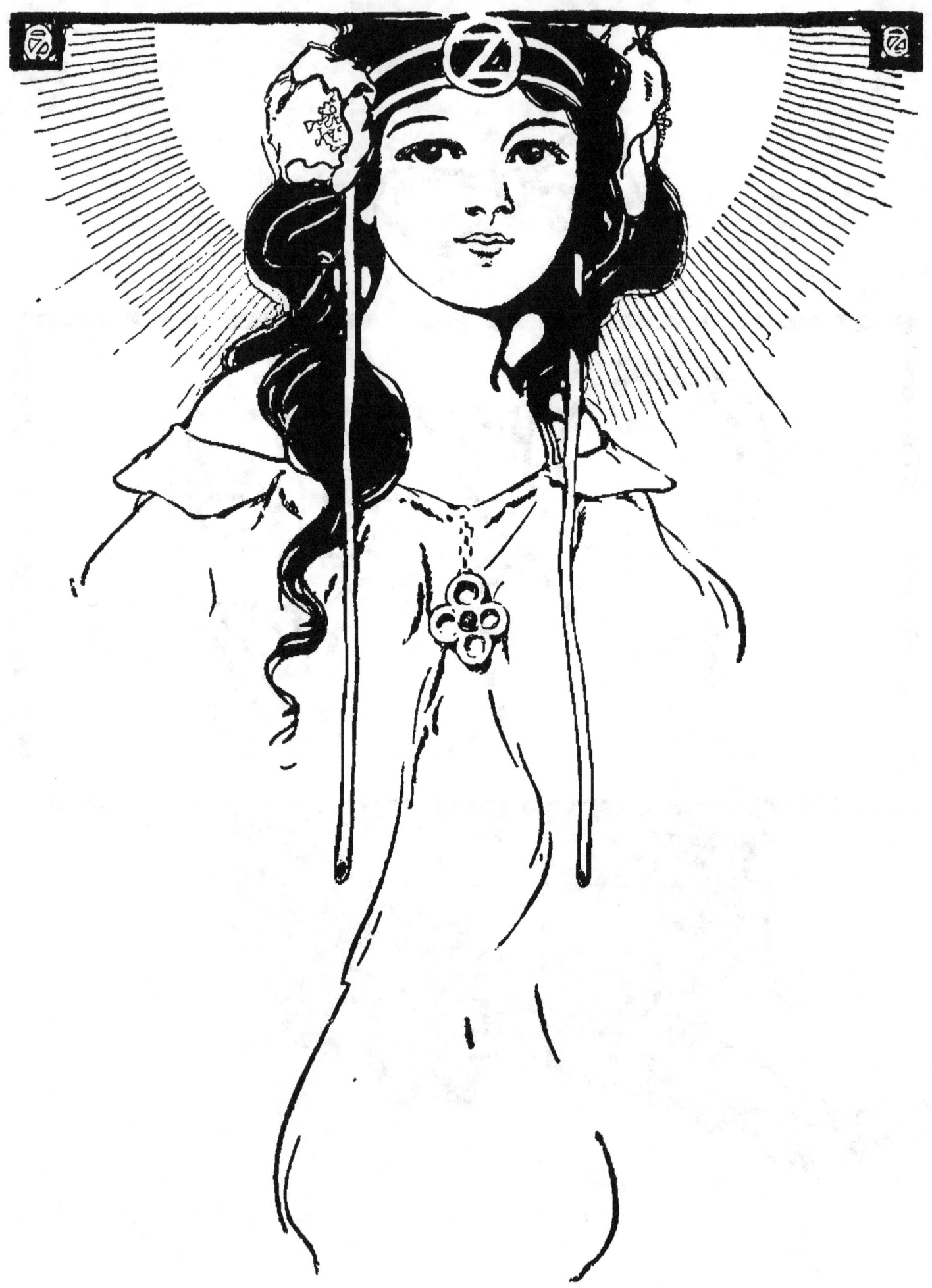

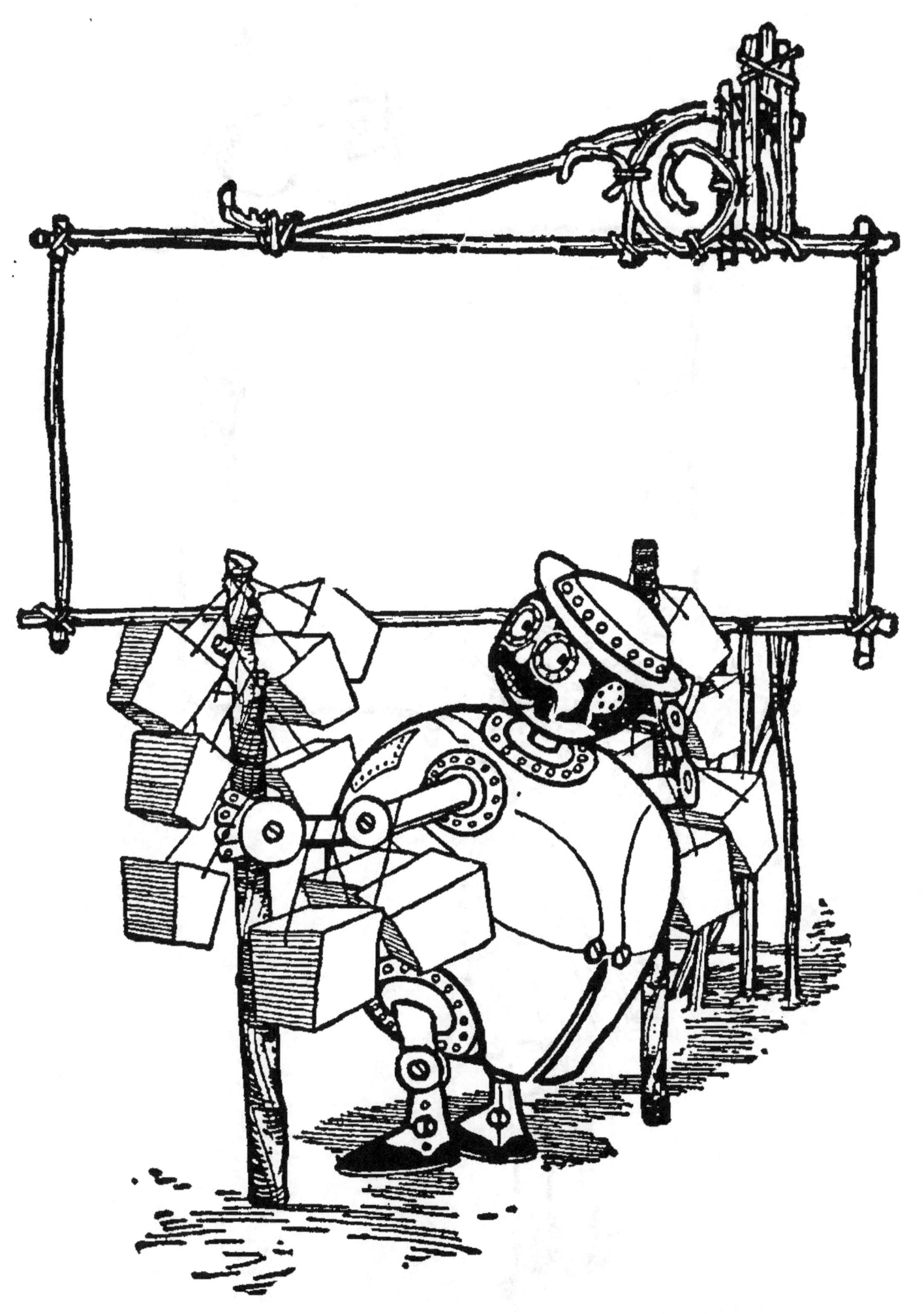

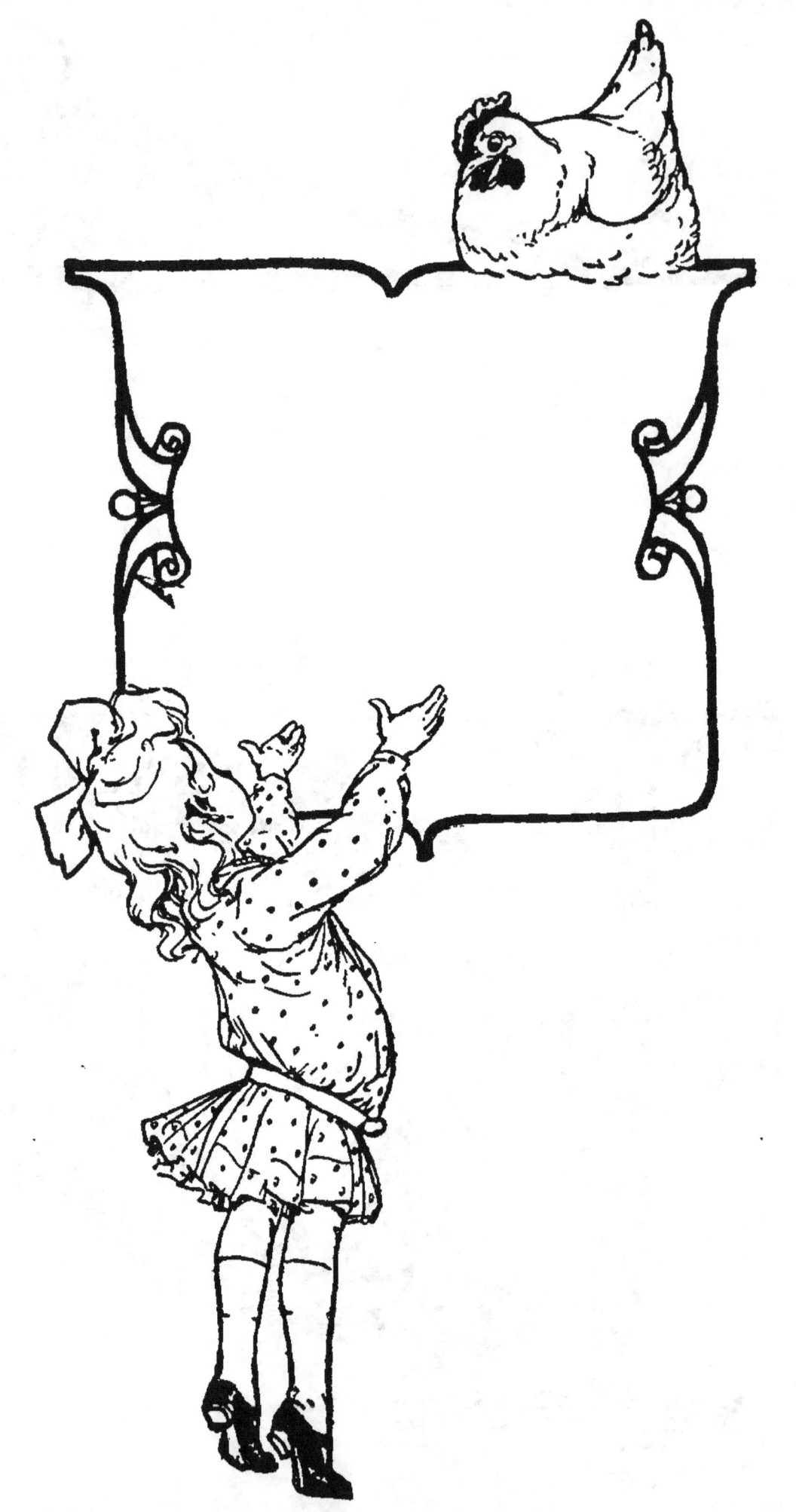

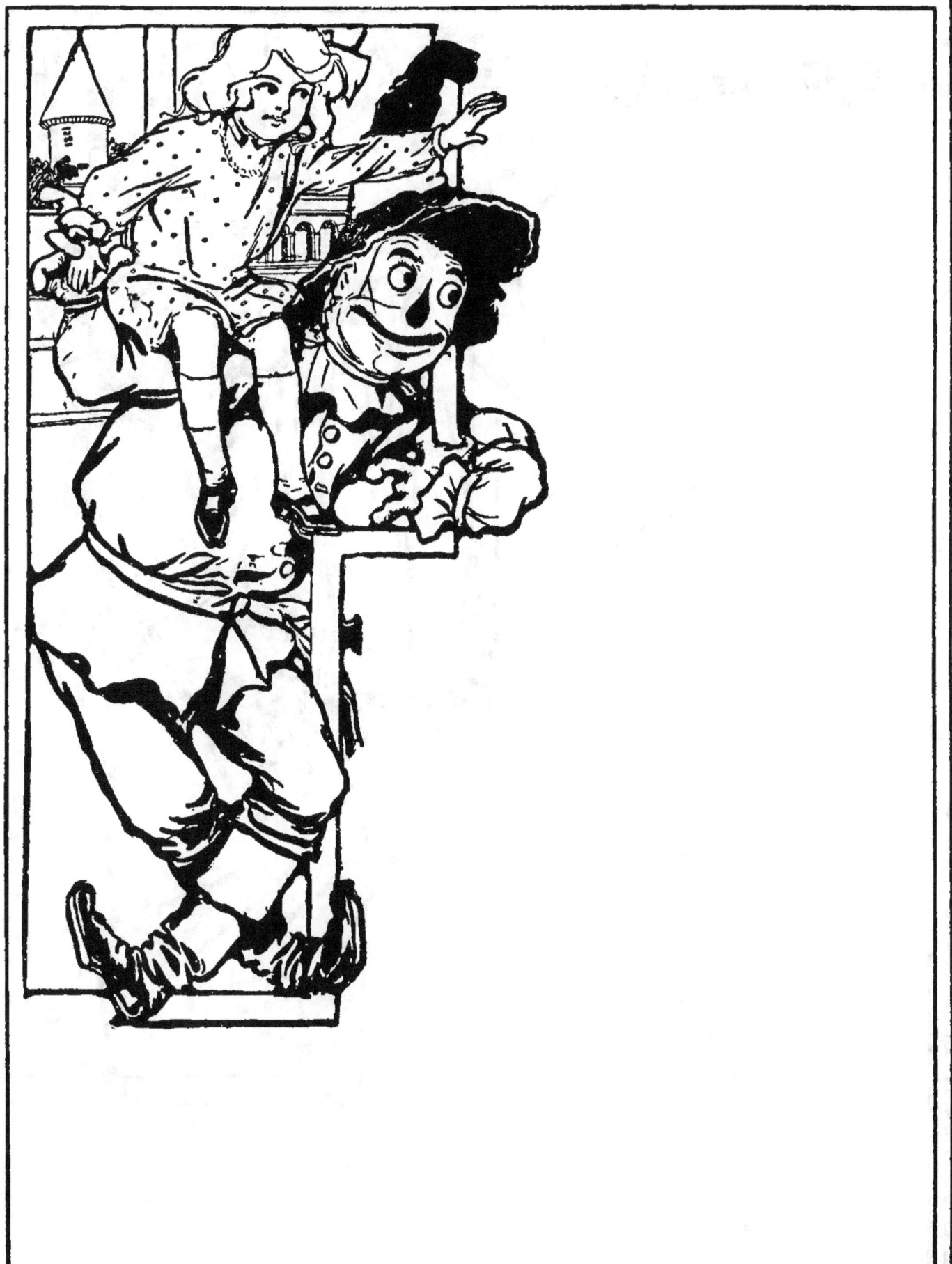

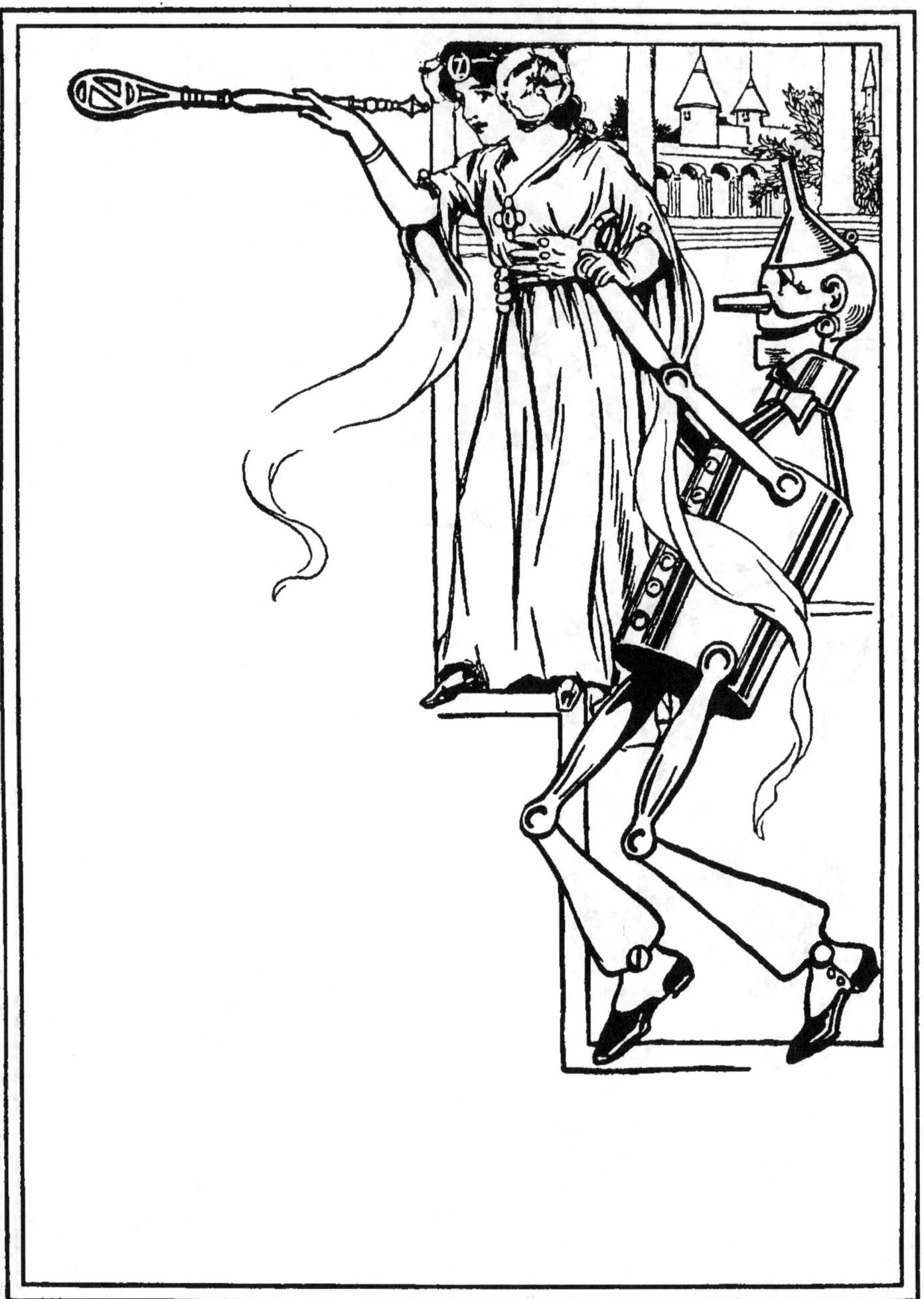

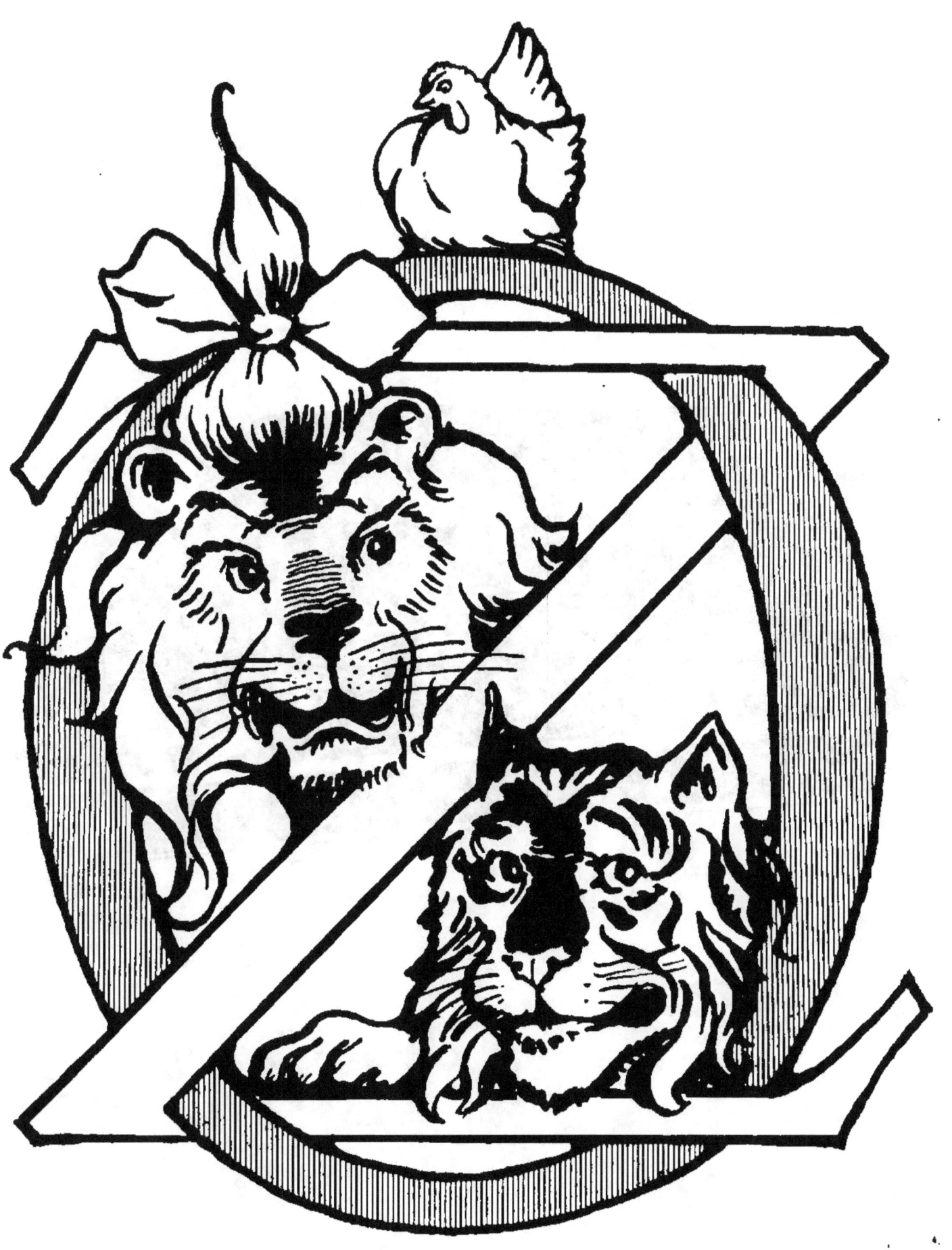

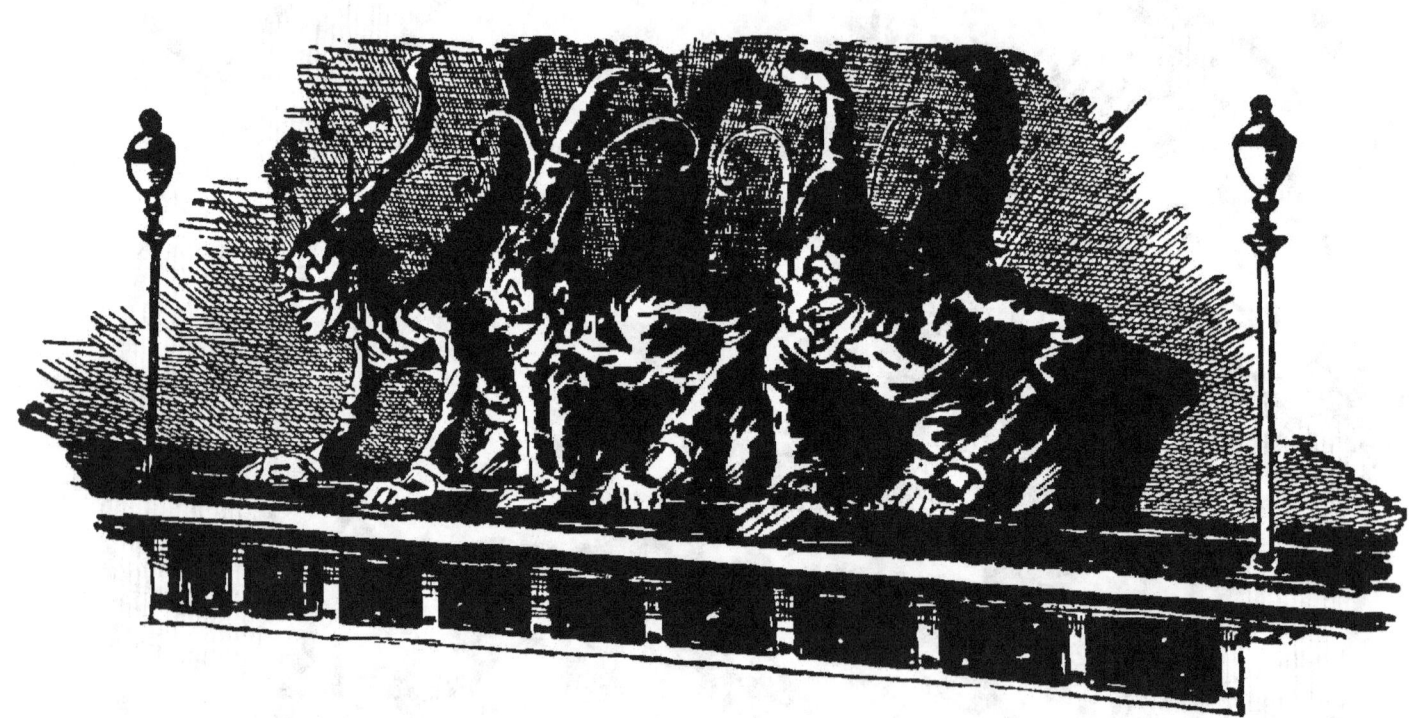

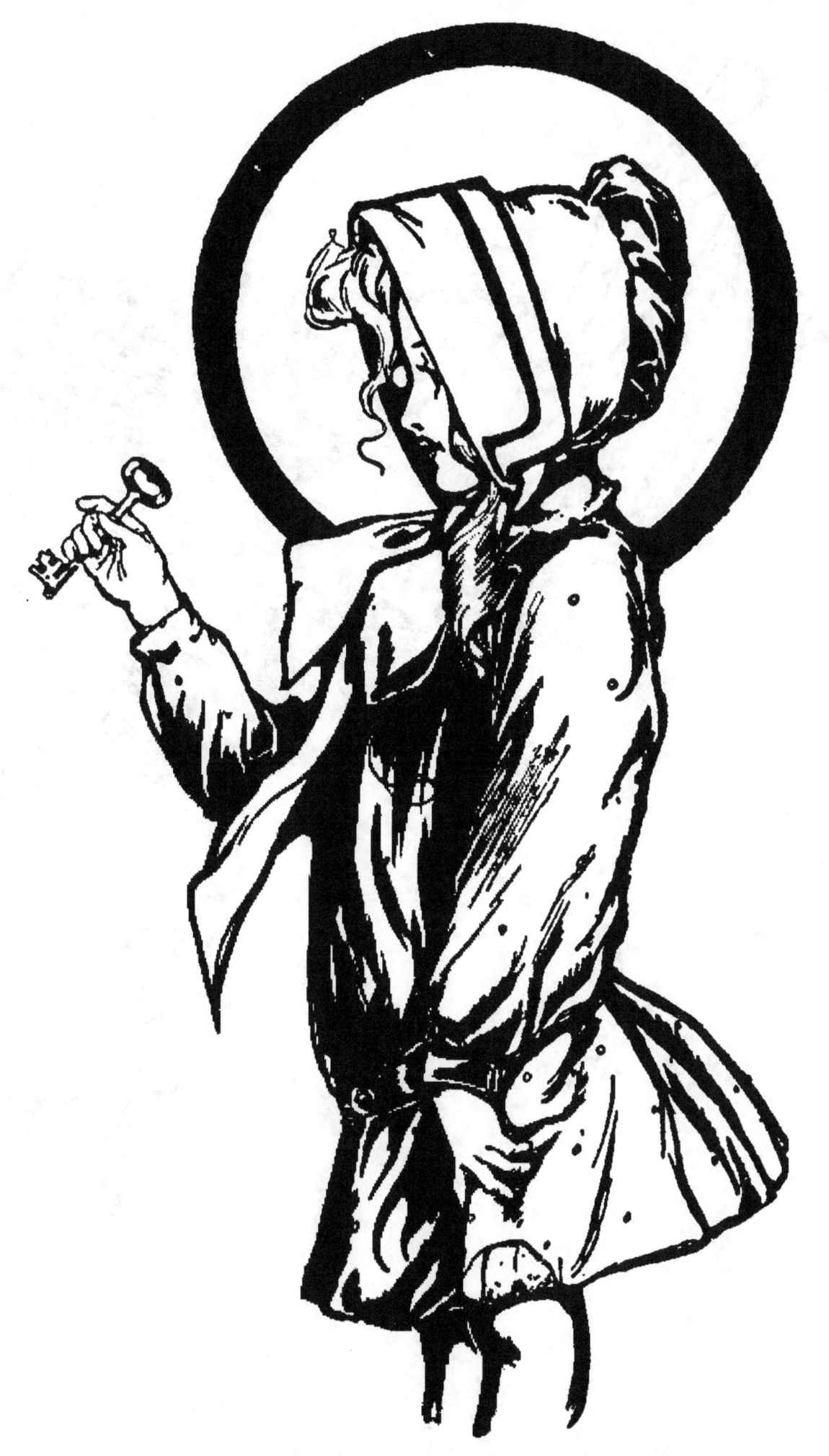

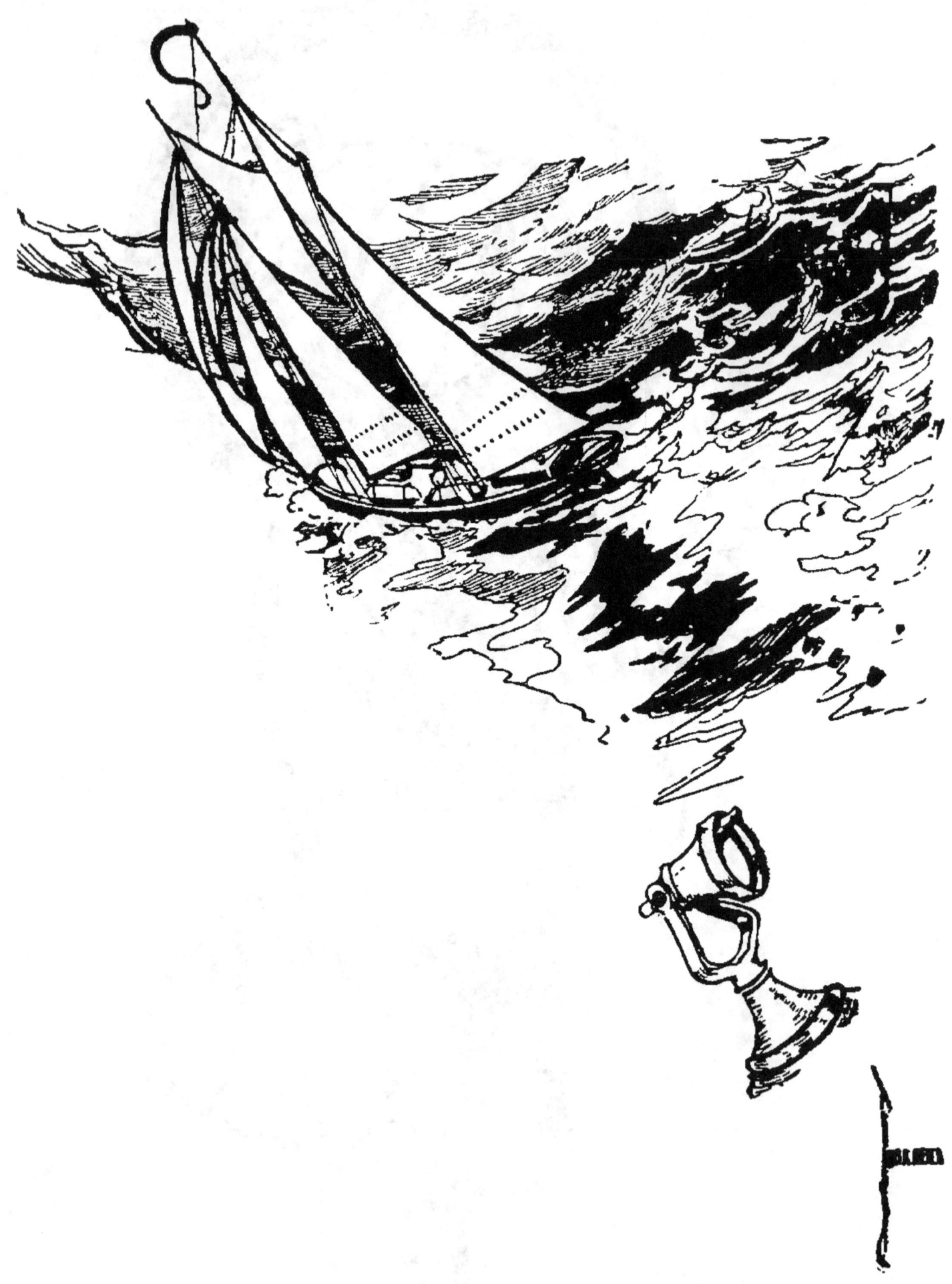

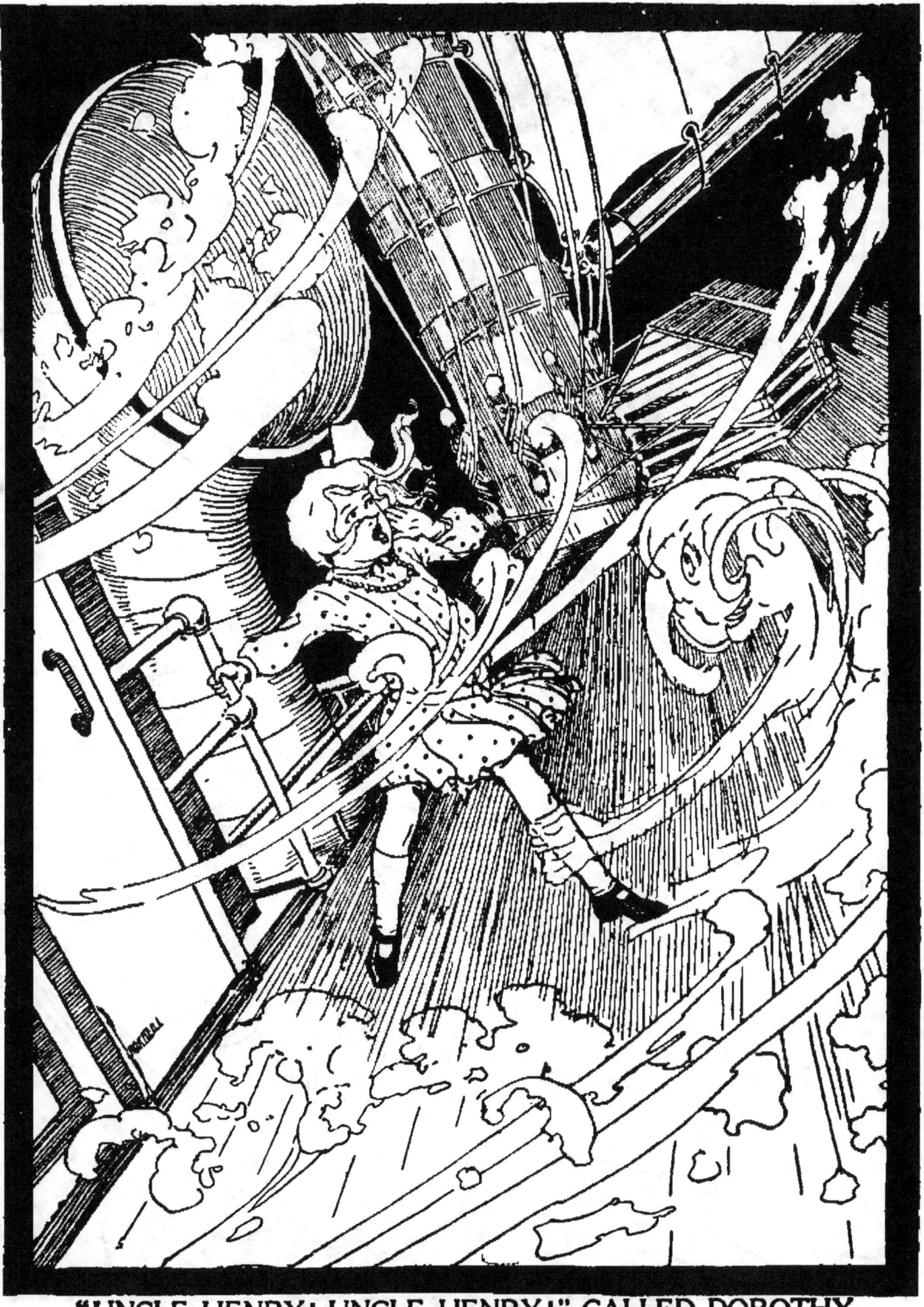

"UNCLE HENRY! UNCLE HENRY!" CALLED DOROTHY

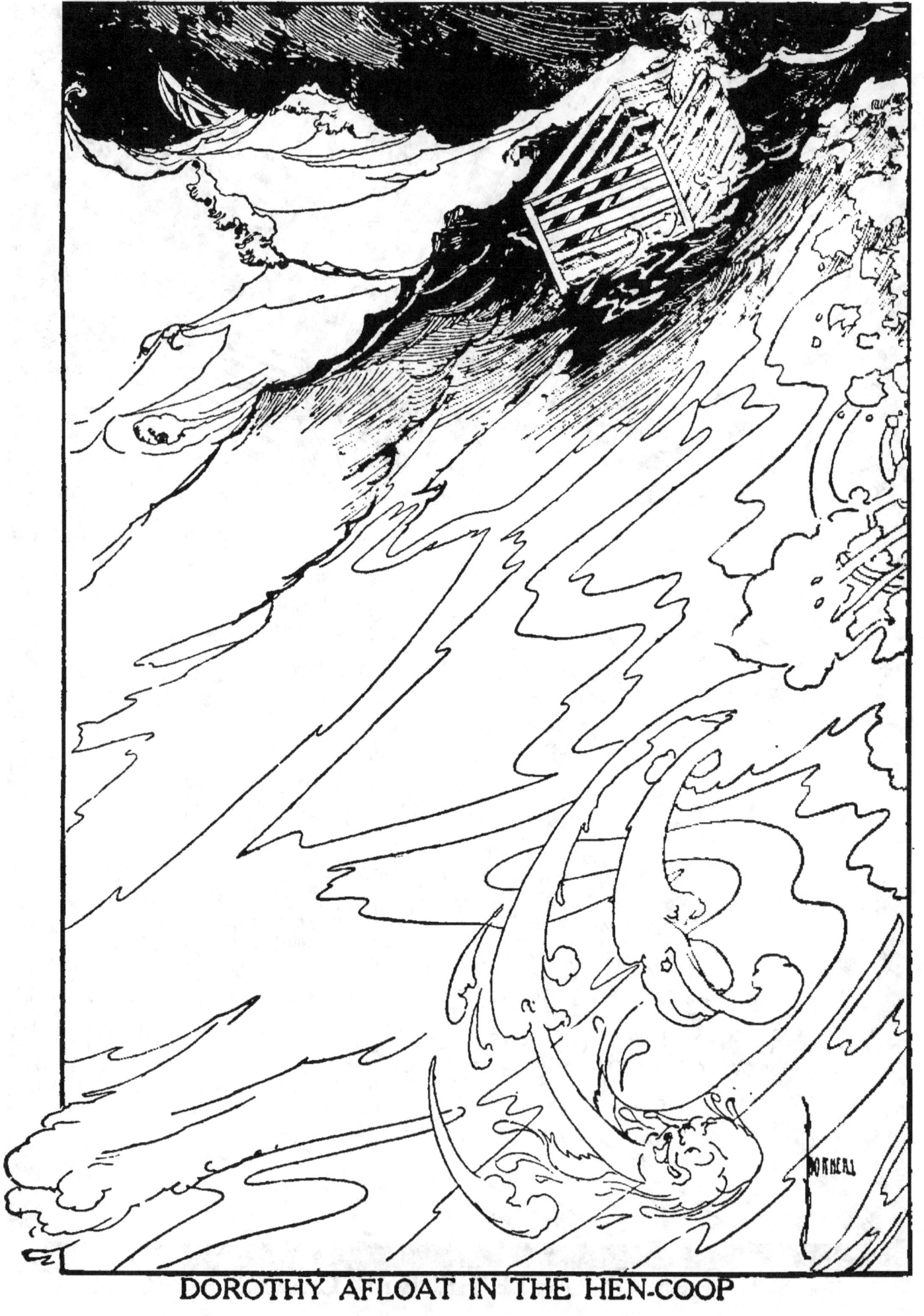

DOROTHY AFLOAT IN THE HEN-COOP

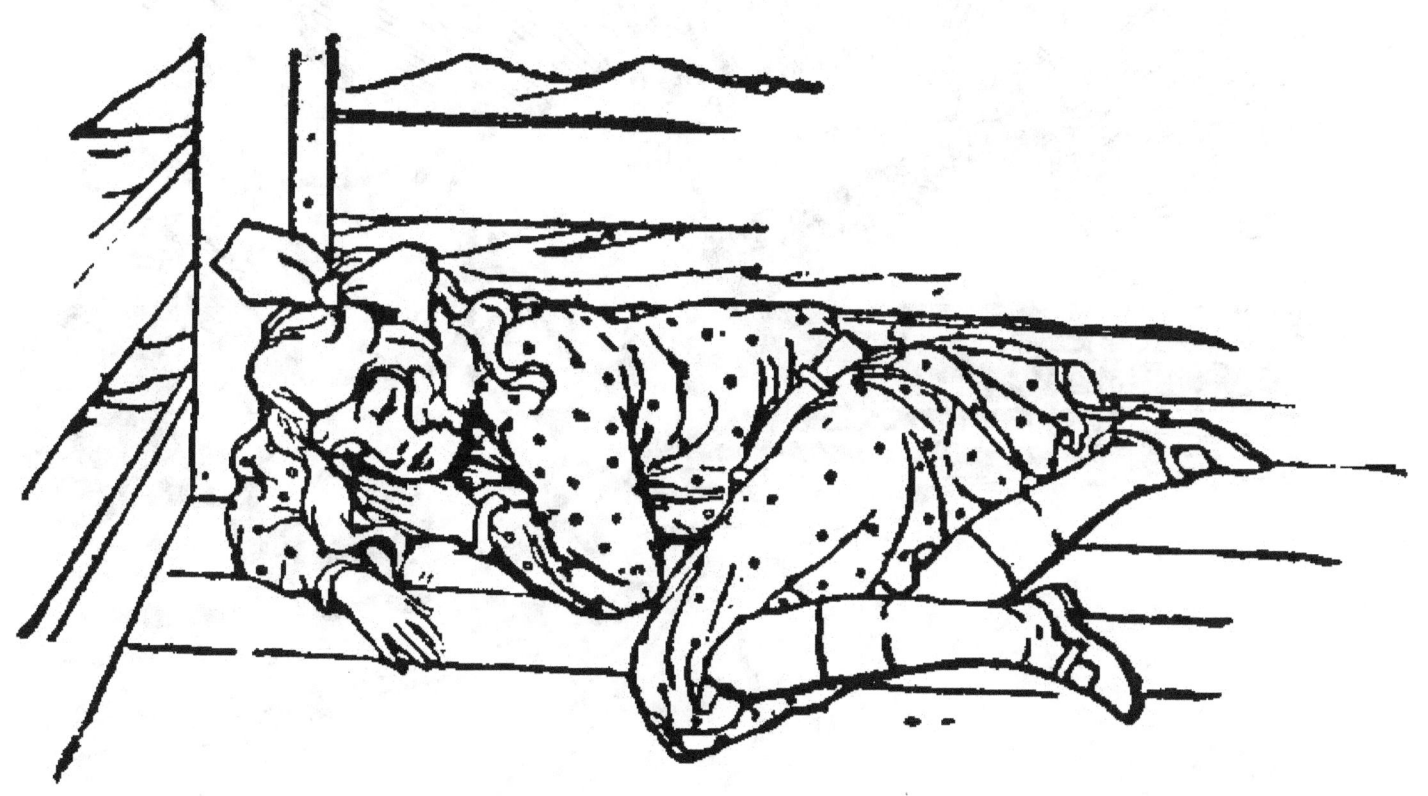

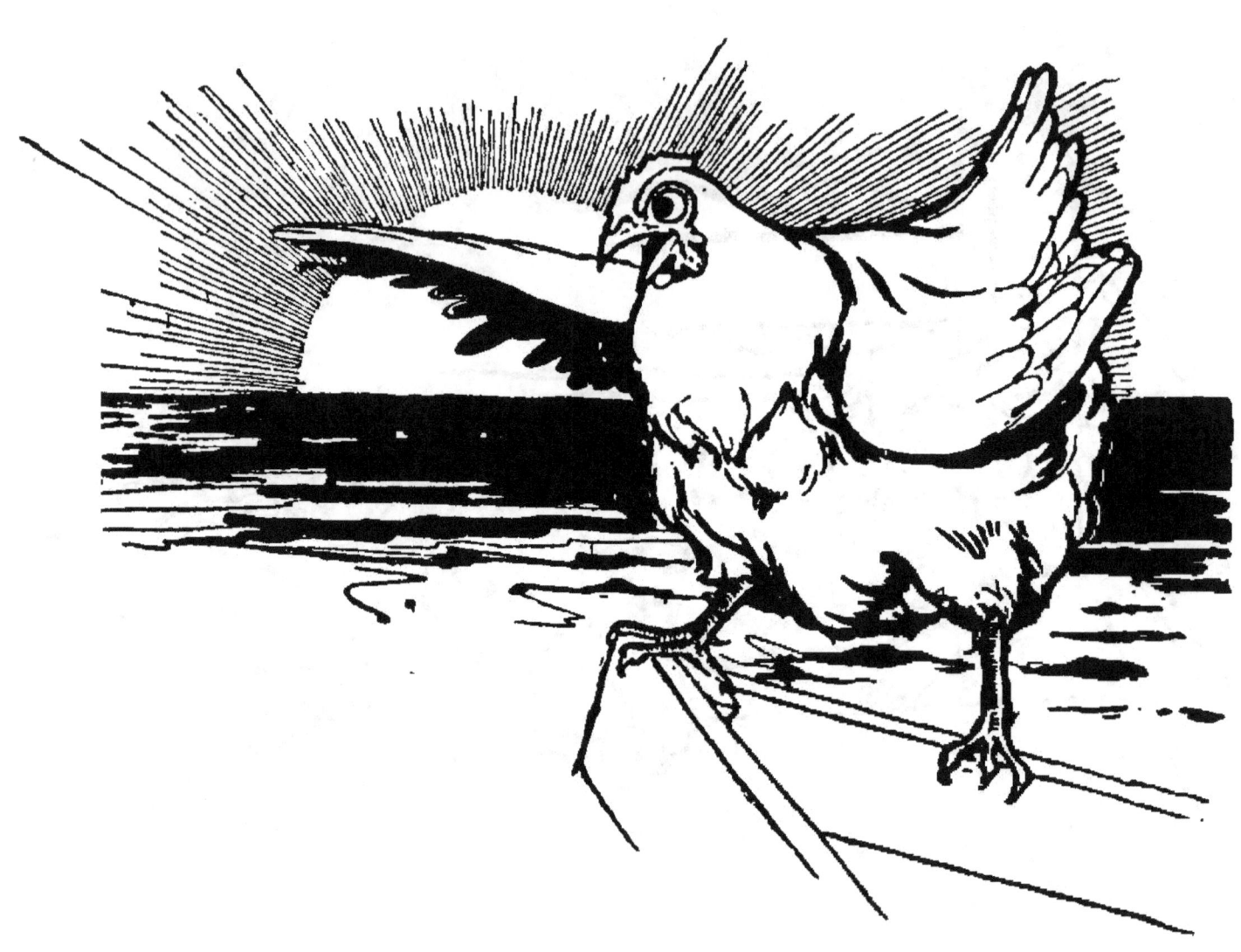

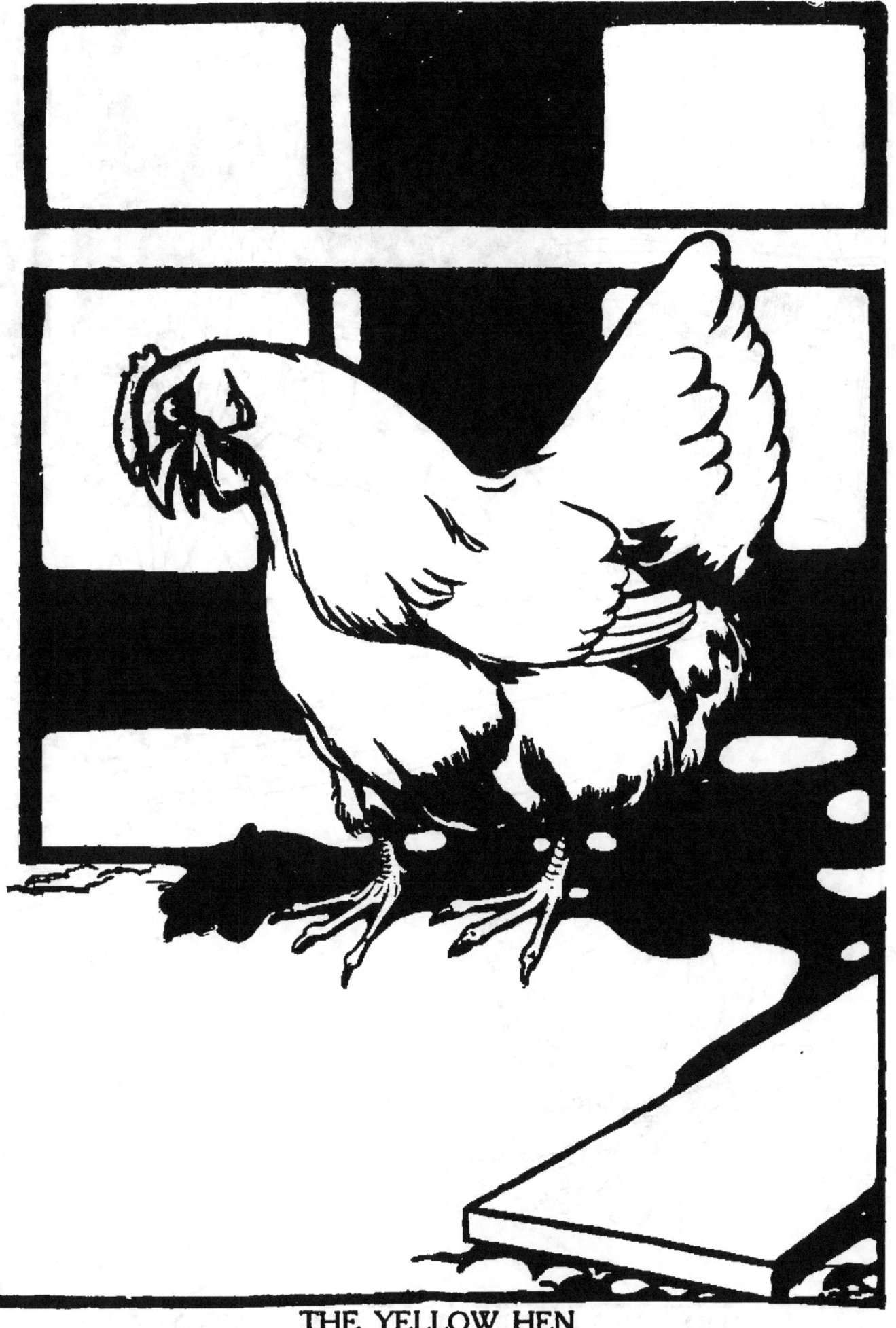

THE YELLOW HEN

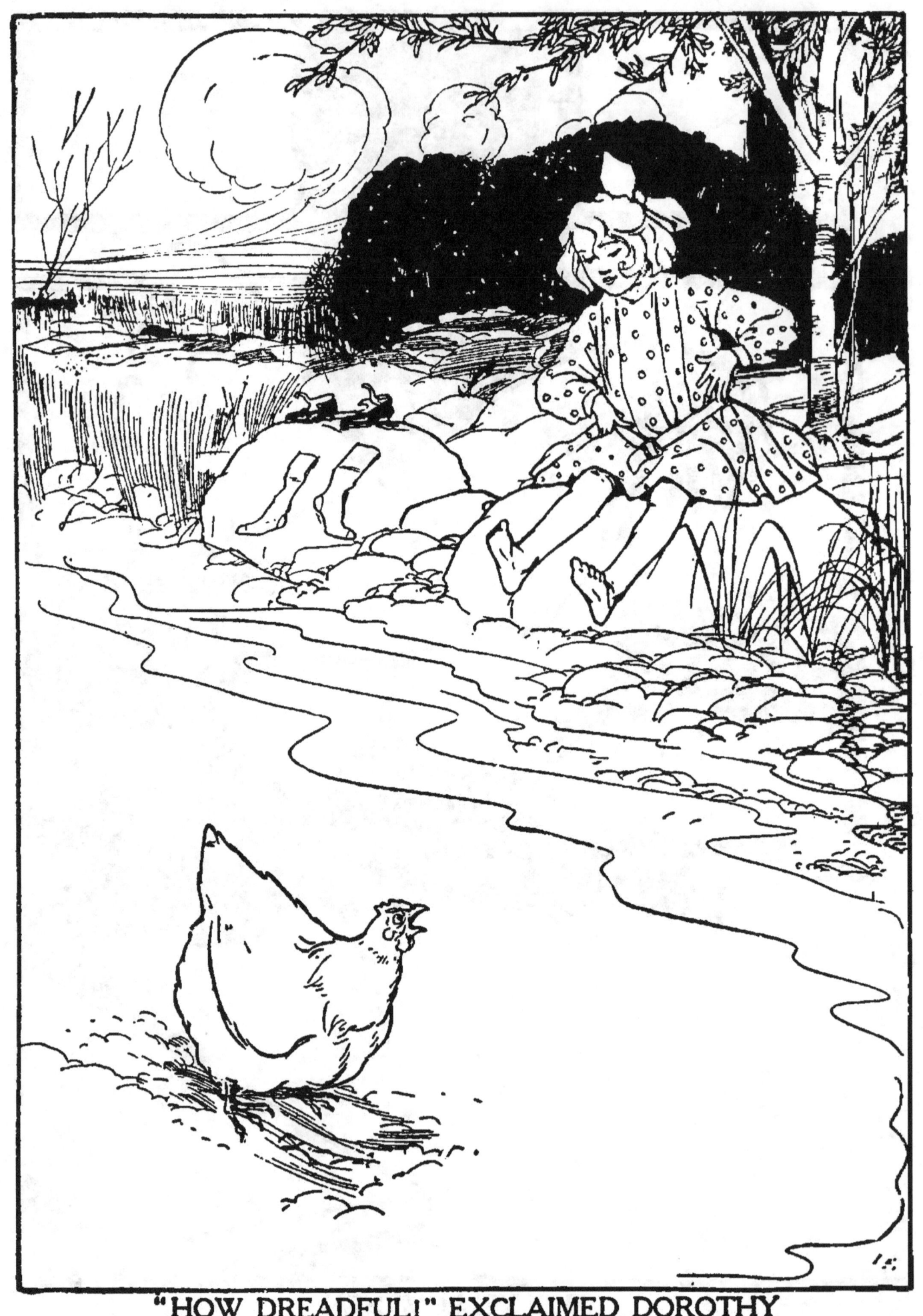

"HOW DREADFUL!" EXCLAIMED DOROTHY

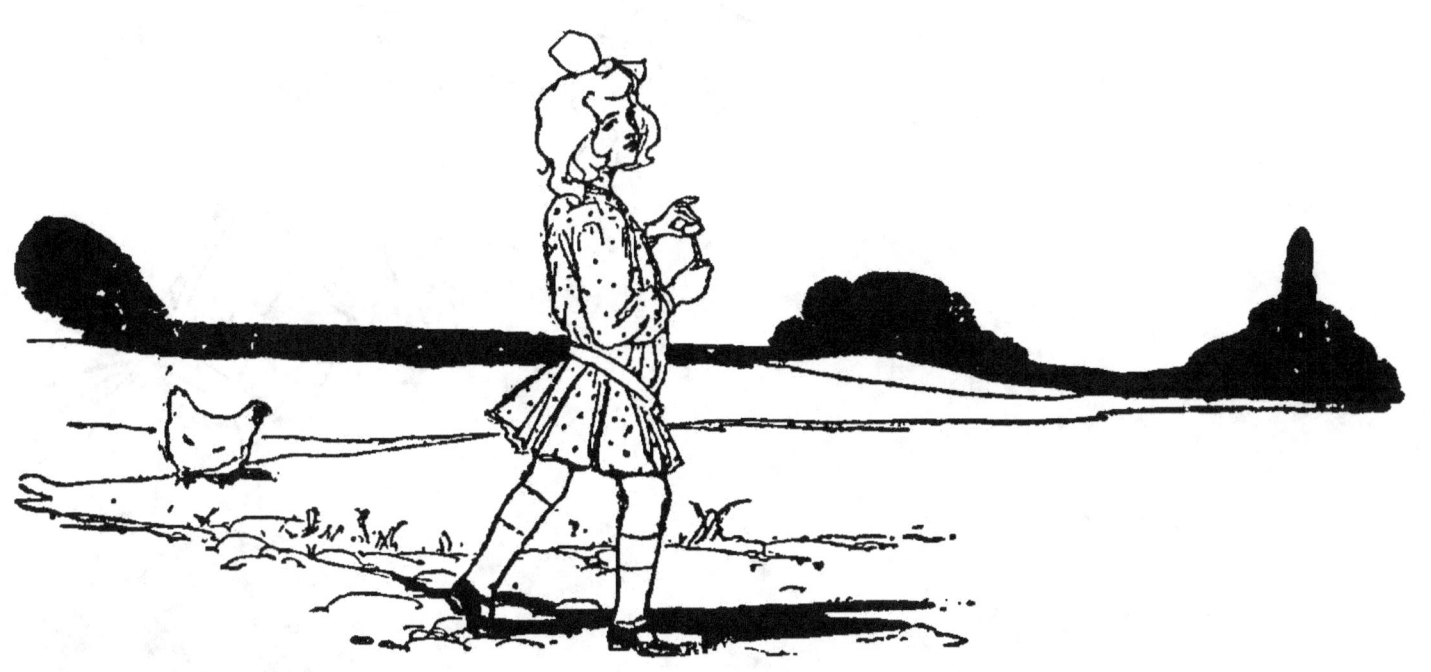

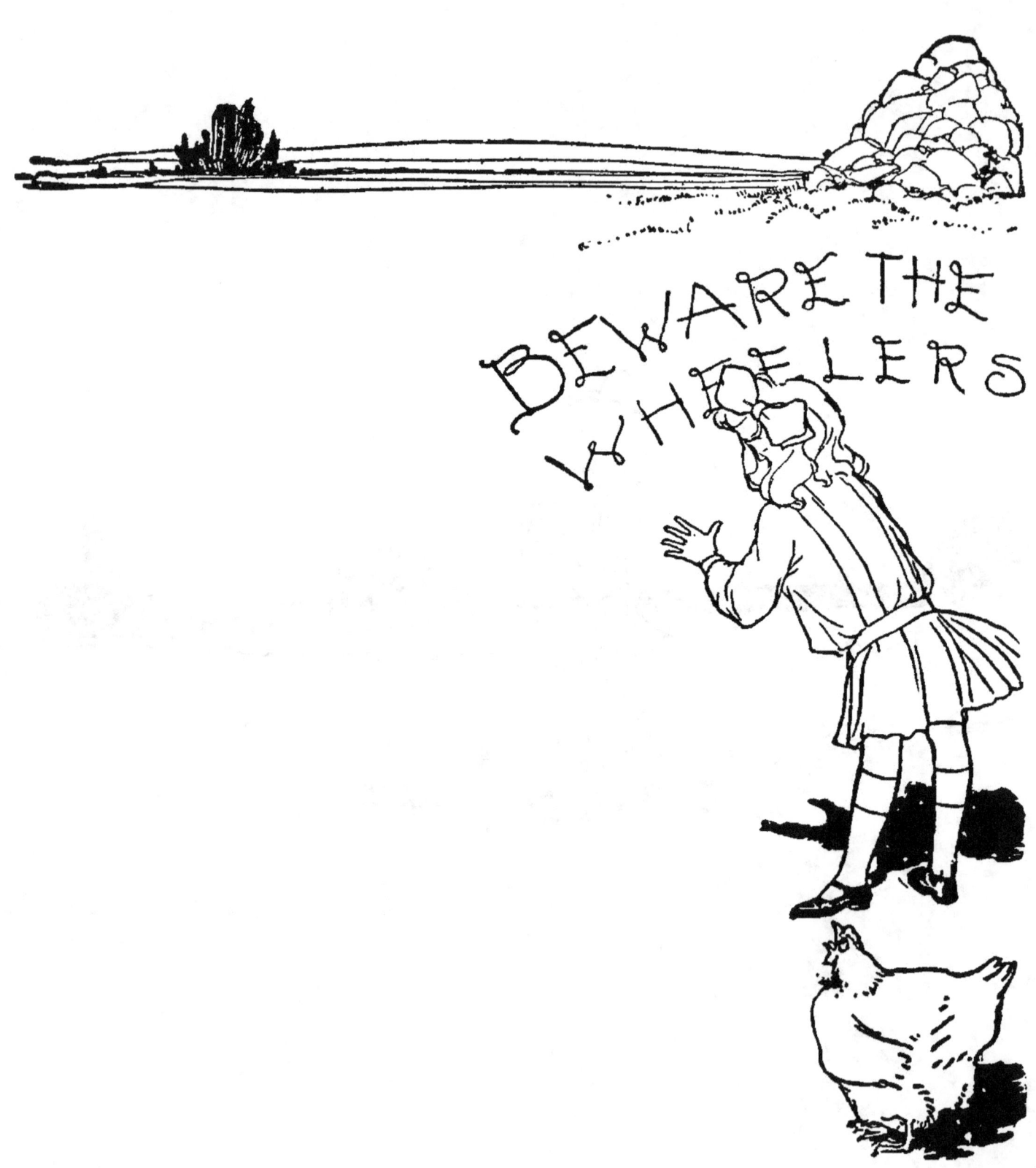

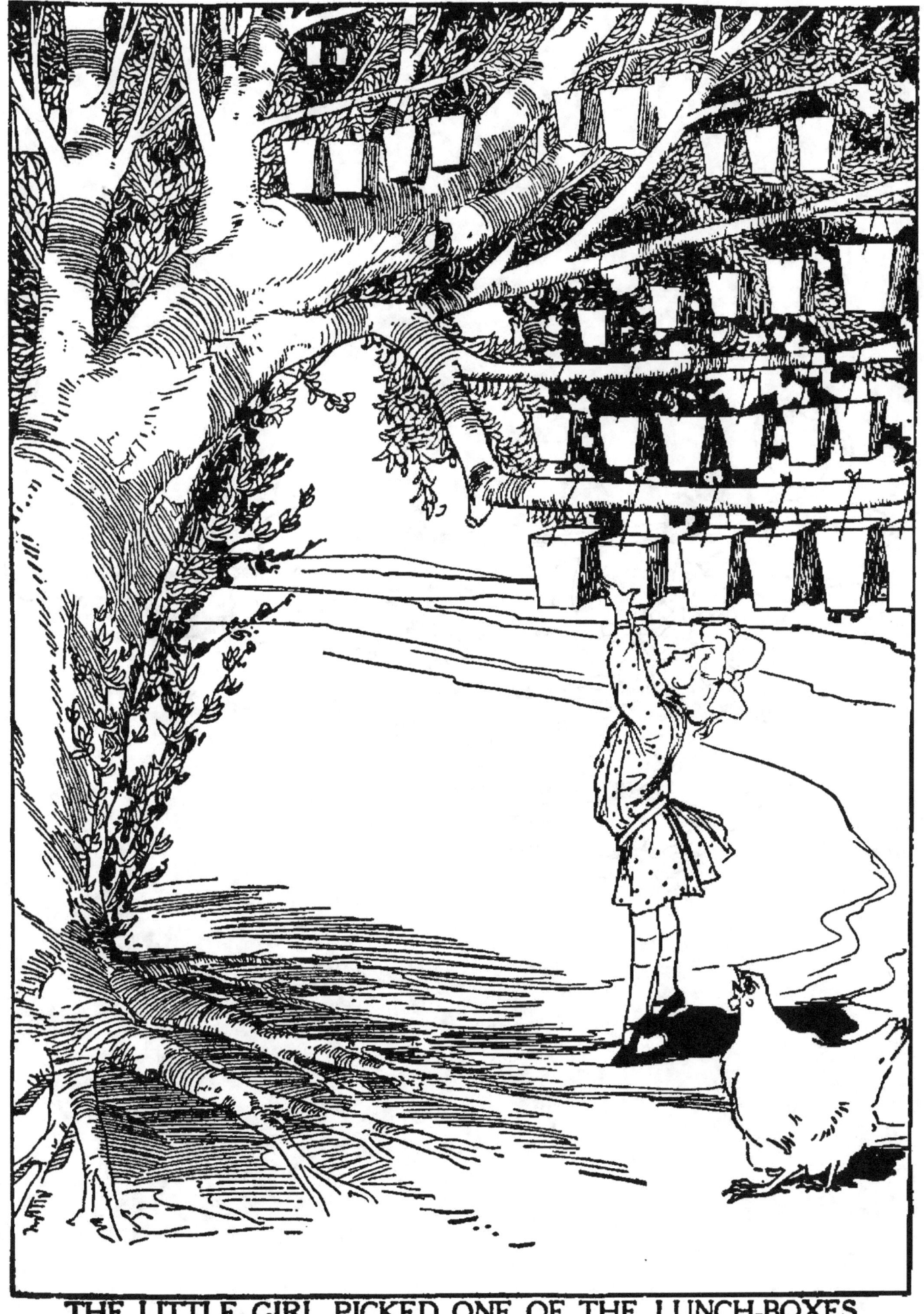

THE LITTLE GIRL PICKED ONE OF THE LUNCH-BOXES

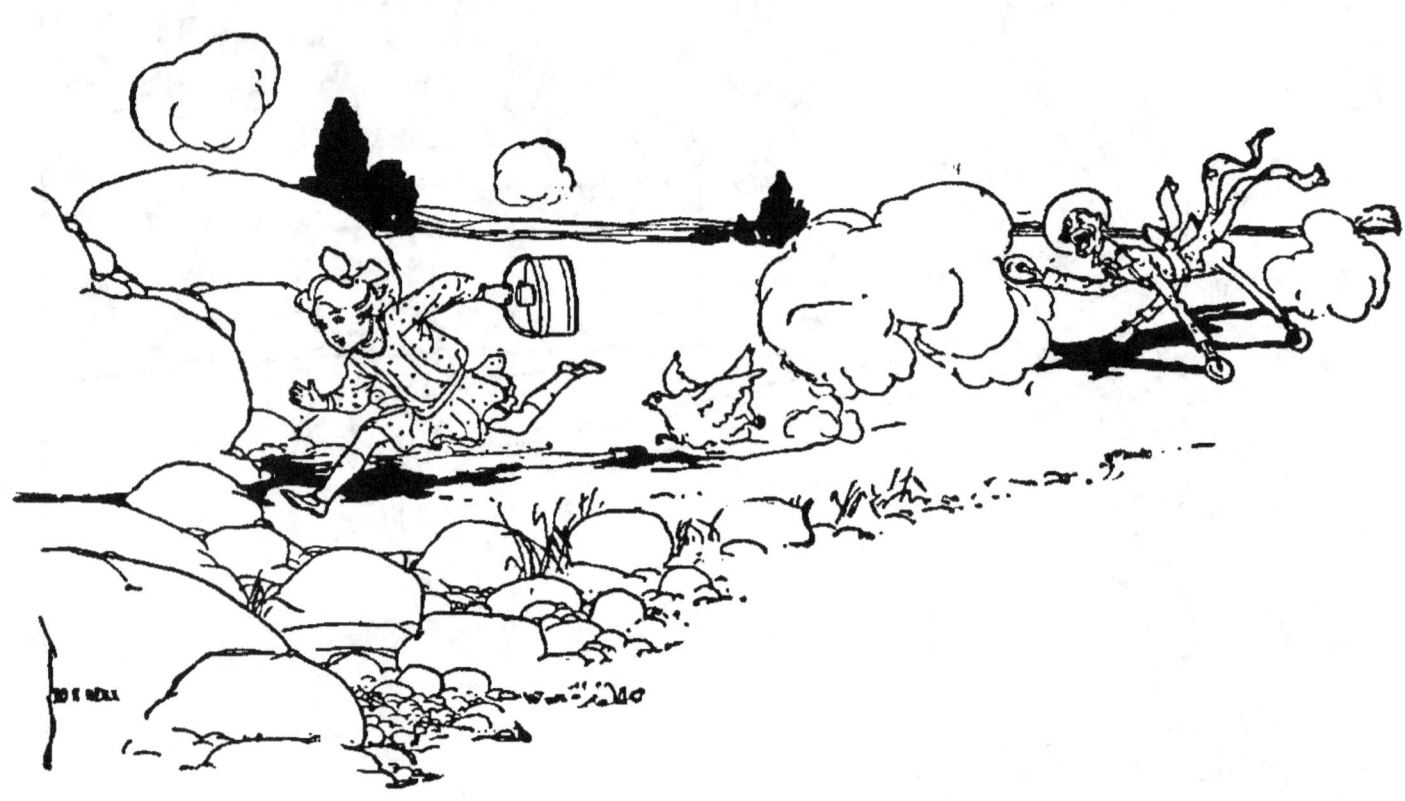

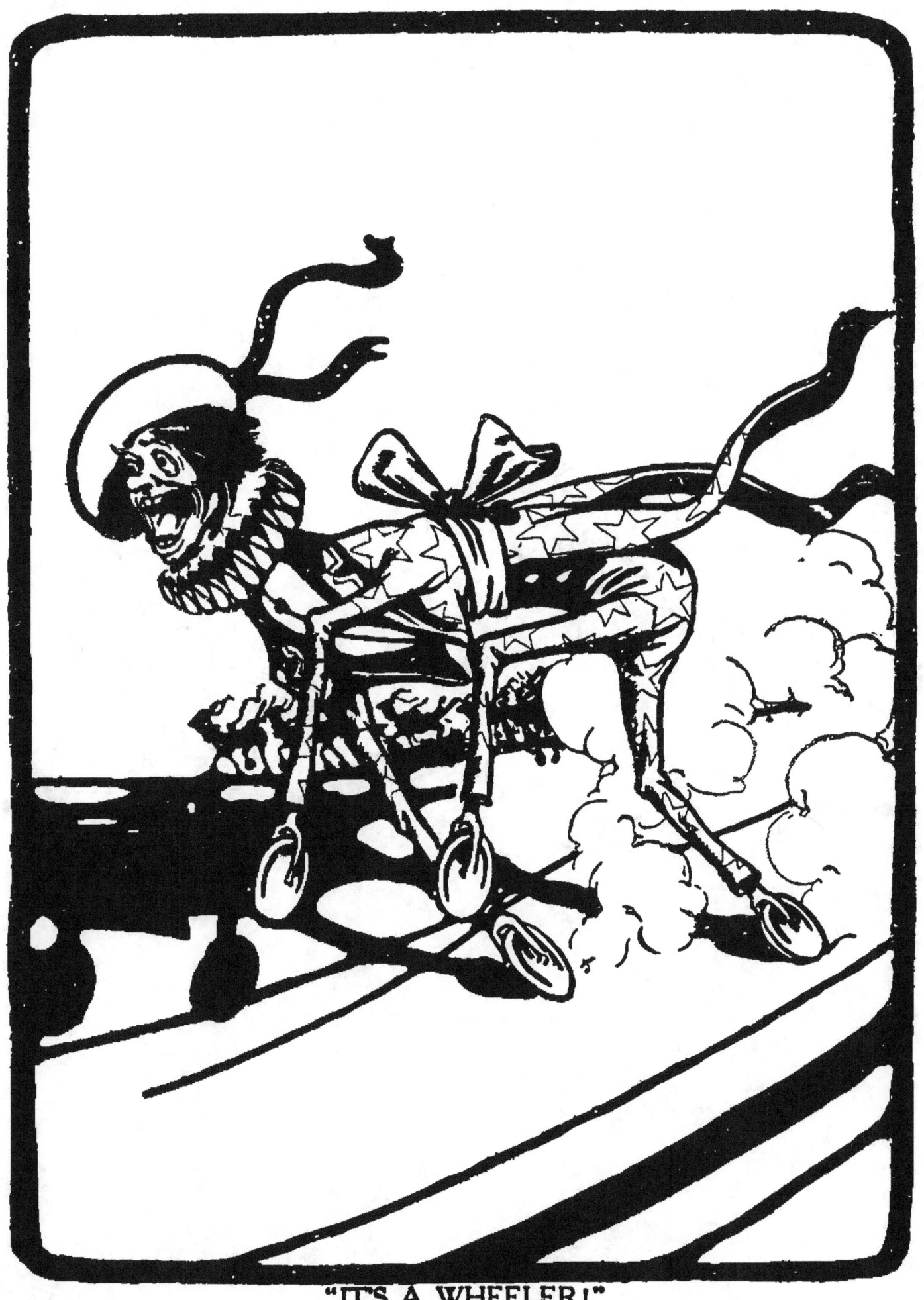

"IT'S A WHEELER!"

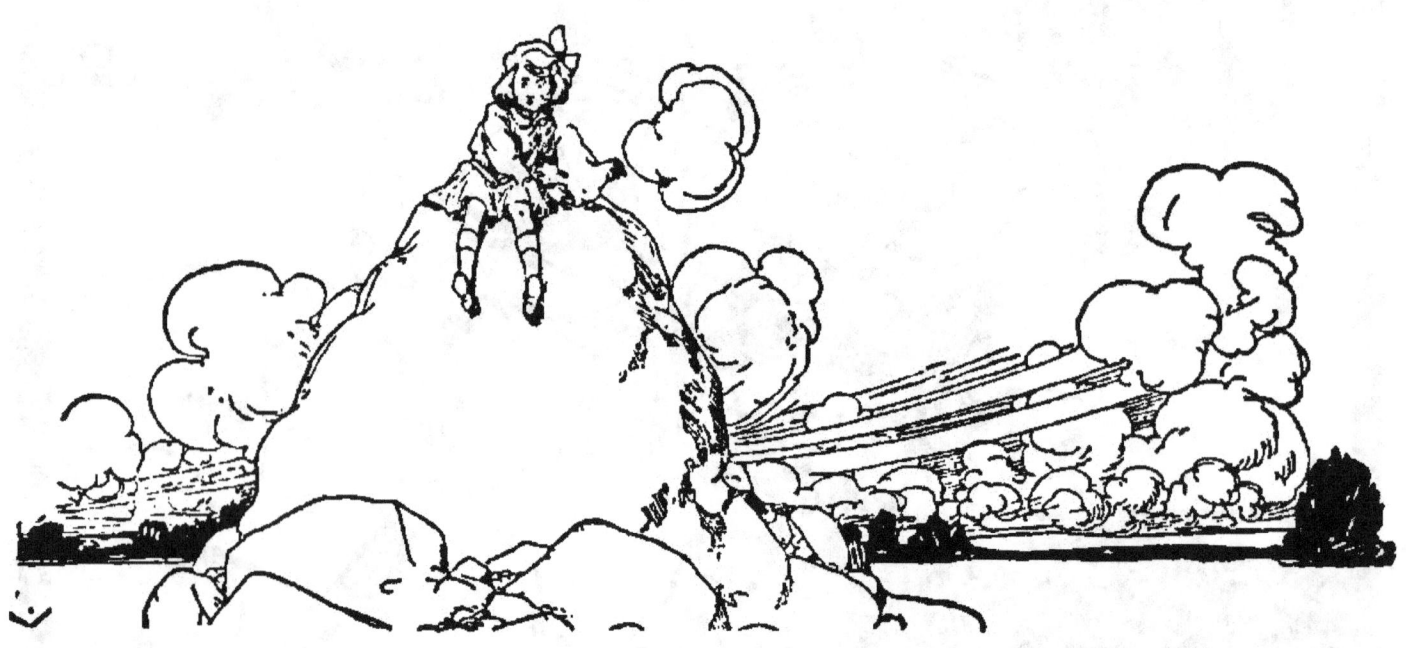

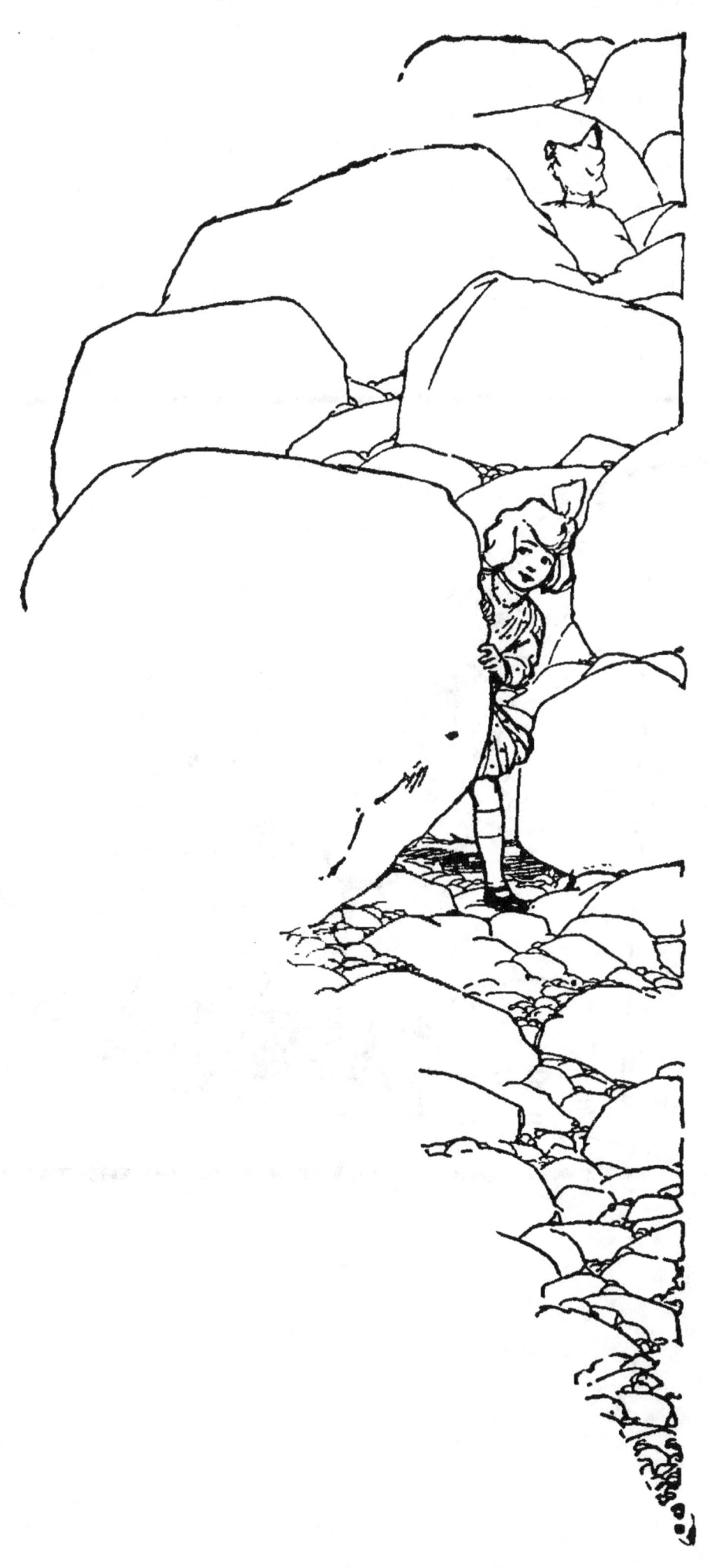

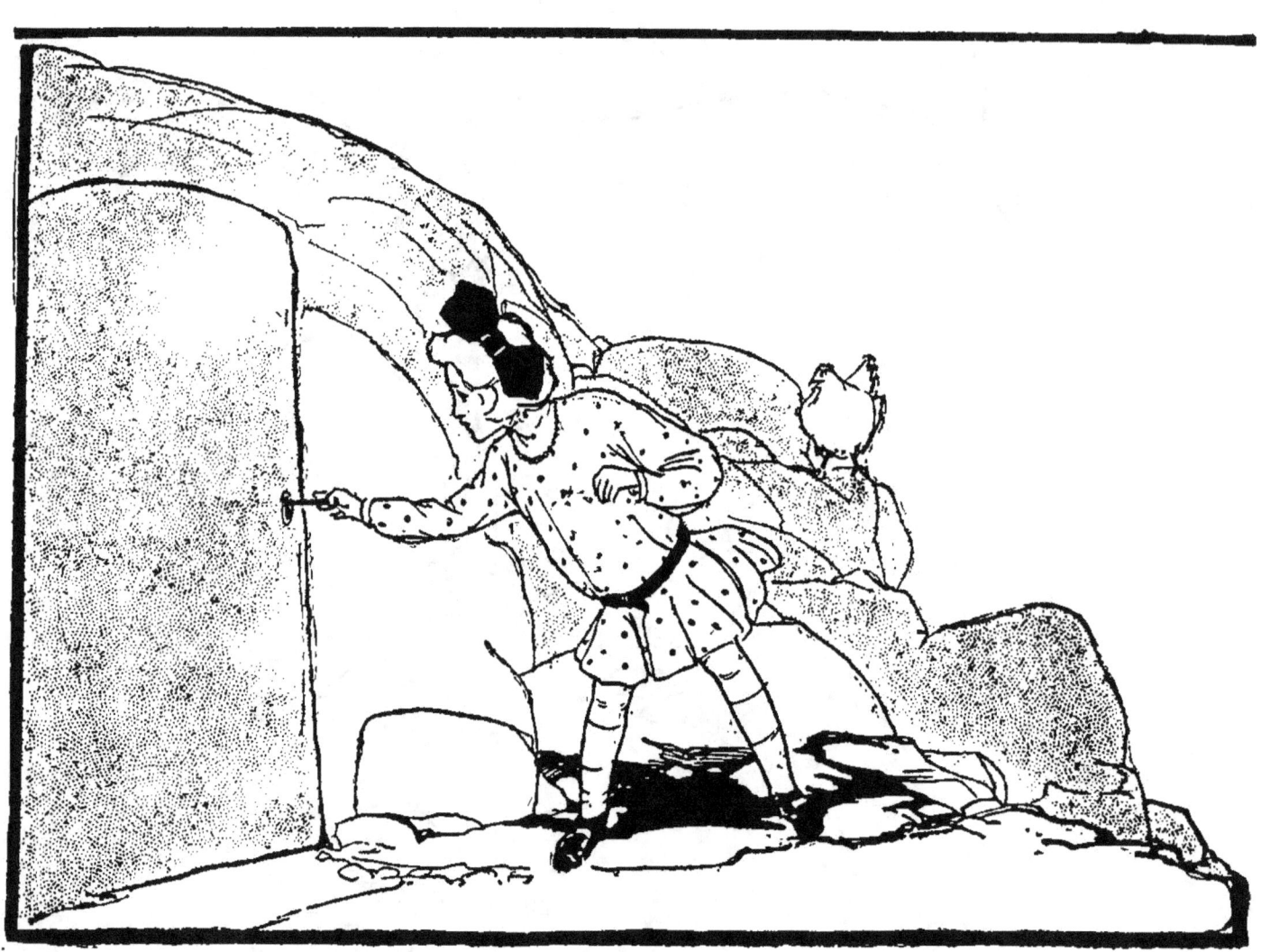

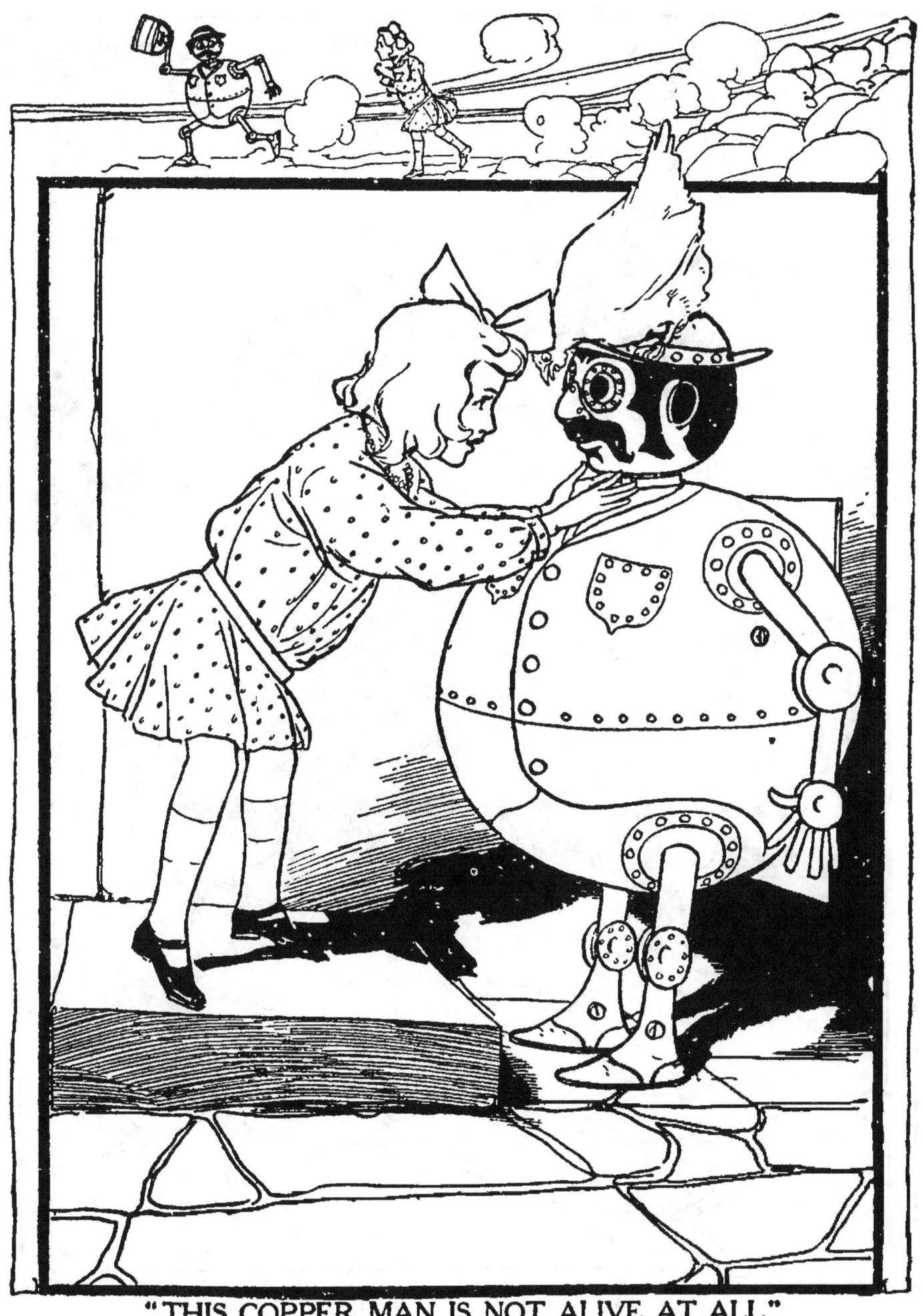

"THIS COPPER MAN IS NOT ALIVE AT ALL"

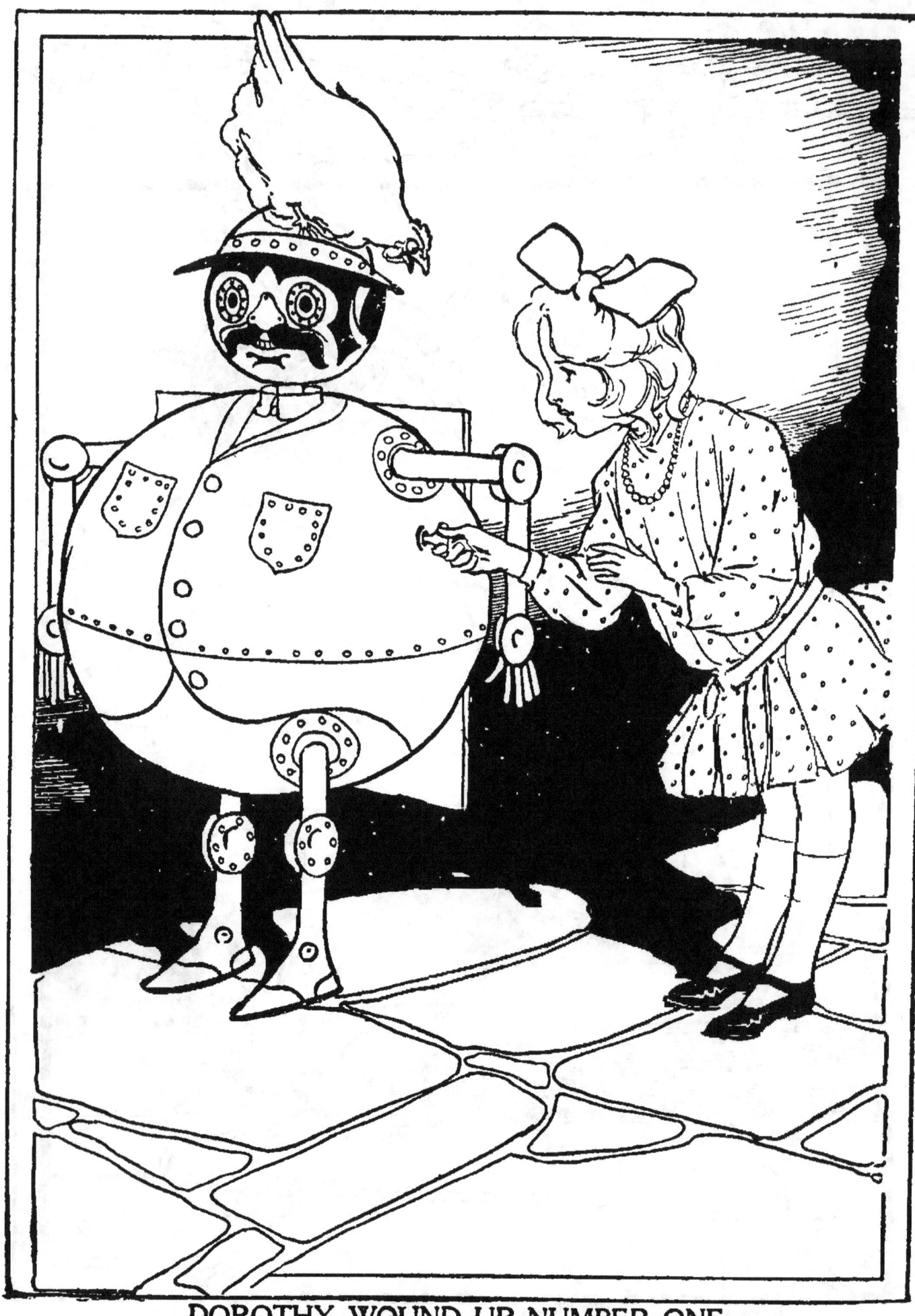

DOROTHY WOUND UP NUMBER ONE

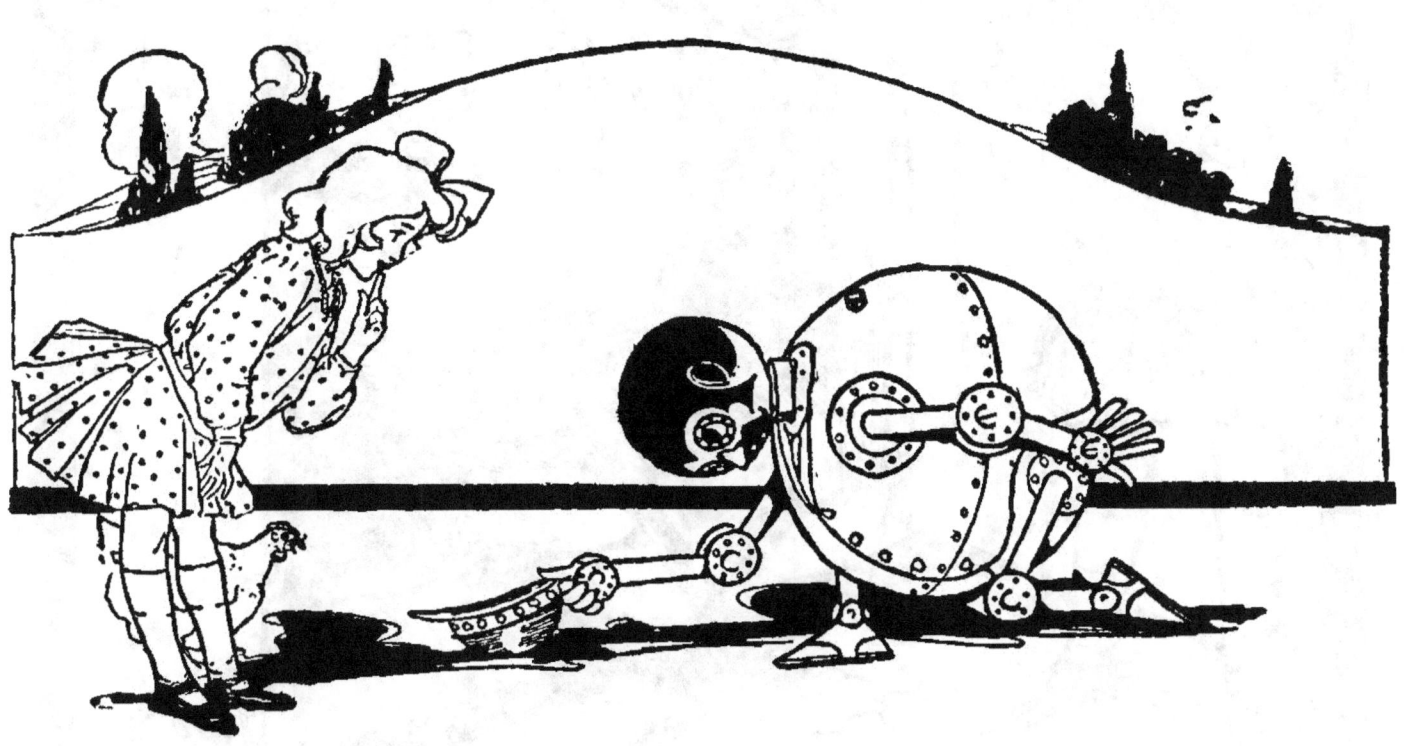

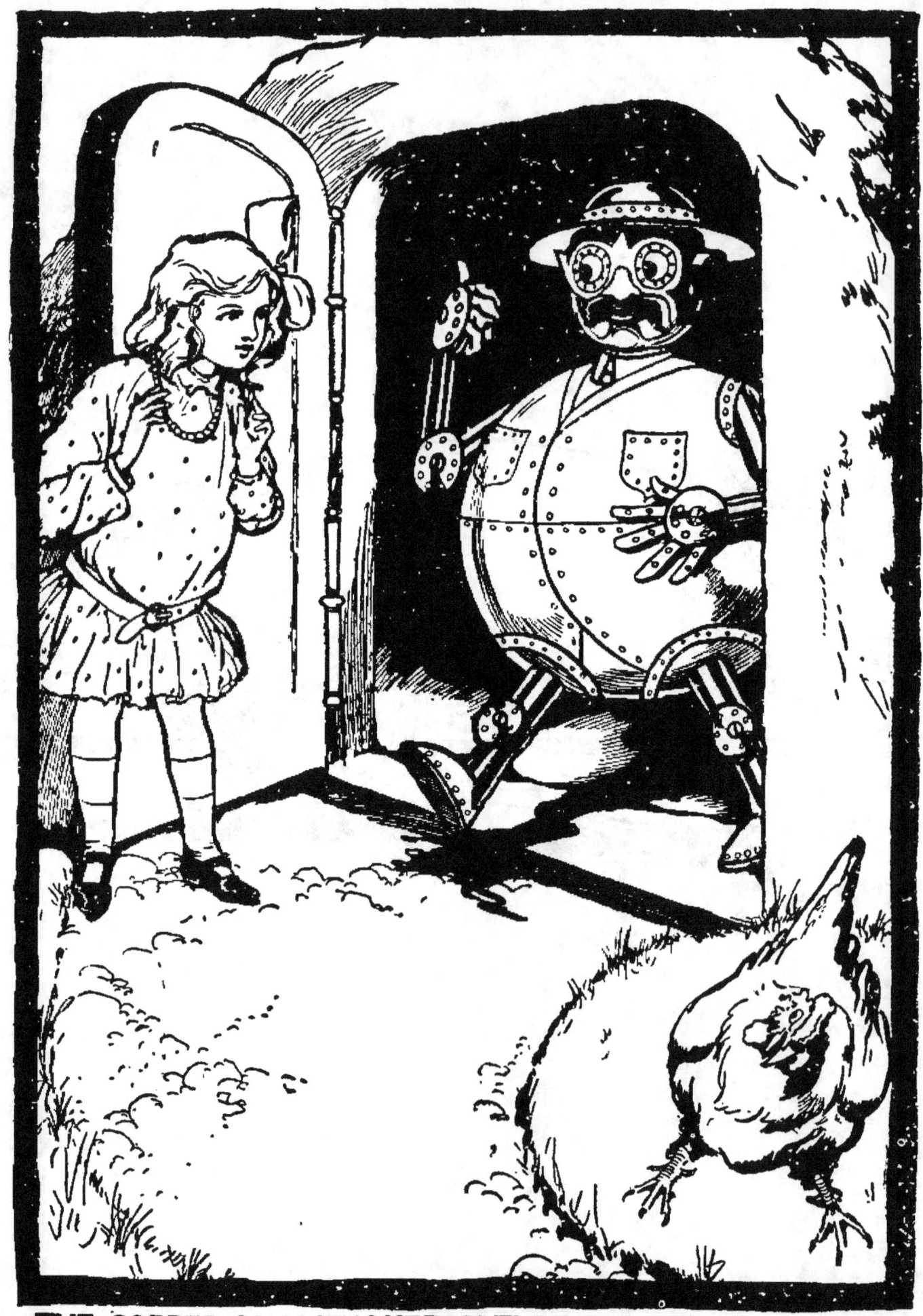

THE COPPER MAN WALKED OUT OF THE ROCKY CAVERN

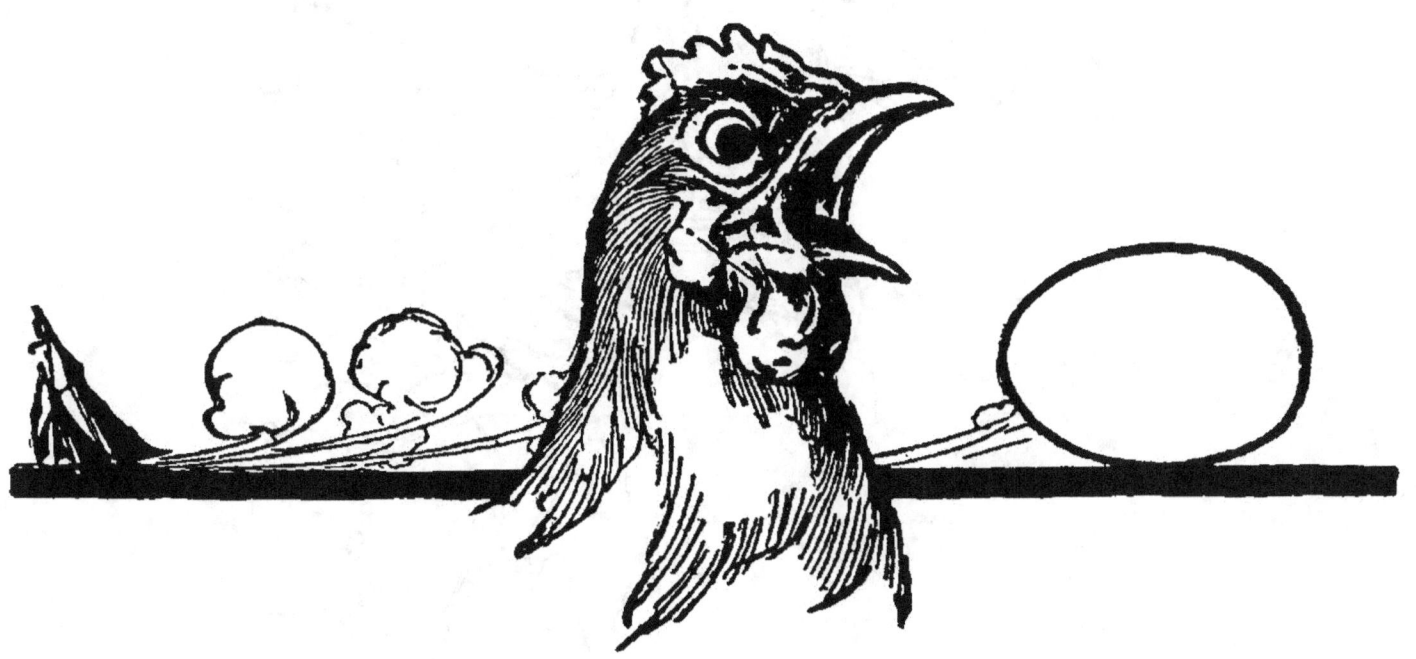

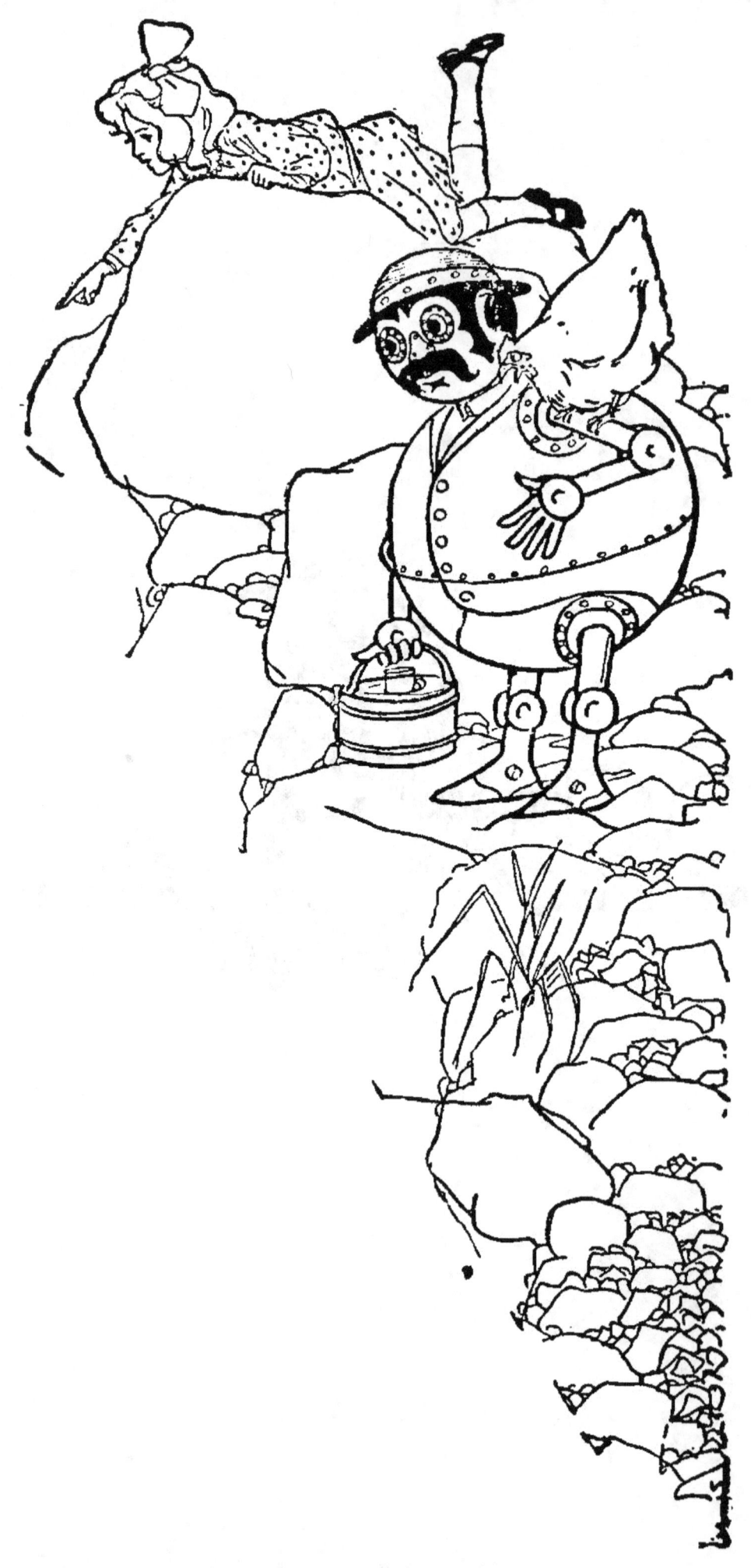

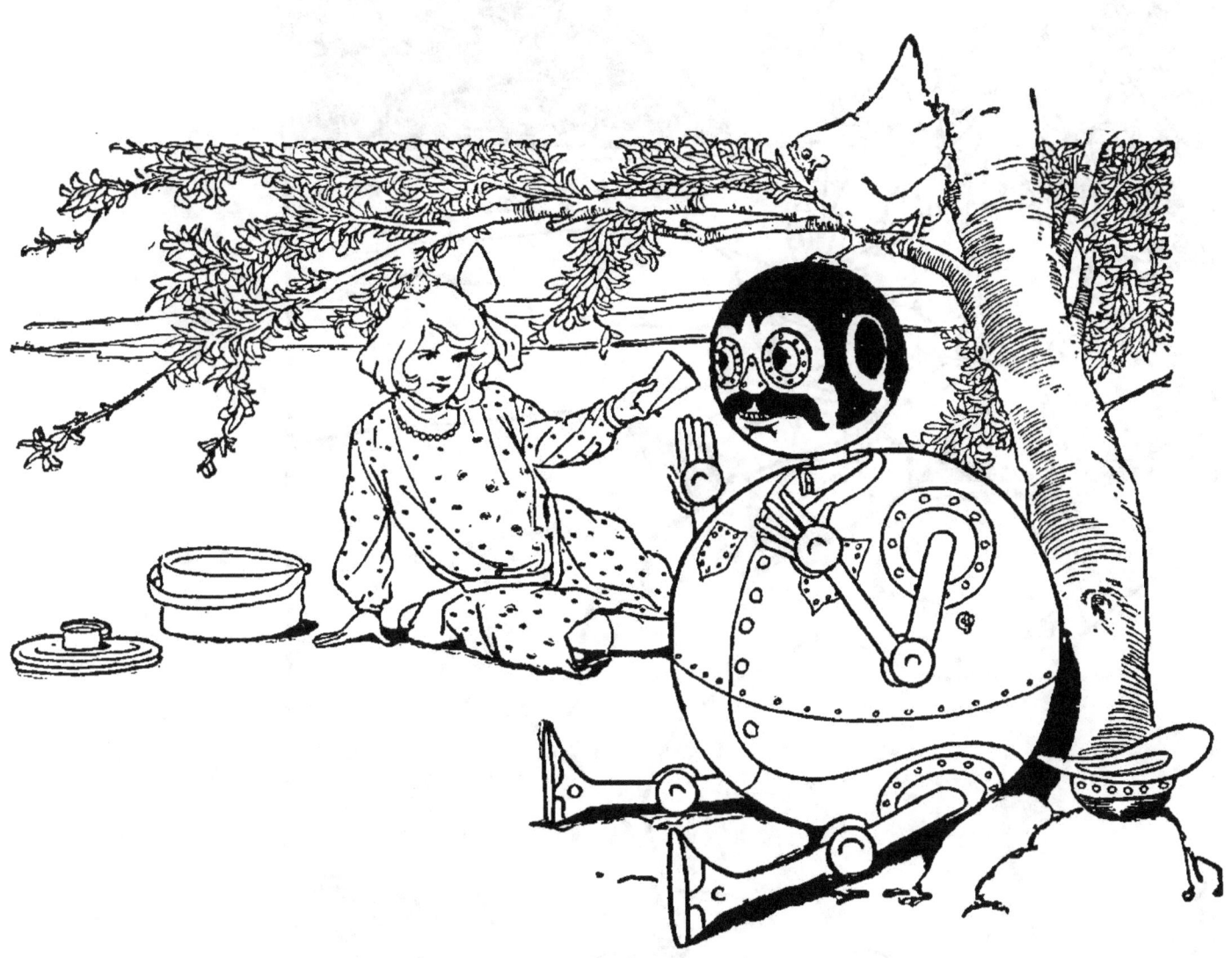

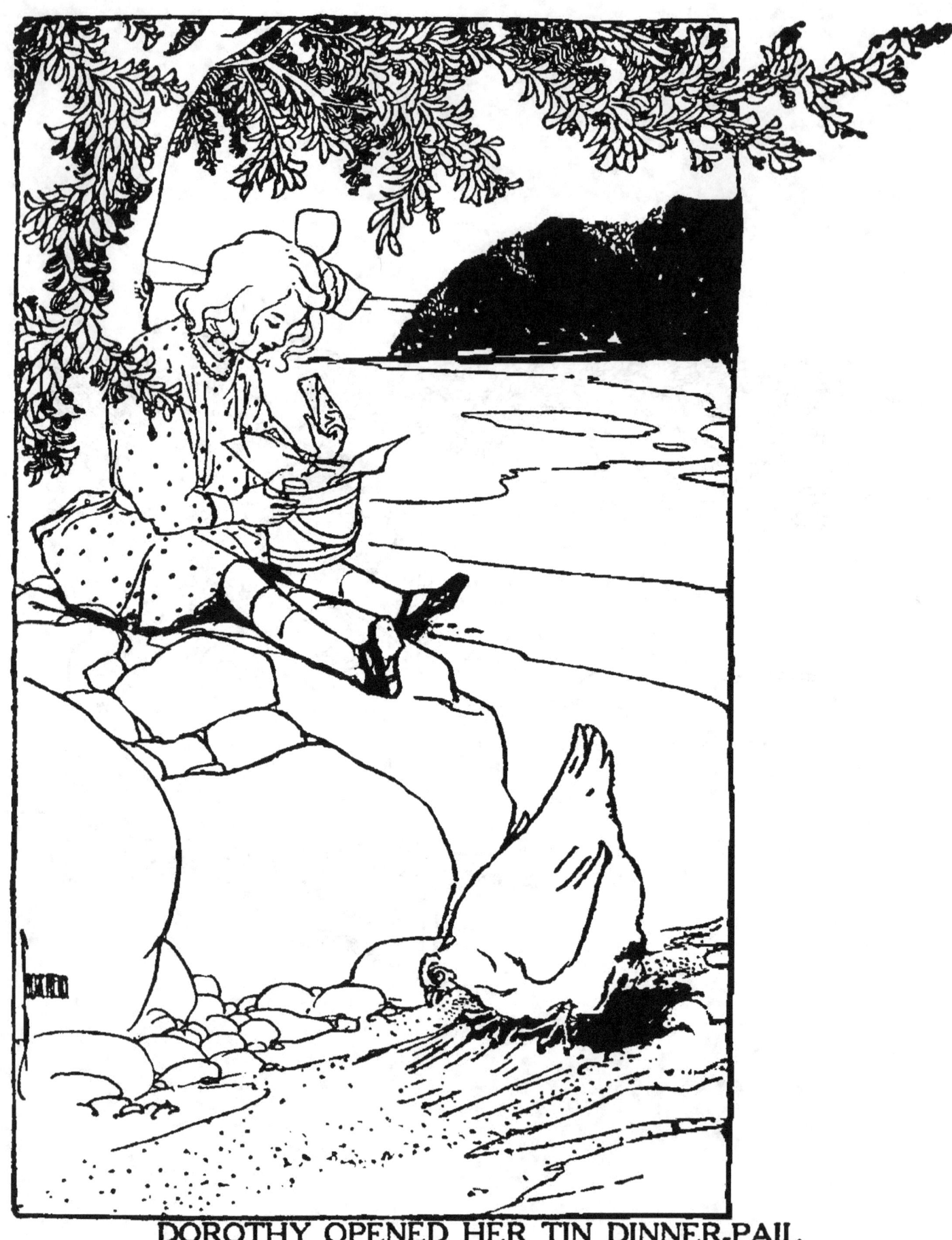

DOROTHY OPENED HER TIN DINNER-PAIL

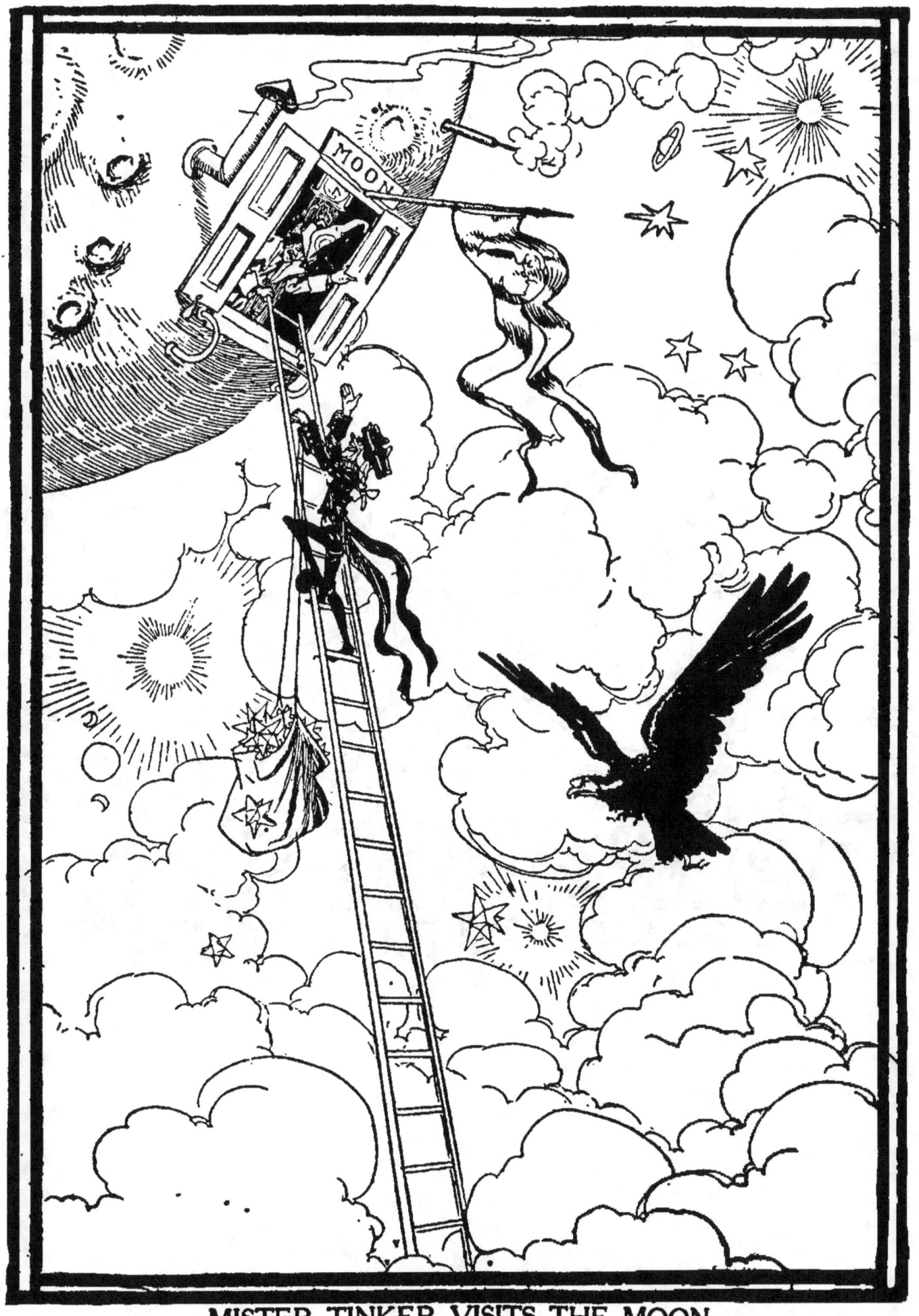

MISTER TINKER VISITS THE MOON

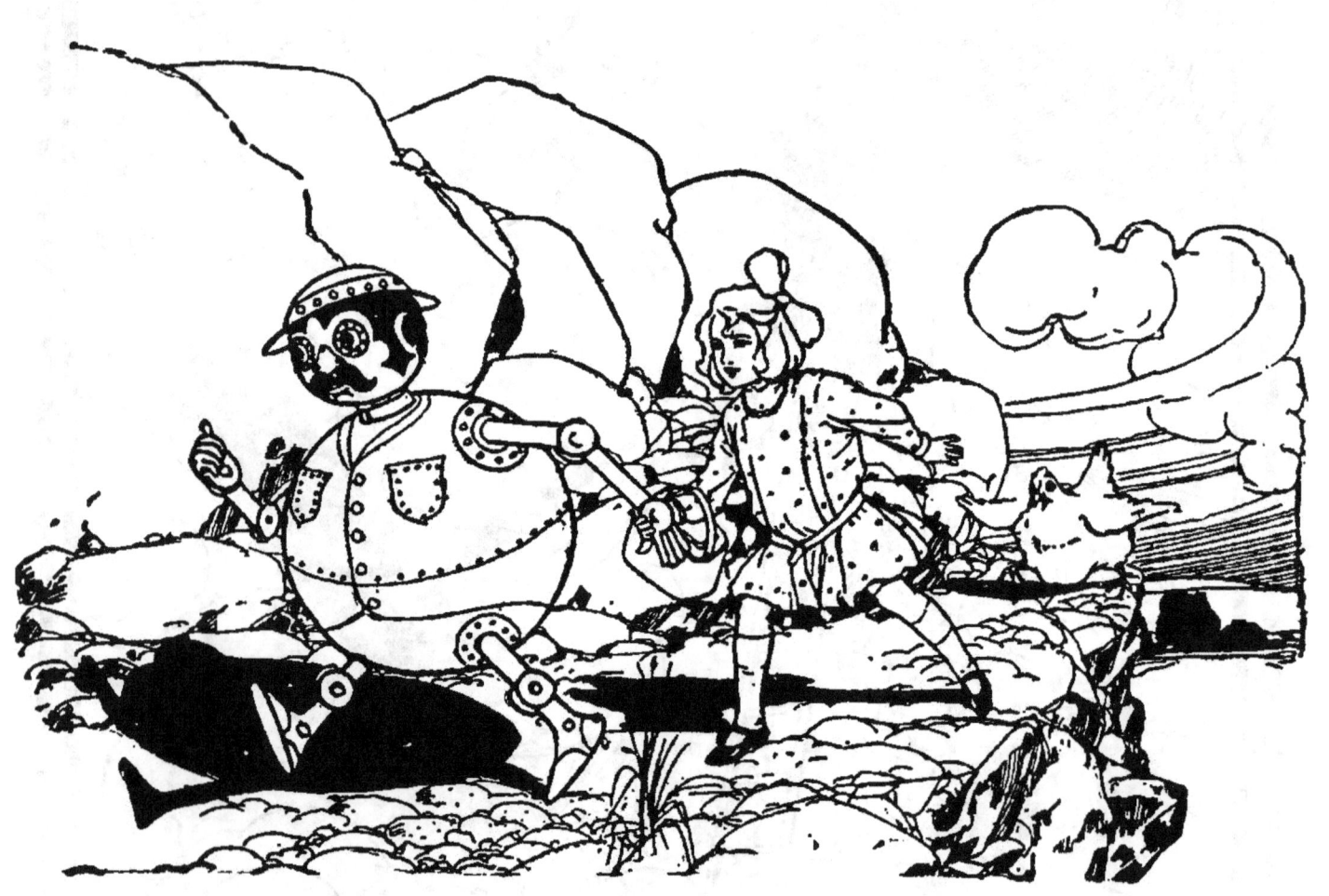

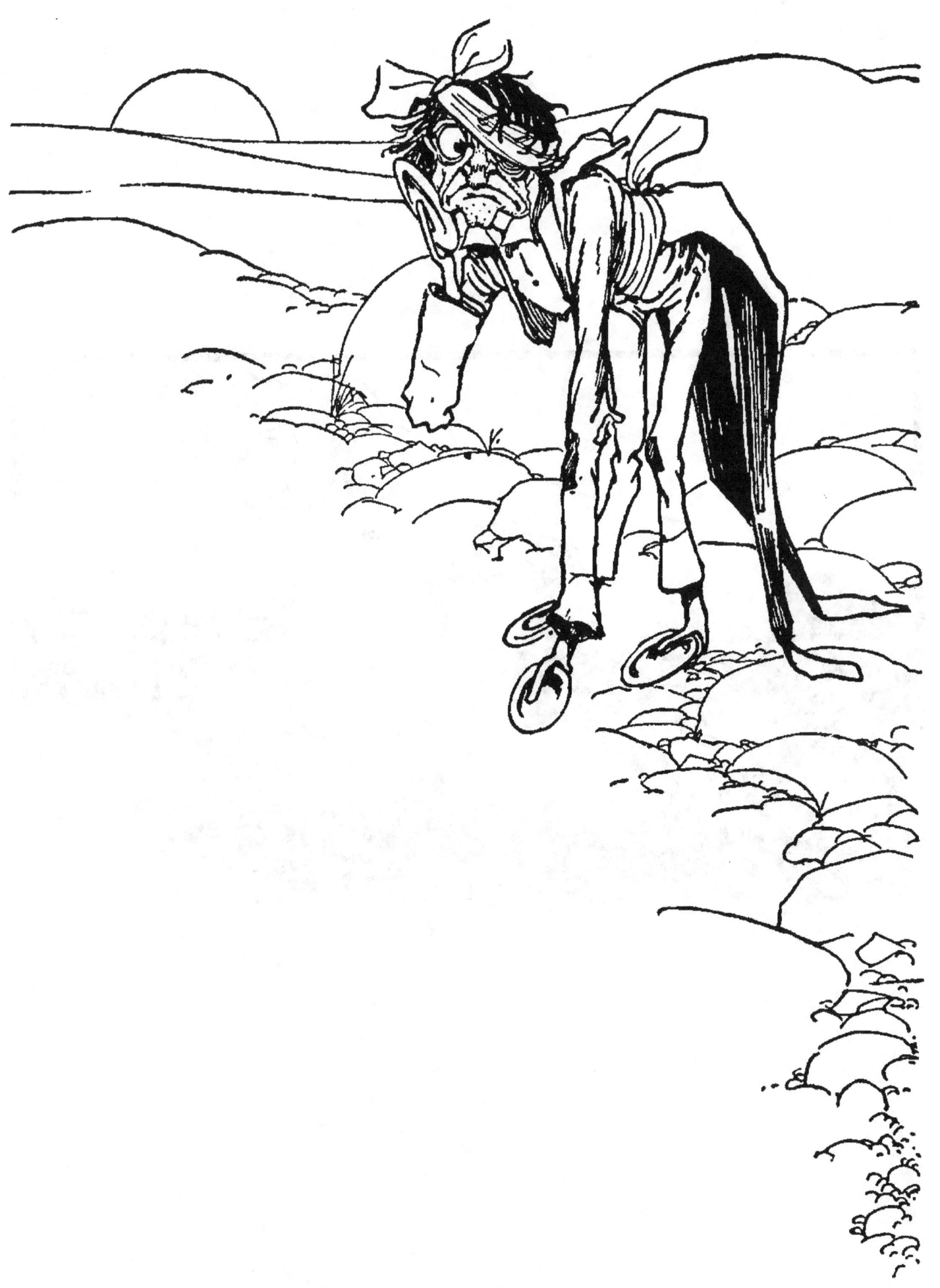

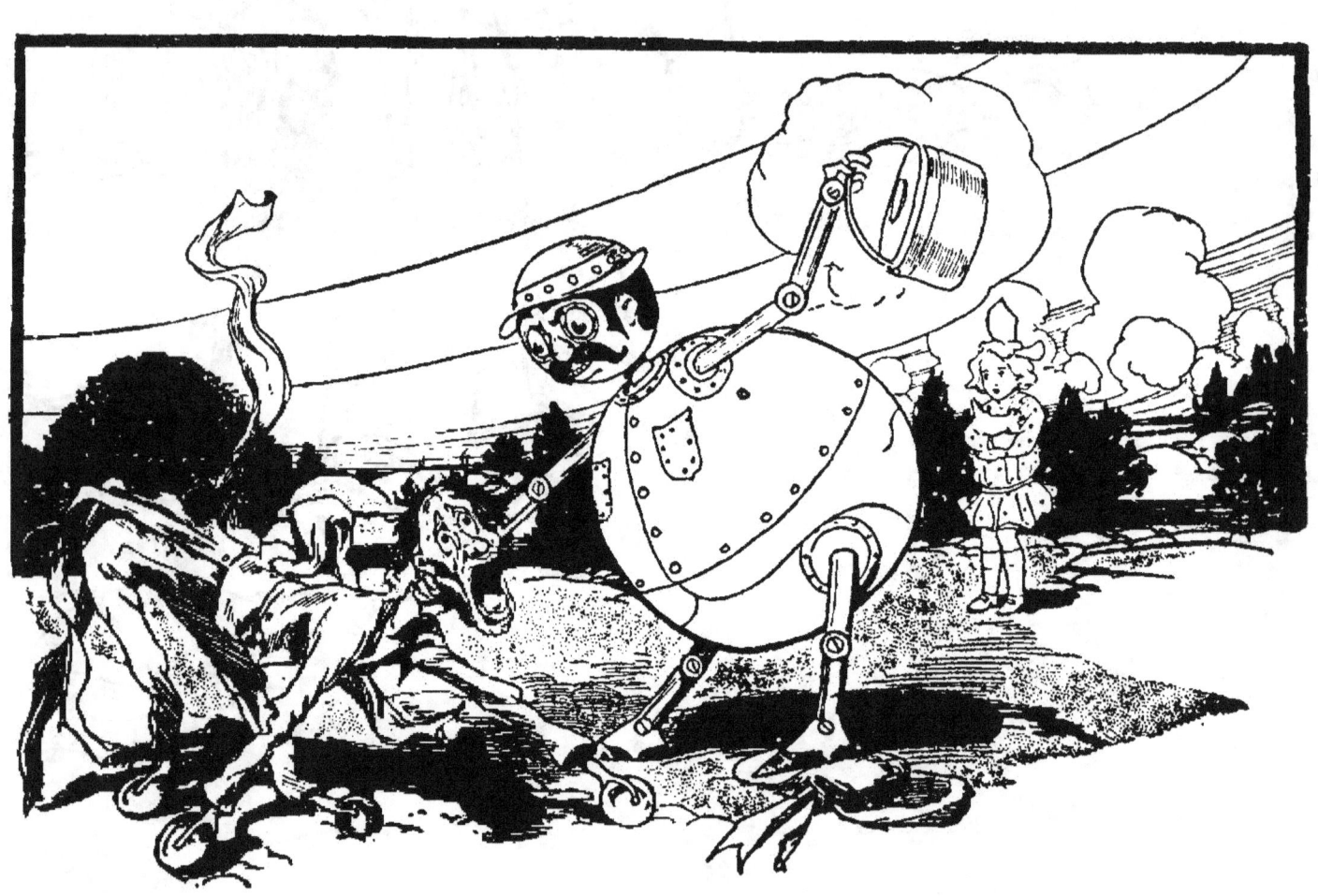

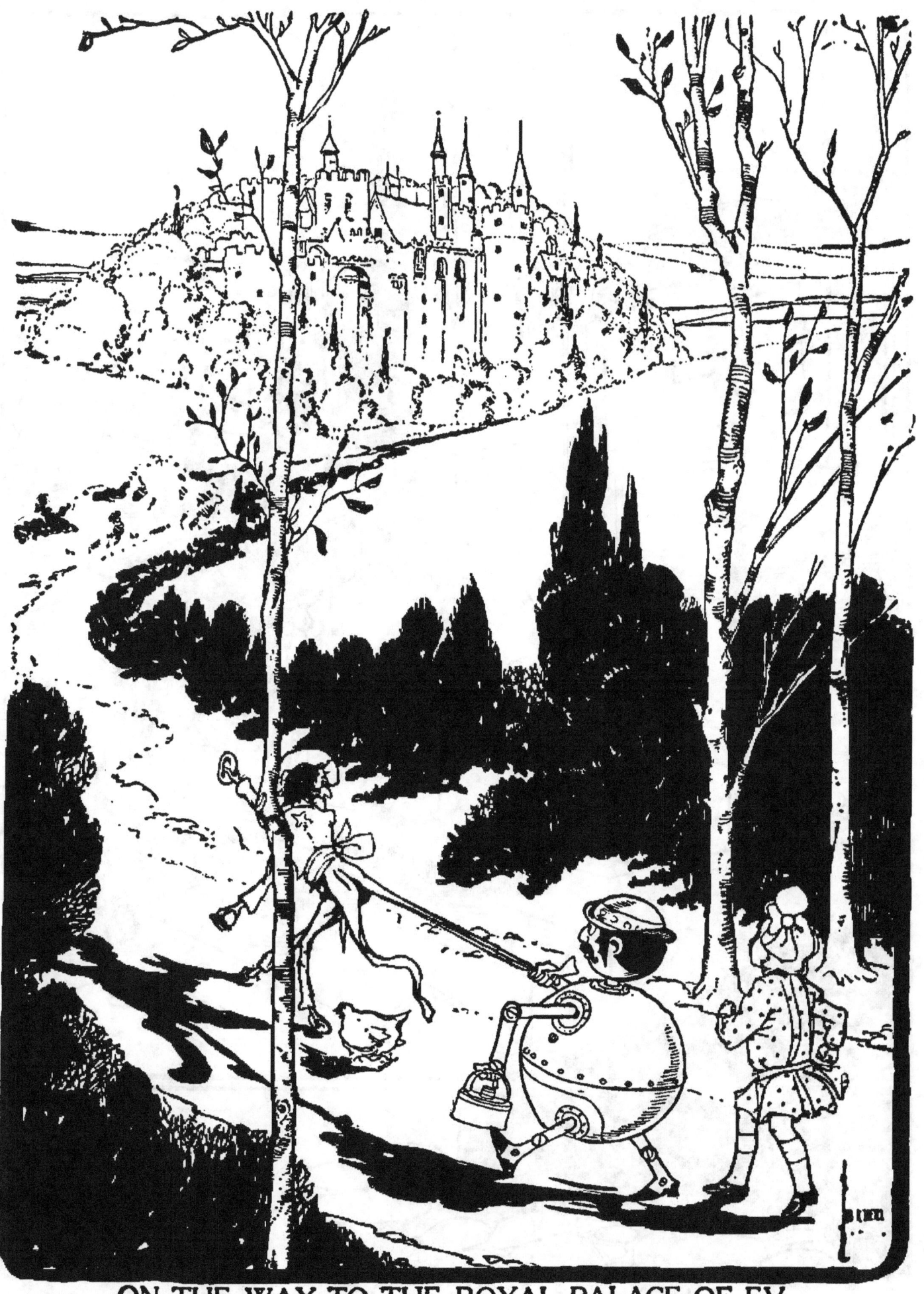

ON THE WAY TO THE ROYAL PALACE OF EV

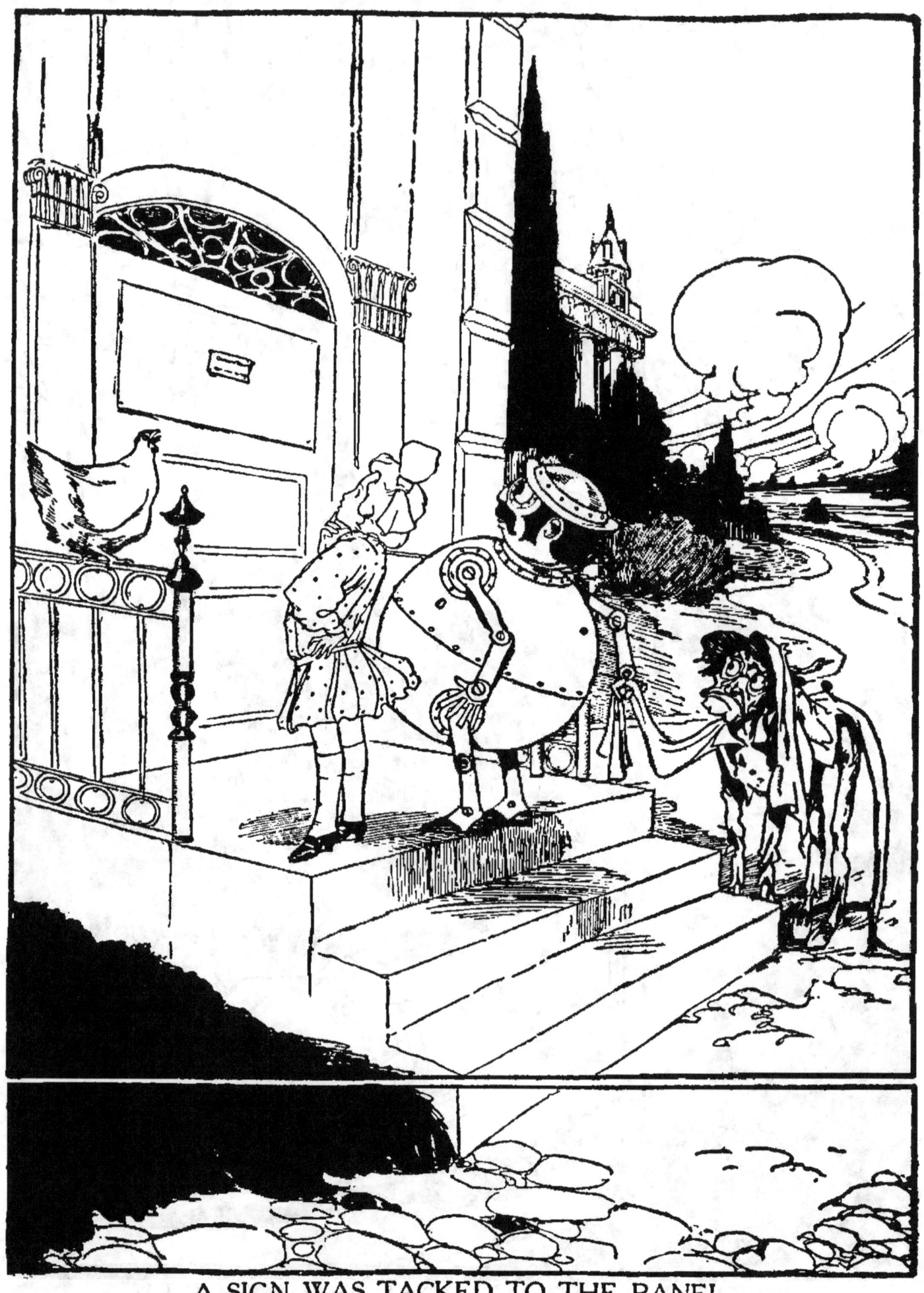

A SIGN WAS TACKED TO THE PANEL

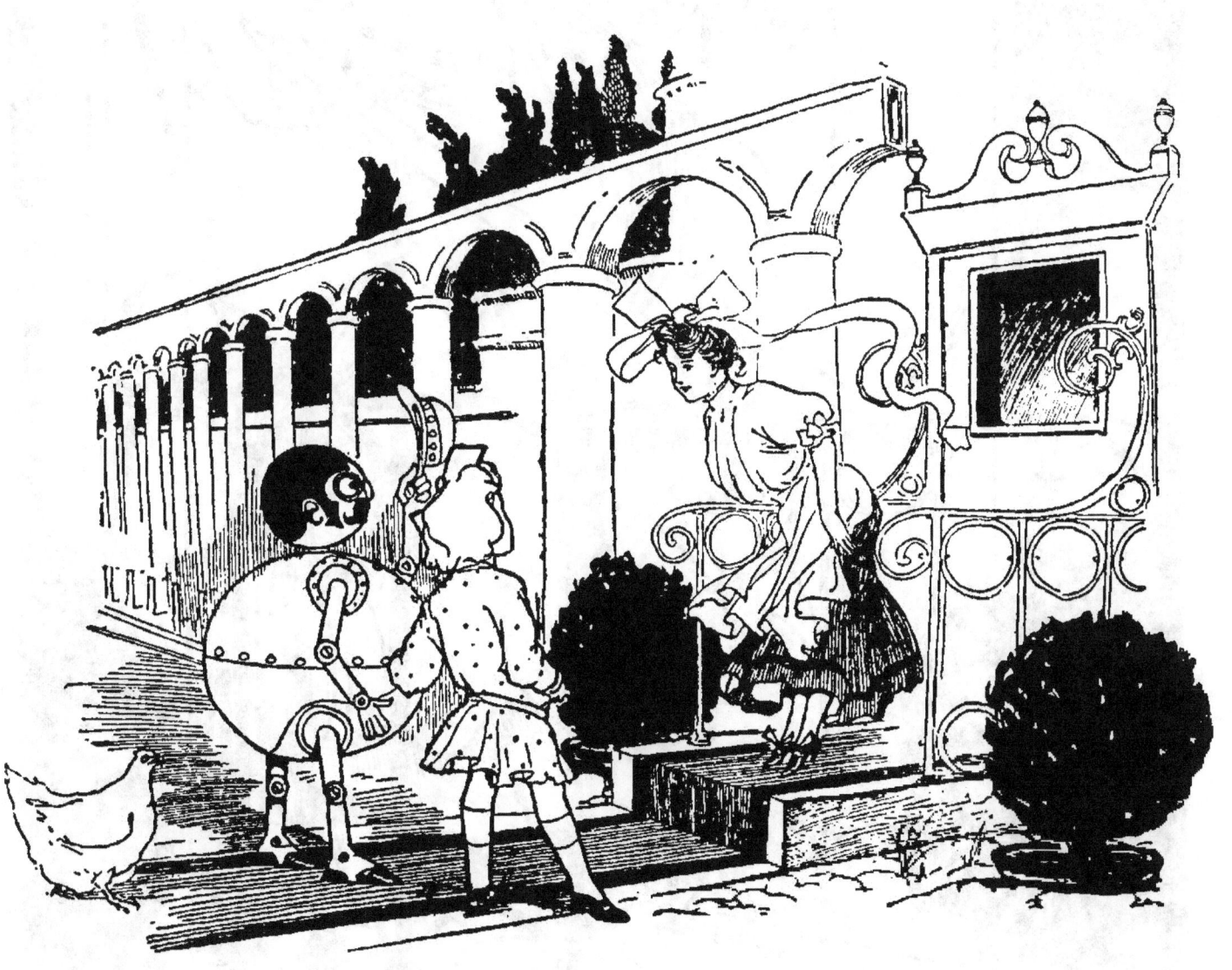

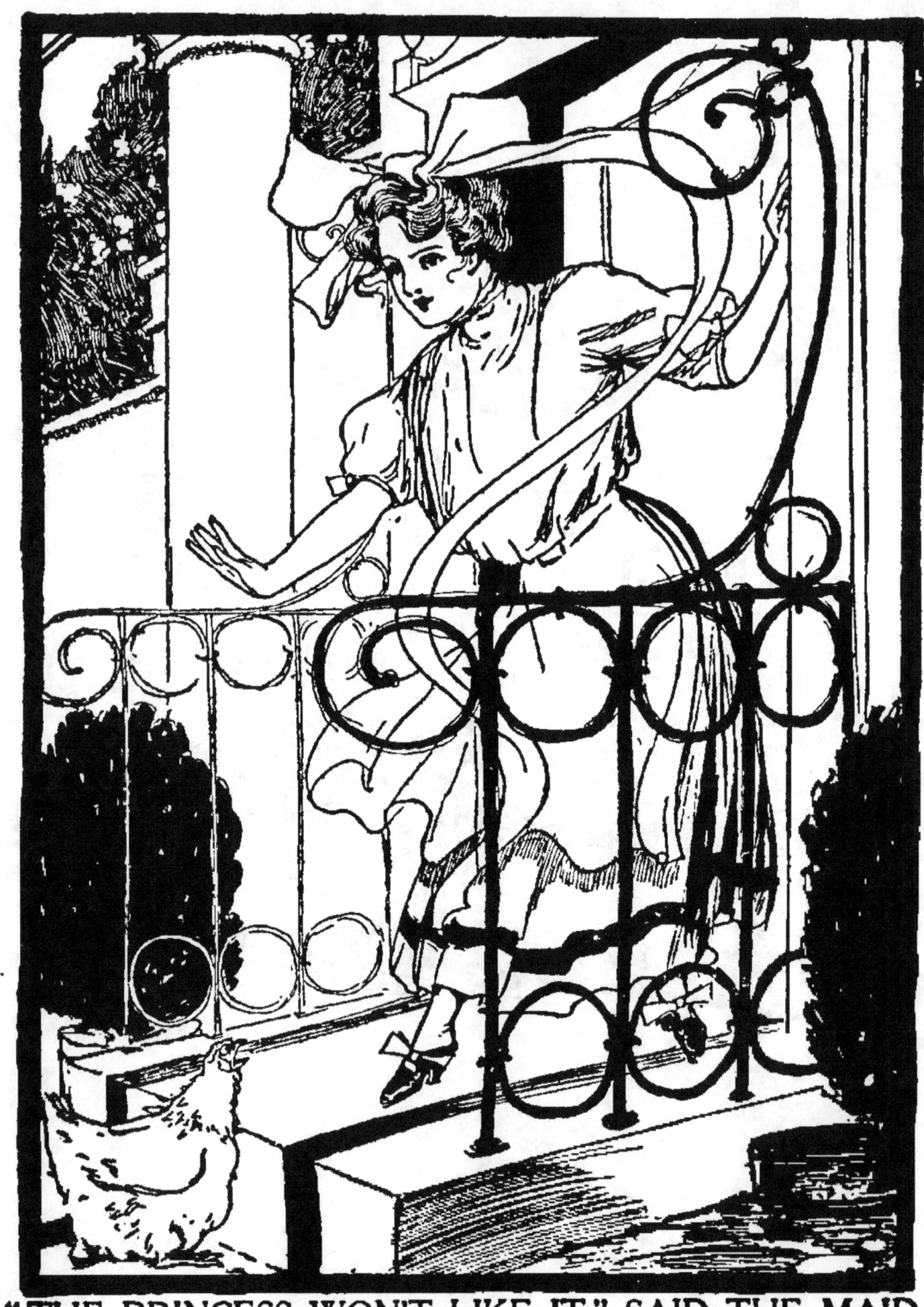

"THE PRINCESS WON'T LIKE IT," SAID THE MAID

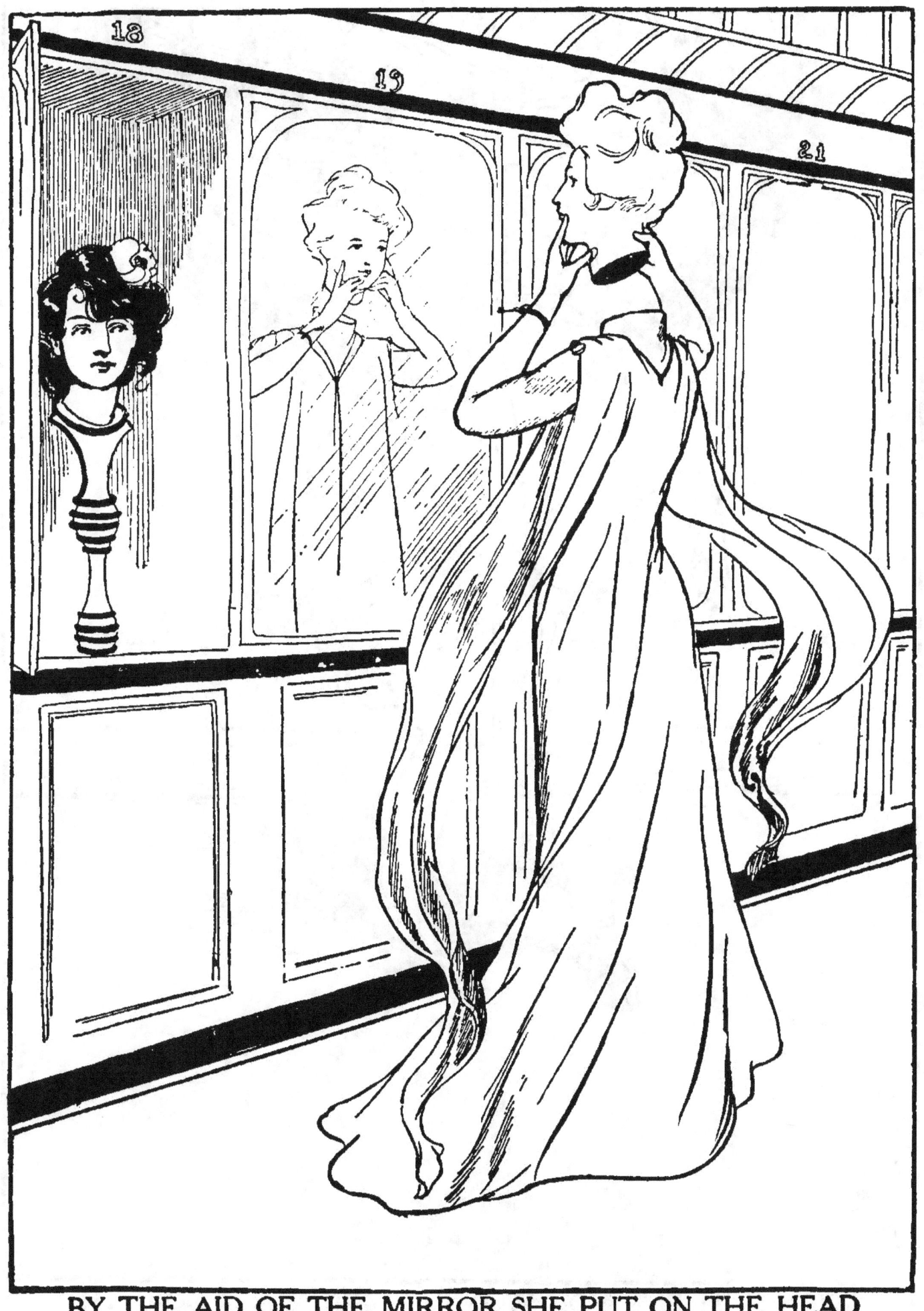

BY THE AID OF THE MIRROR SHE PUT ON THE HEAD

"WELL I B'LIEVE YOU WON'T!" EXCLAIMED DOROTHY

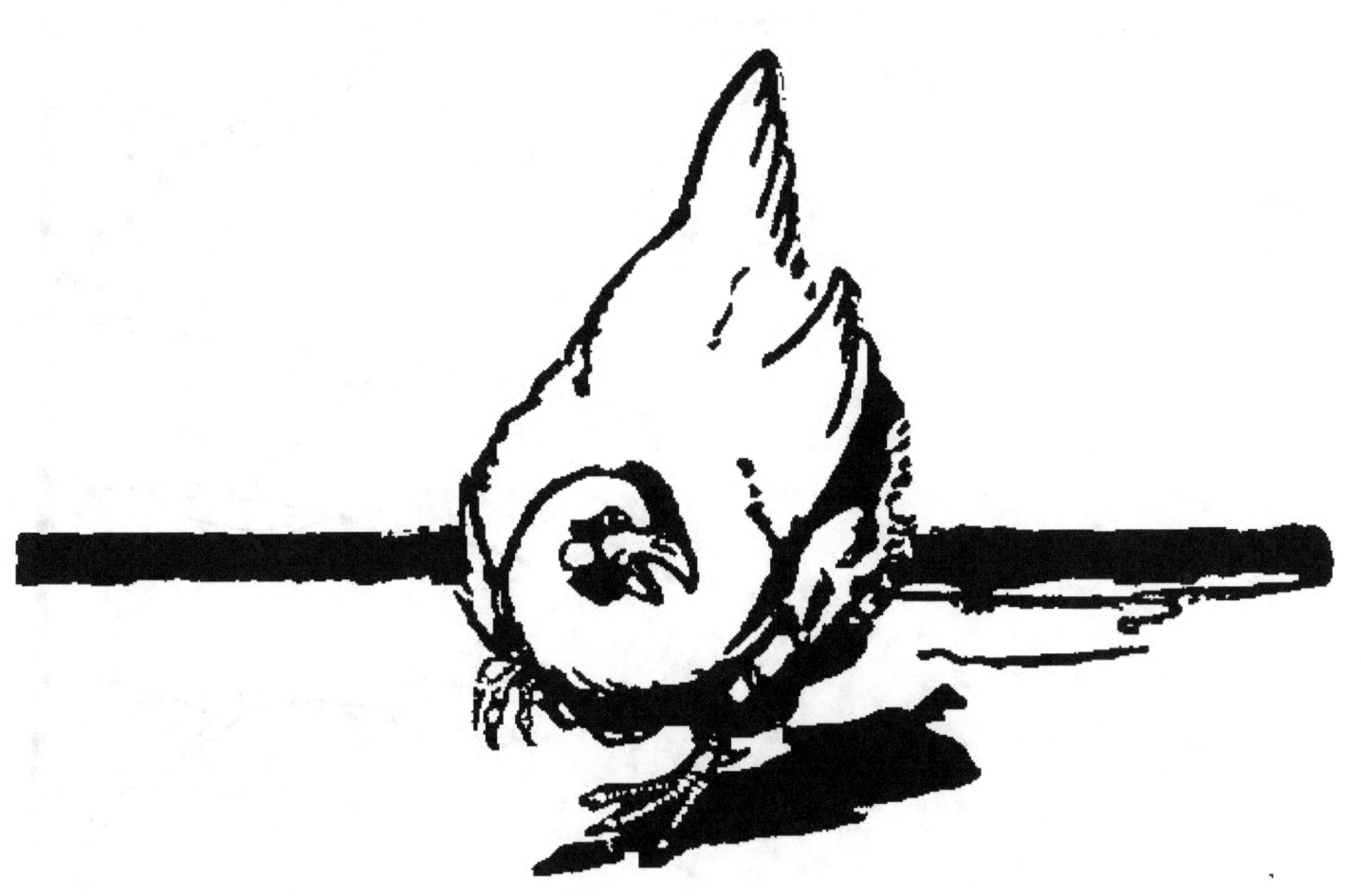

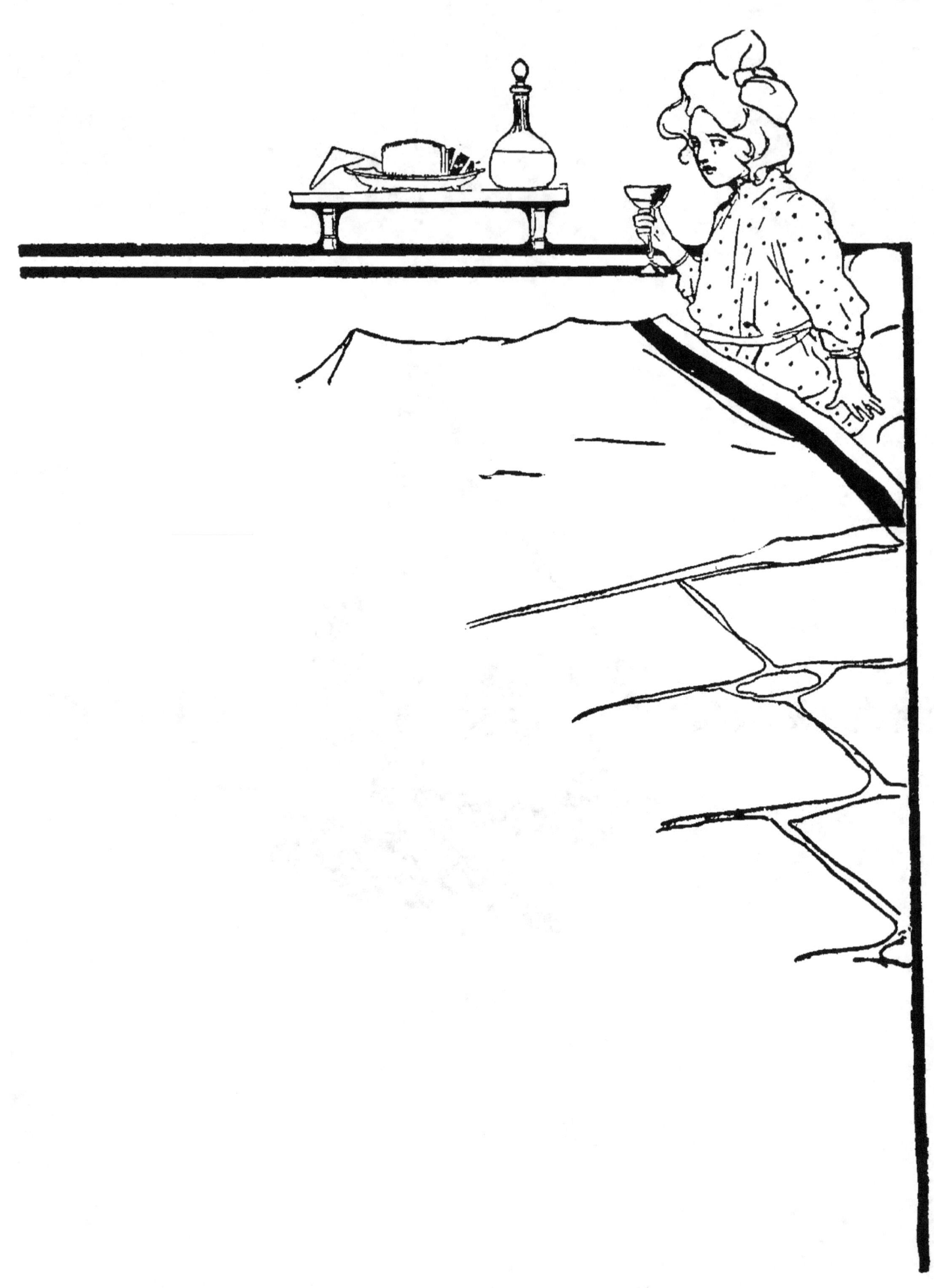

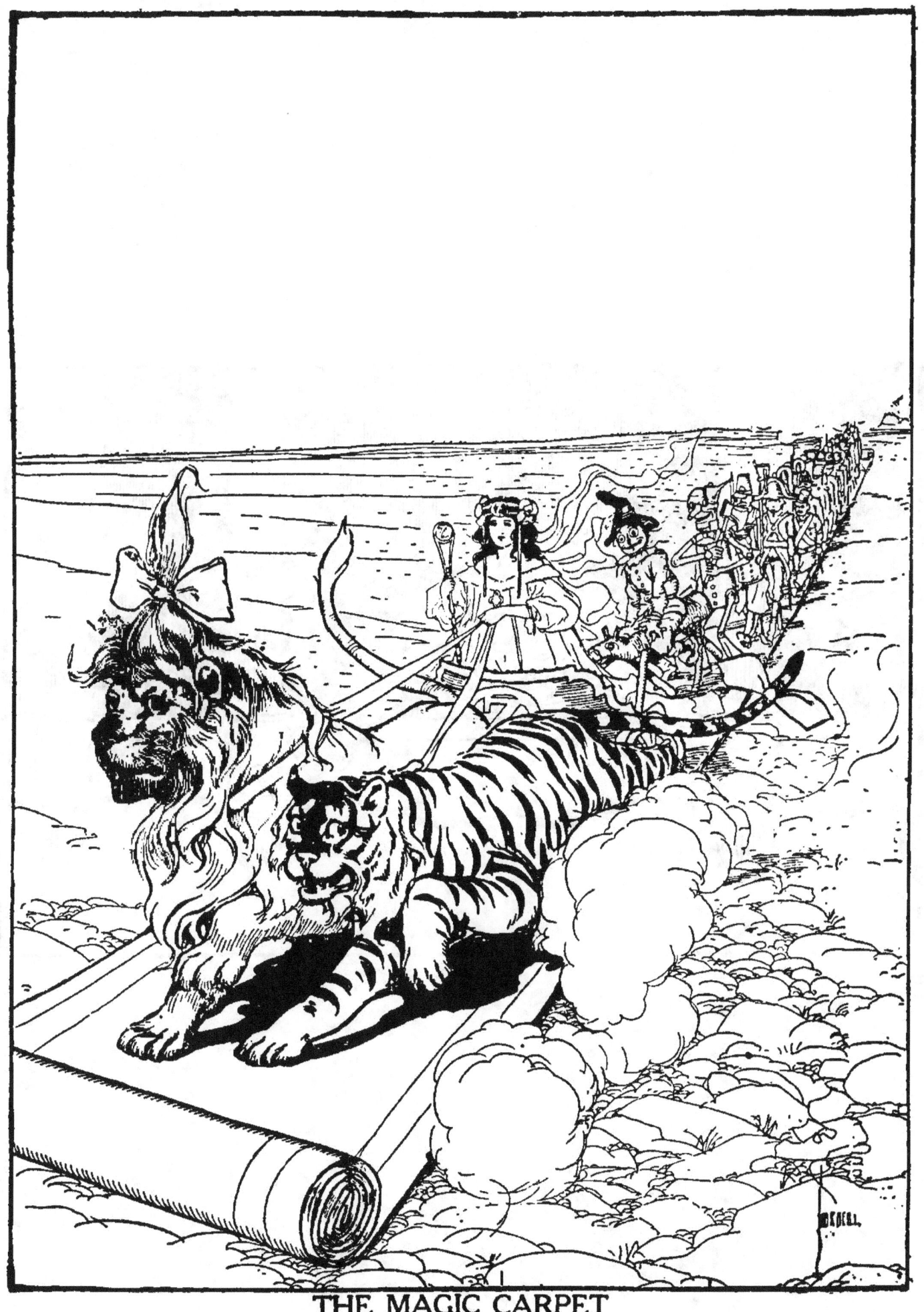

THE MAGIC CARPET

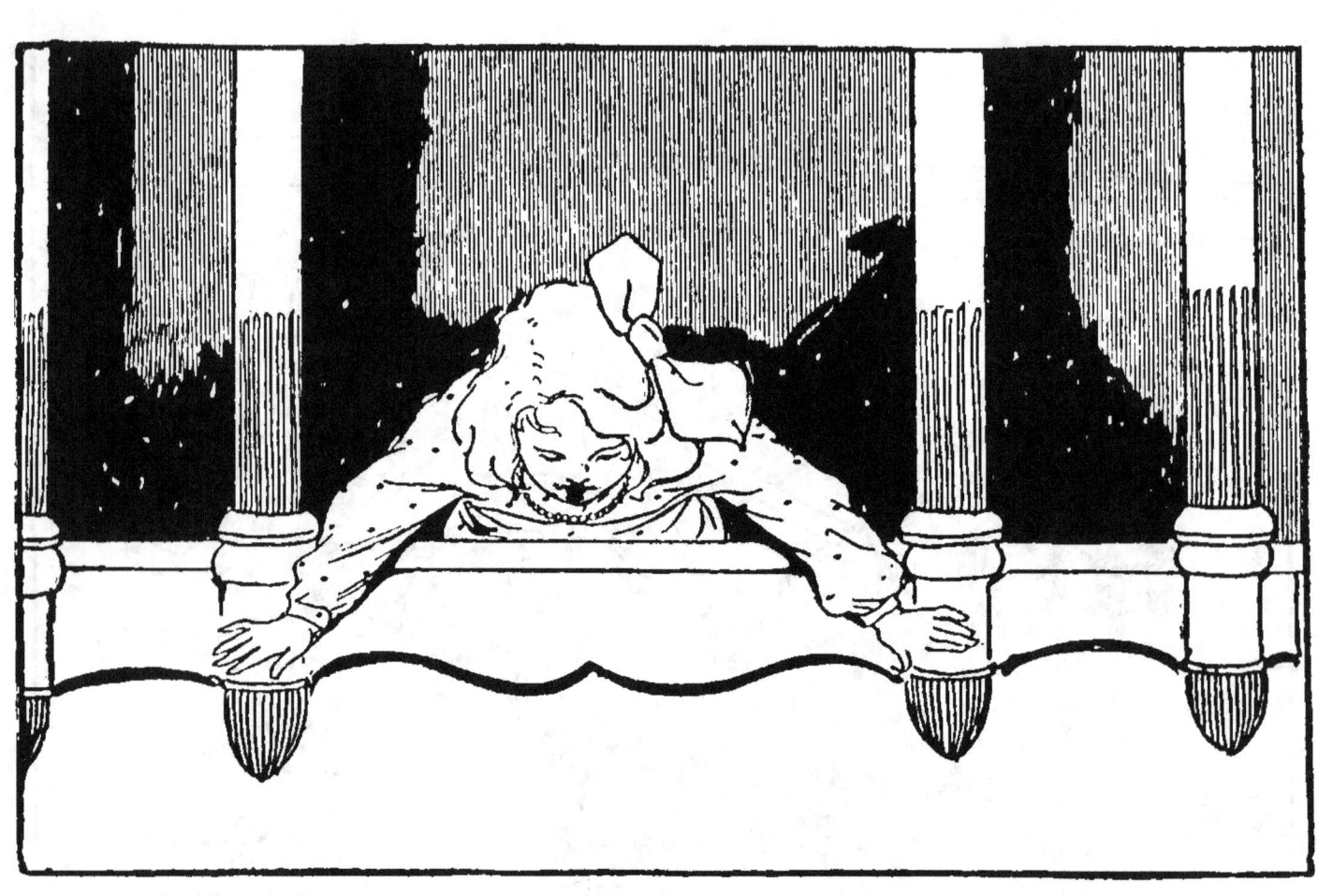

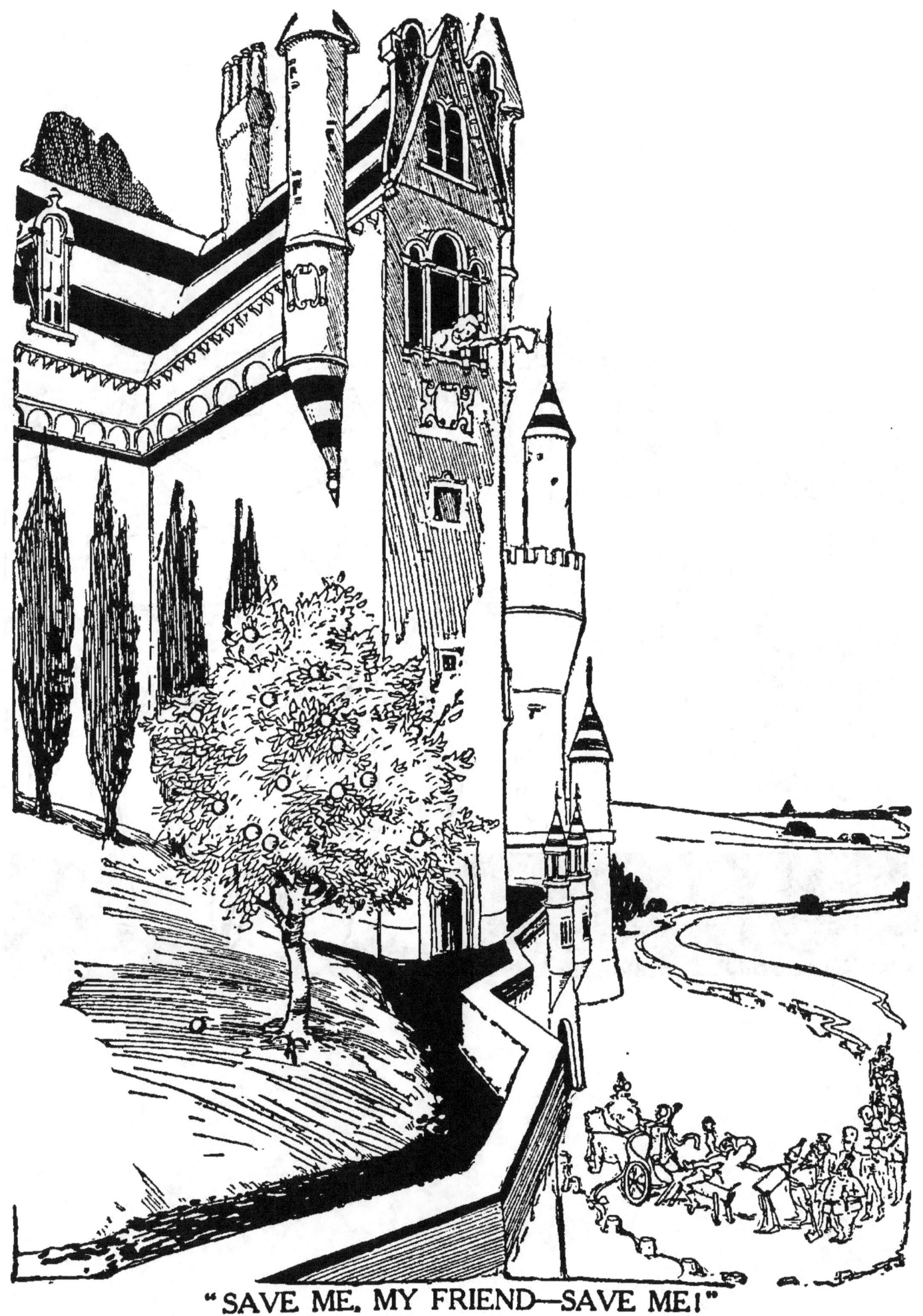

"SAVE ME, MY FRIEND—SAVE ME!"

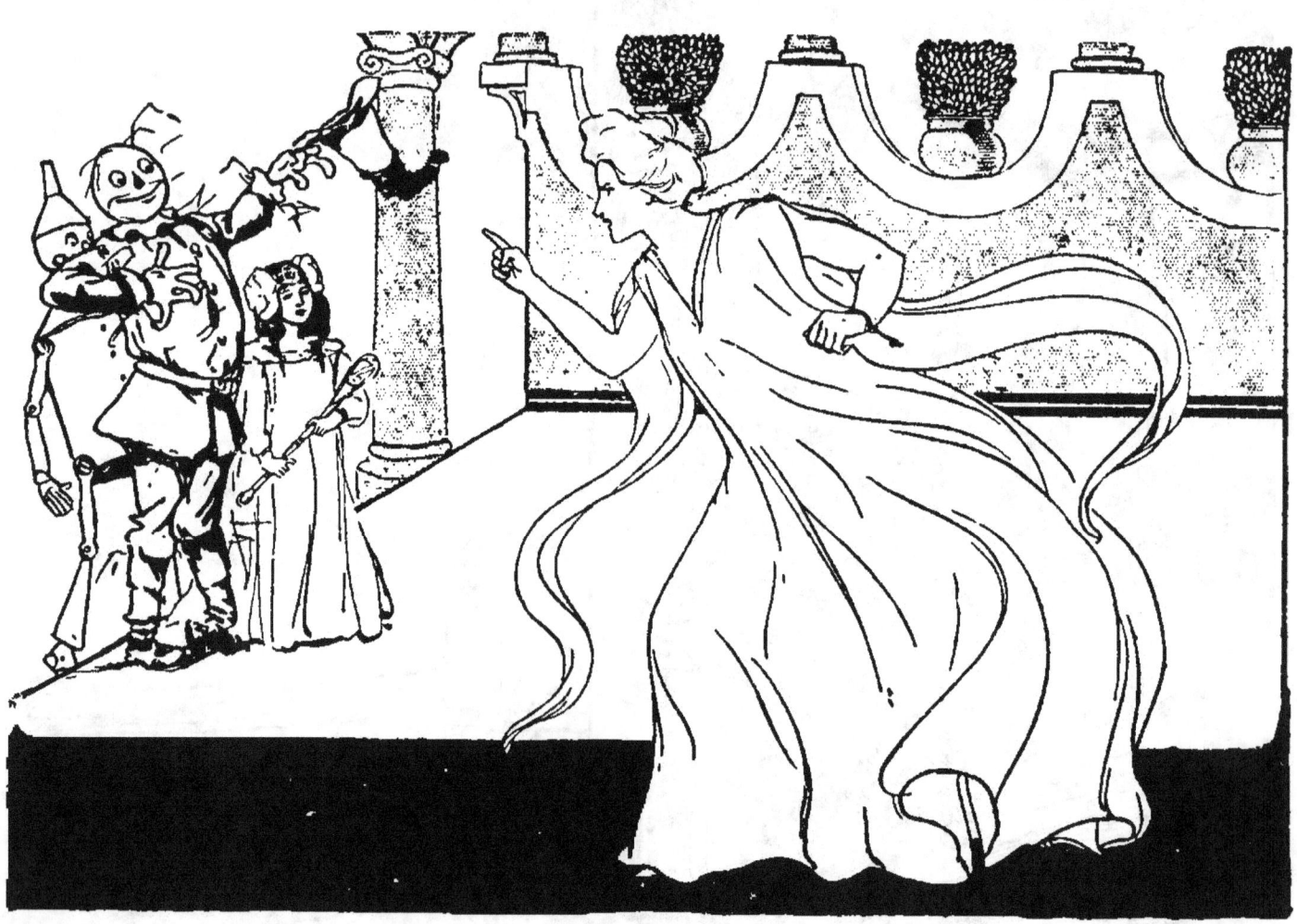

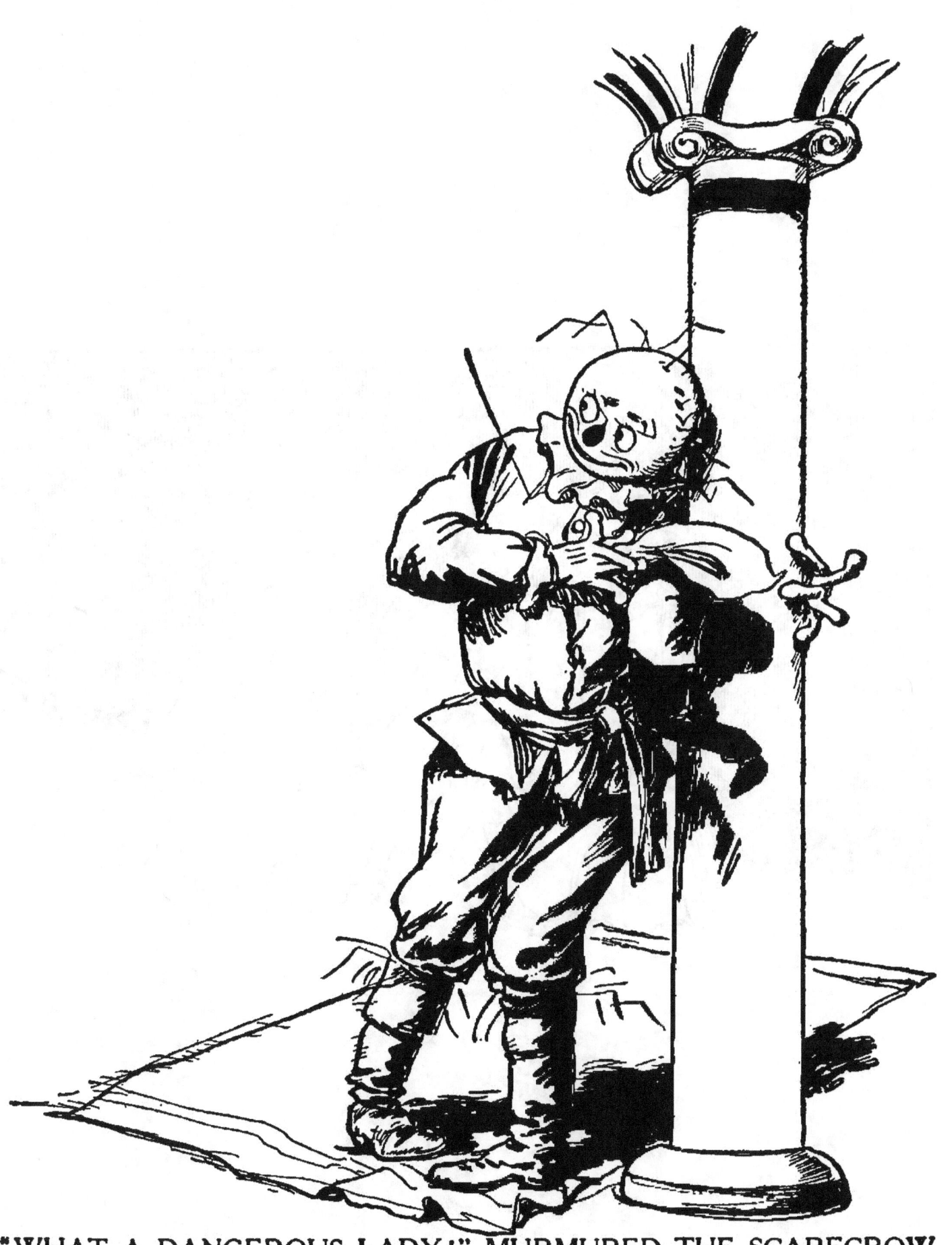

"WHAT A DANGEROUS LADY!" MURMURED THE SCARECROW

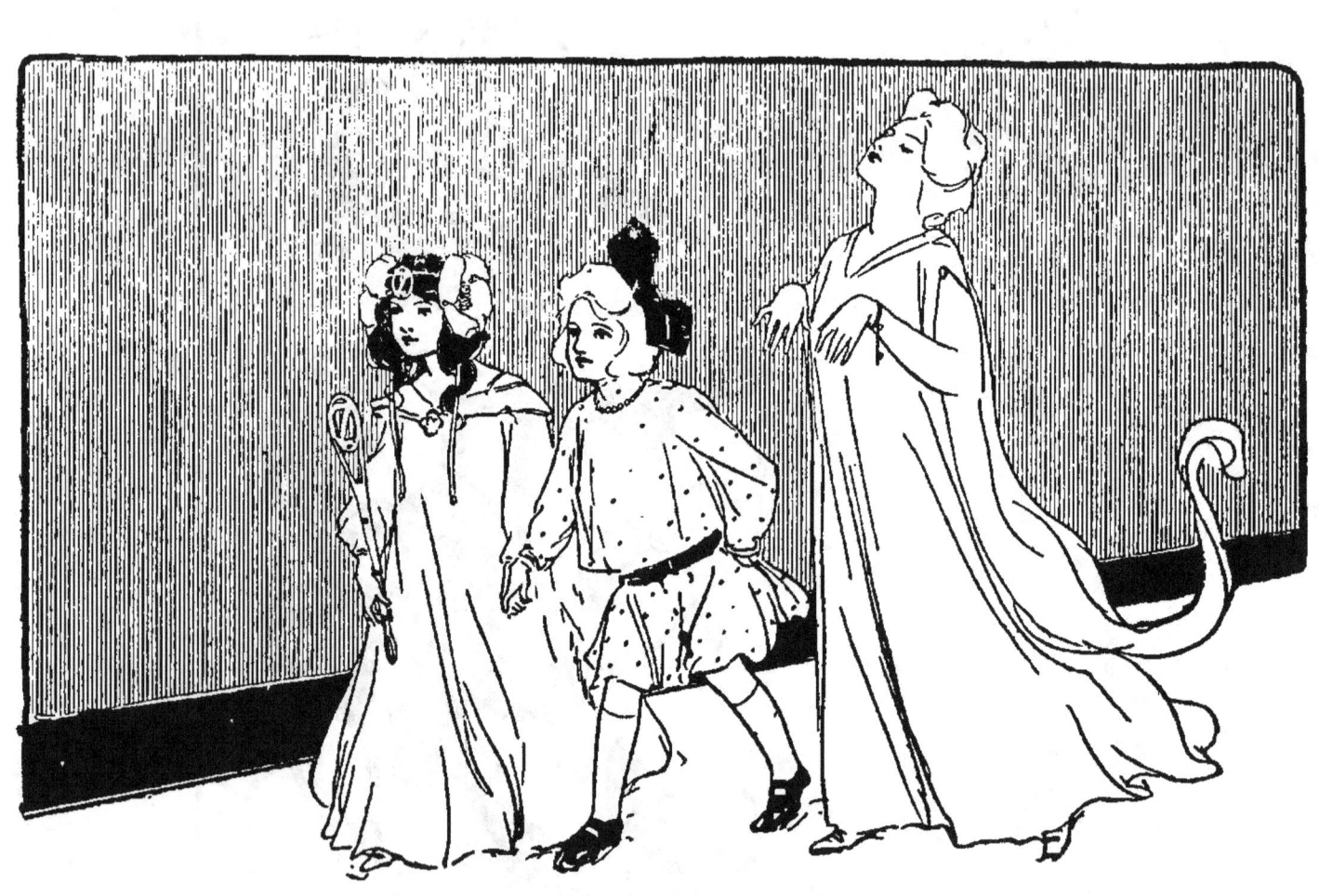

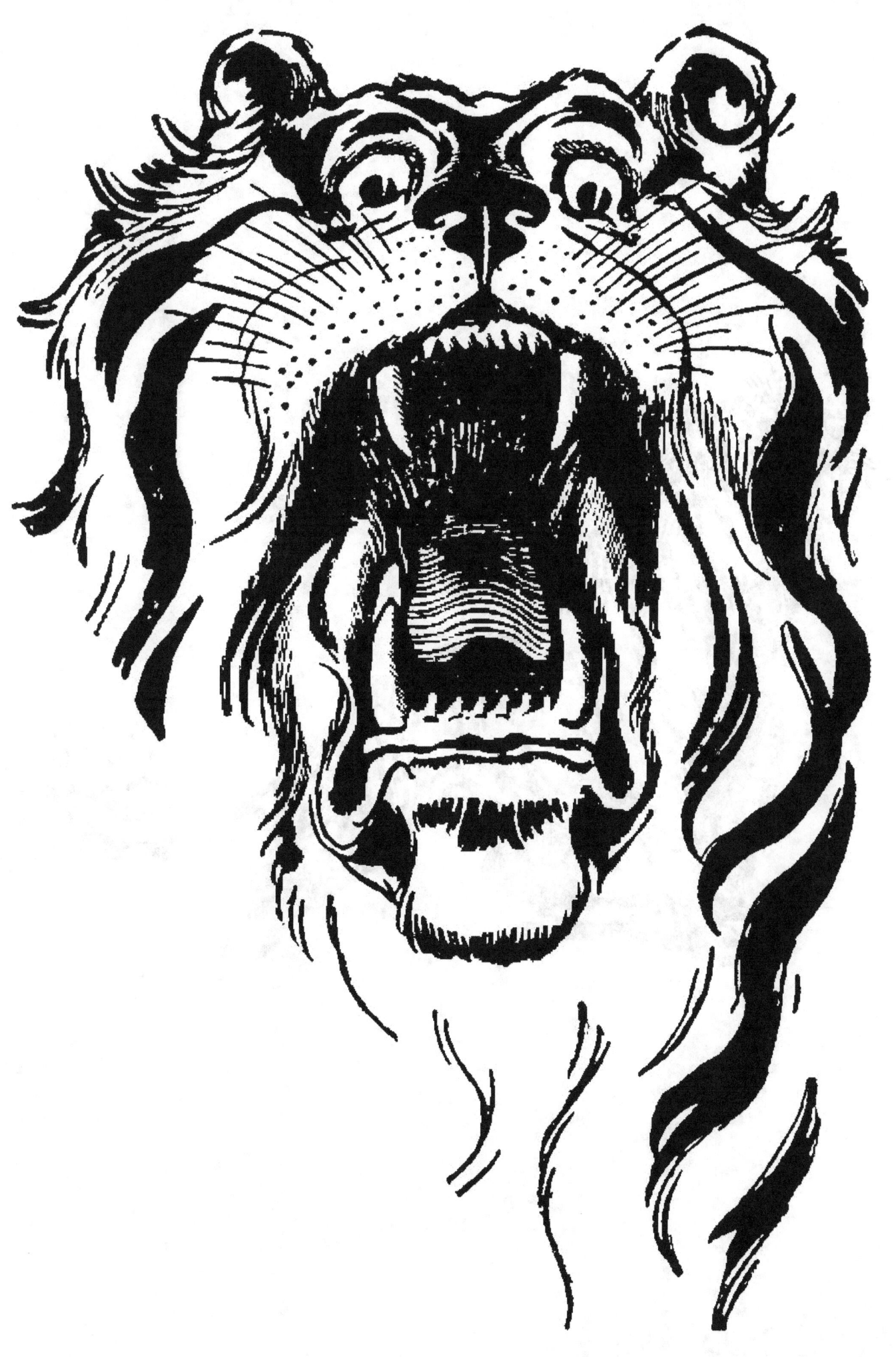

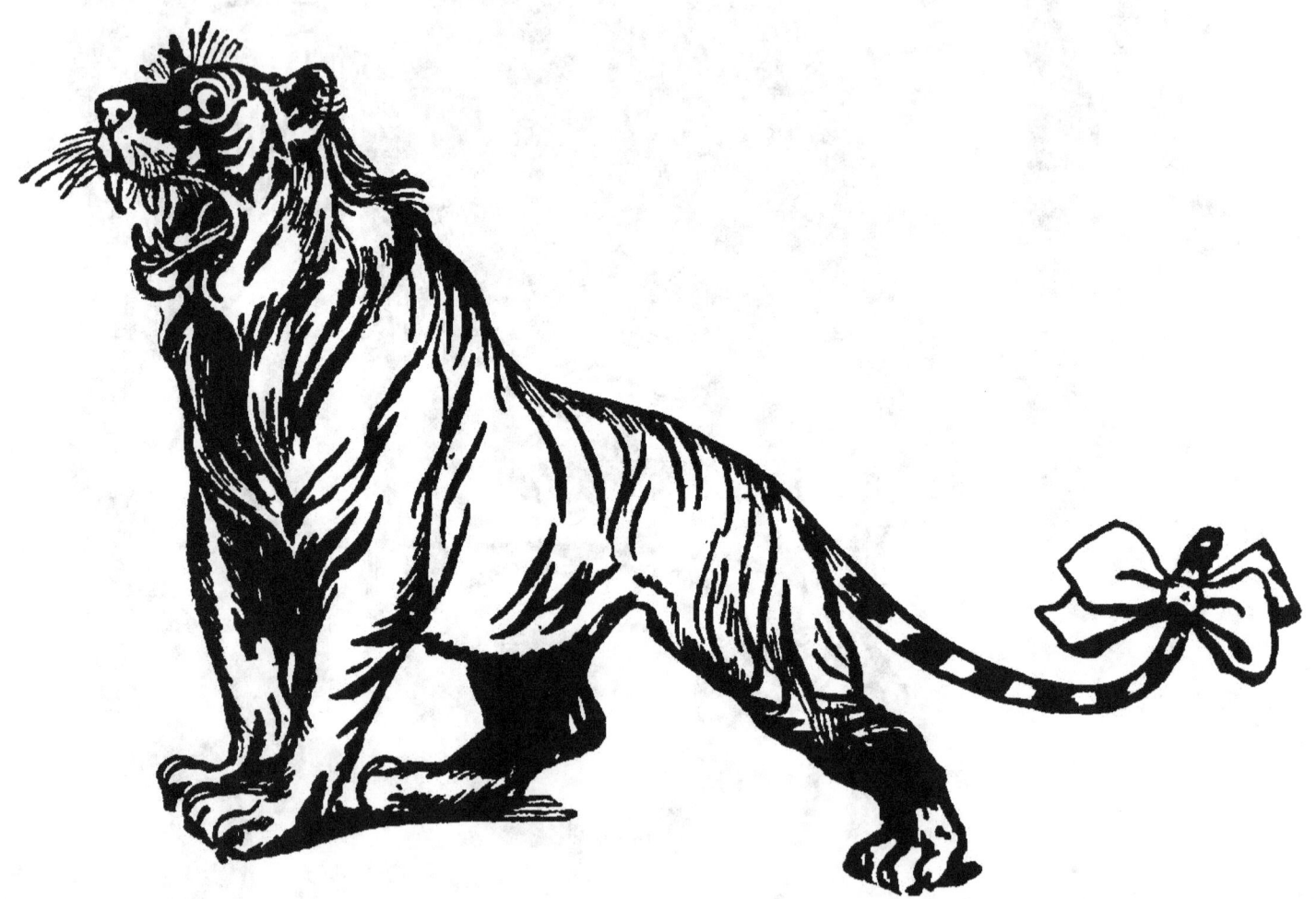

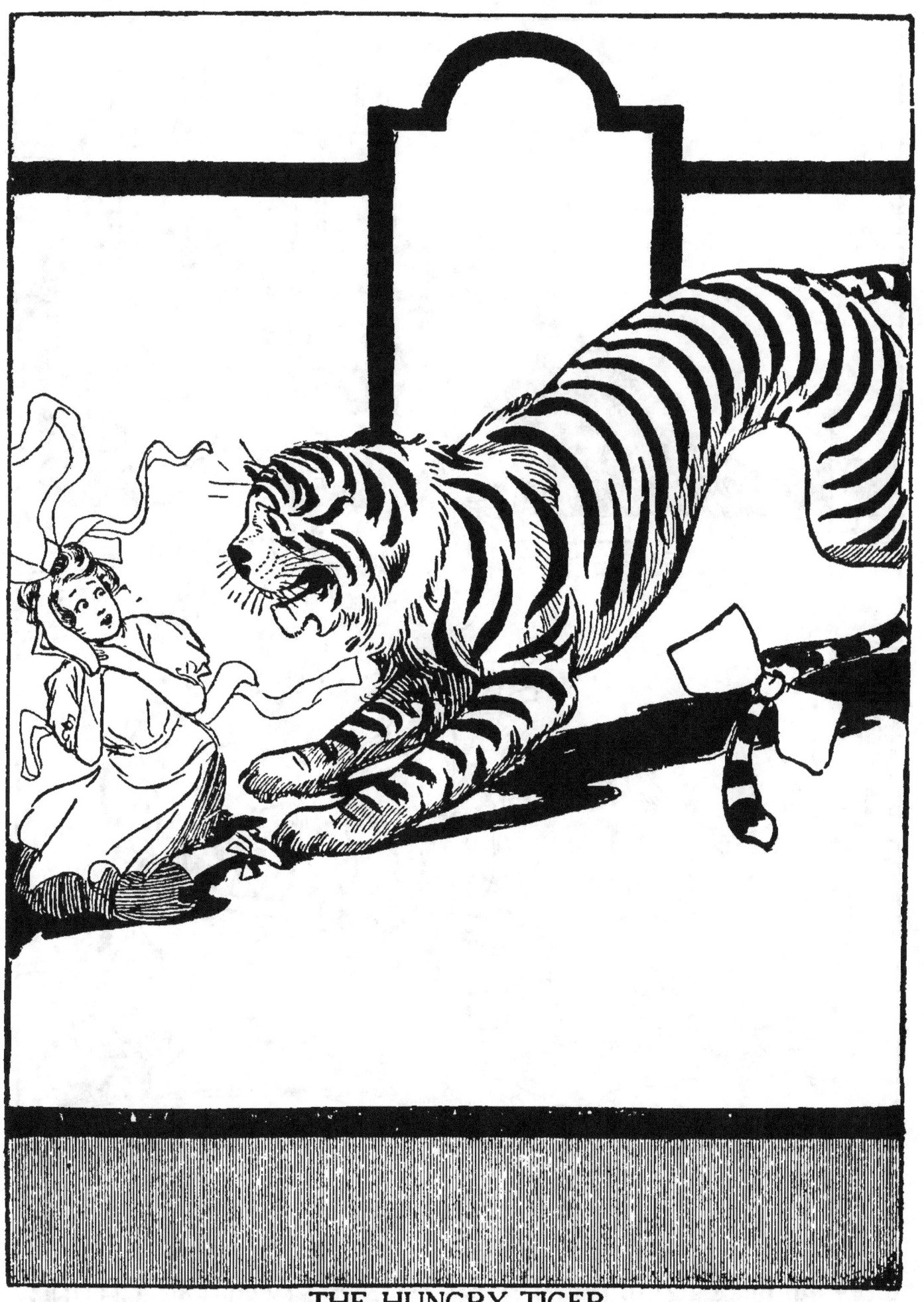

THE HUNGRY TIGER

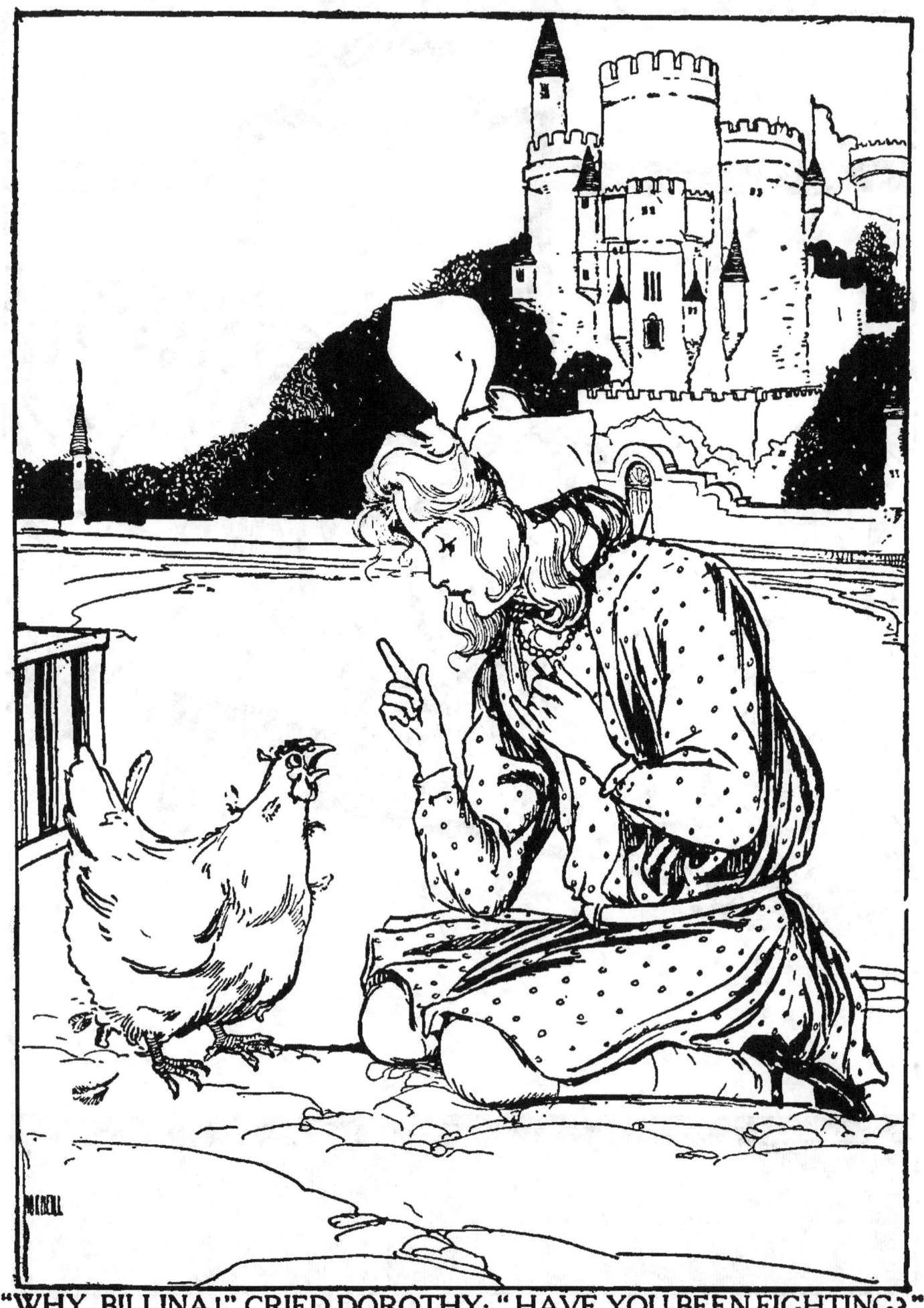

"WHY, BILLINA!" CRIED DOROTHY; "HAVE YOU BEEN FIGHTING?"

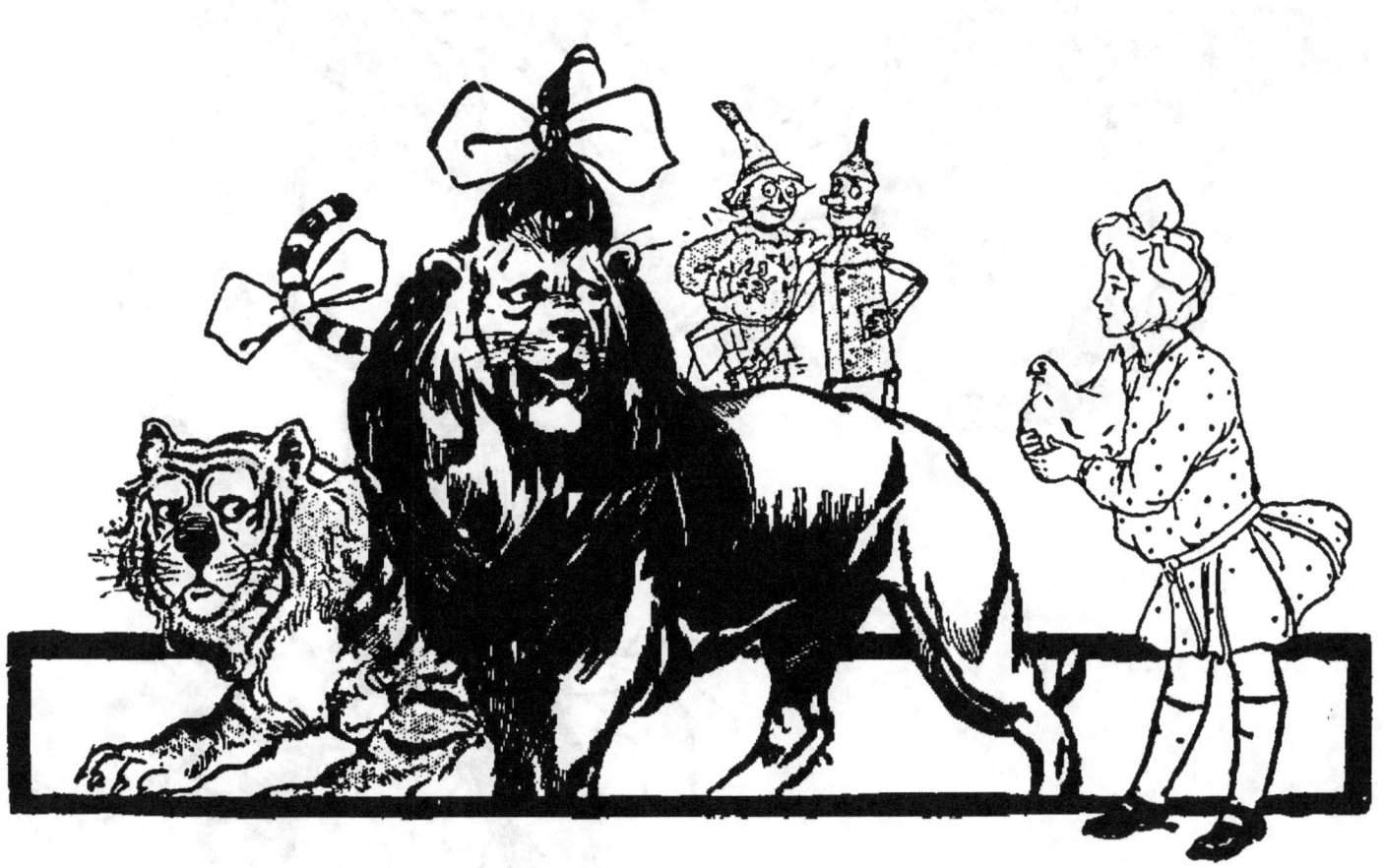

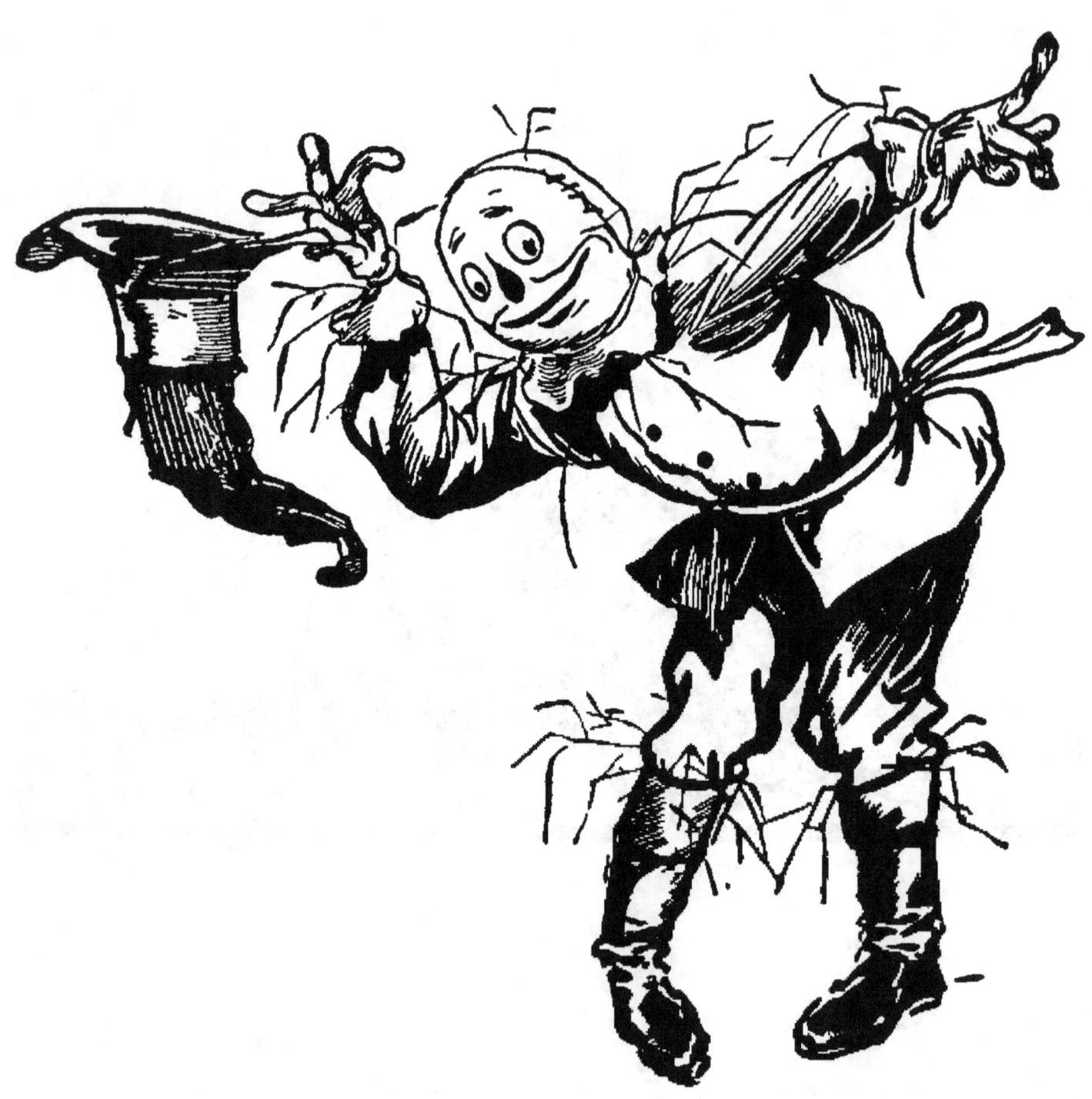

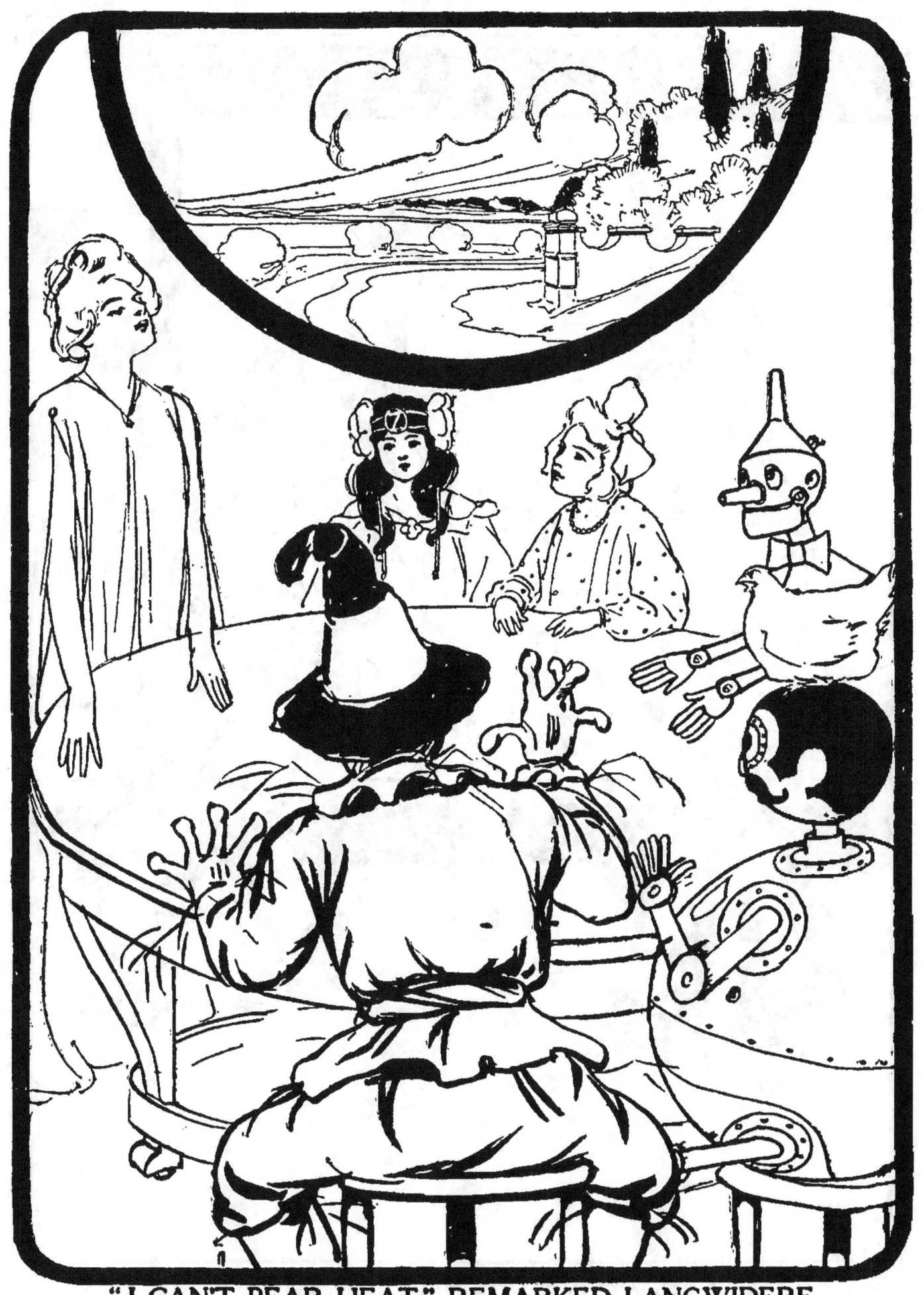

"I CAN'T BEAR HEAT," REMARKED LANGWIDERE

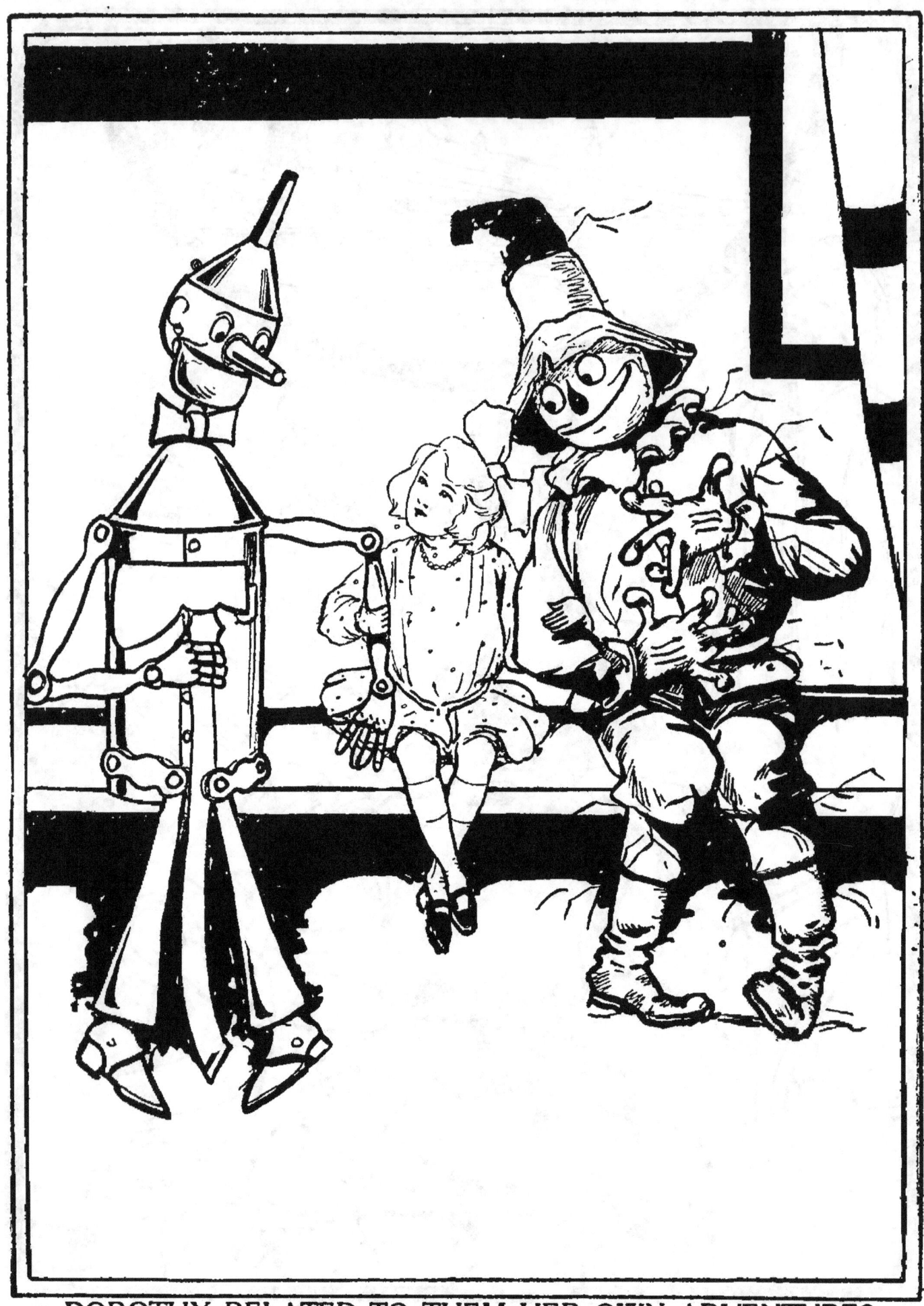

DOROTHY RELATED TO THEM HER OWN ADVENTURES

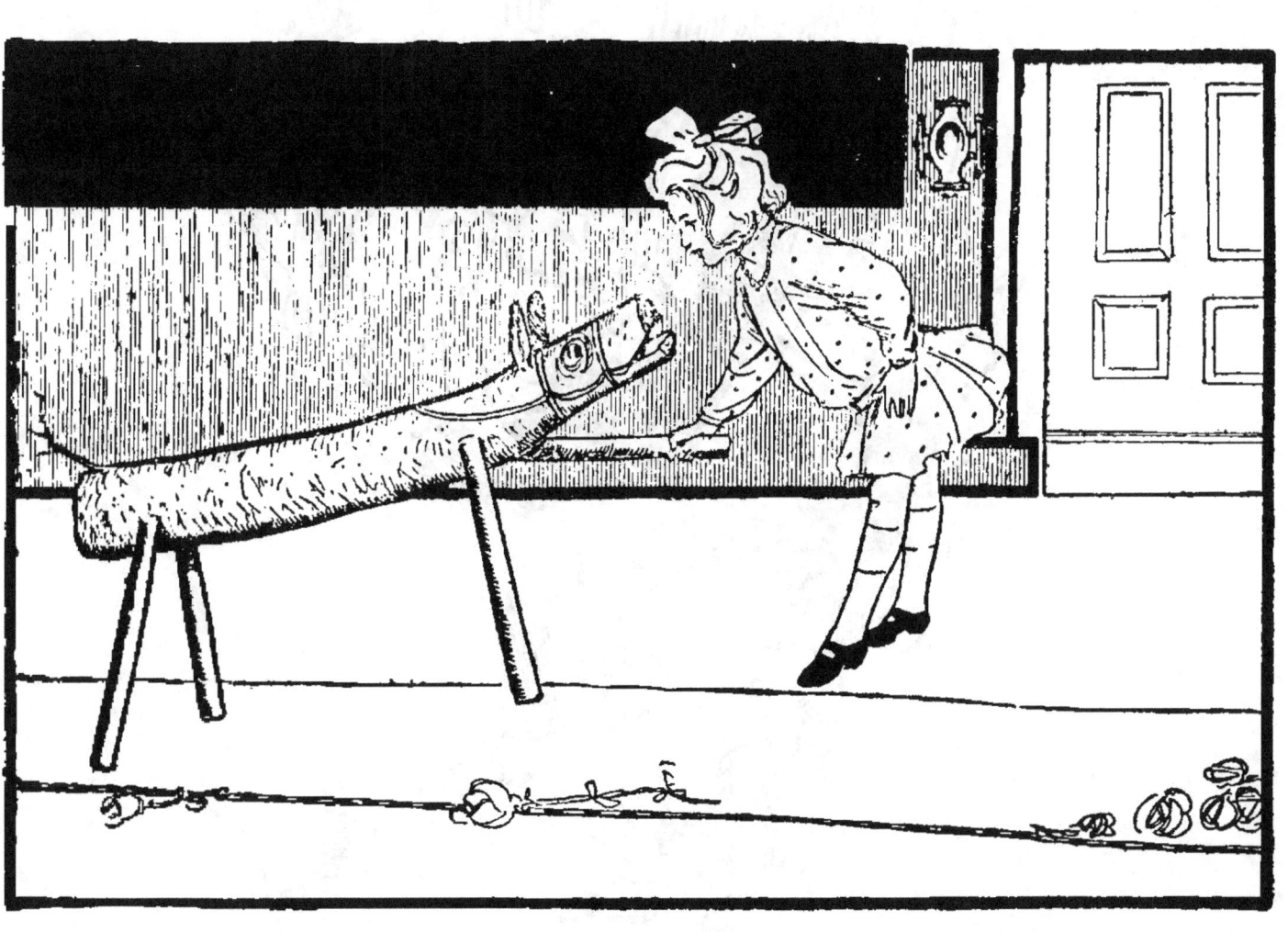

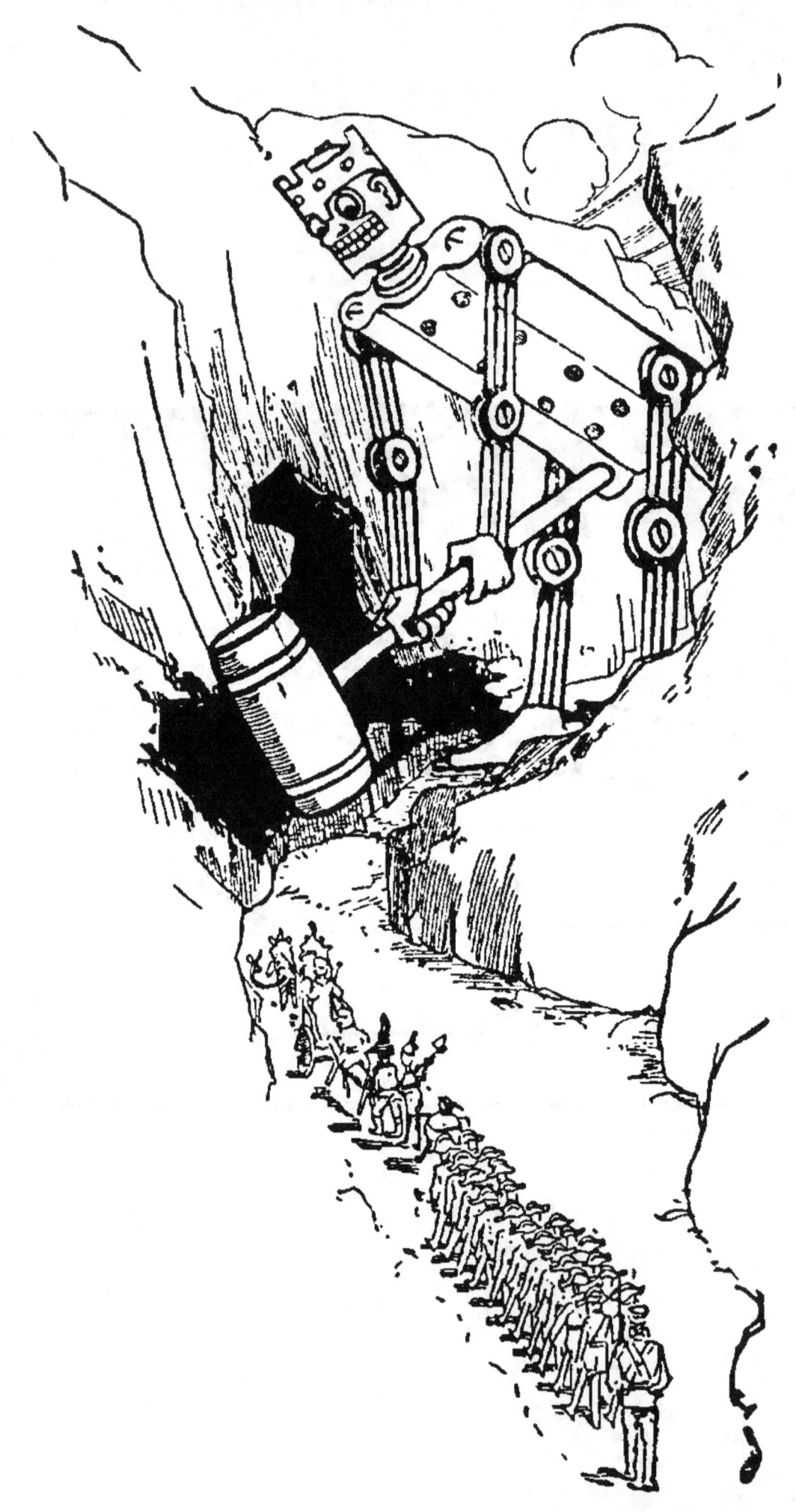

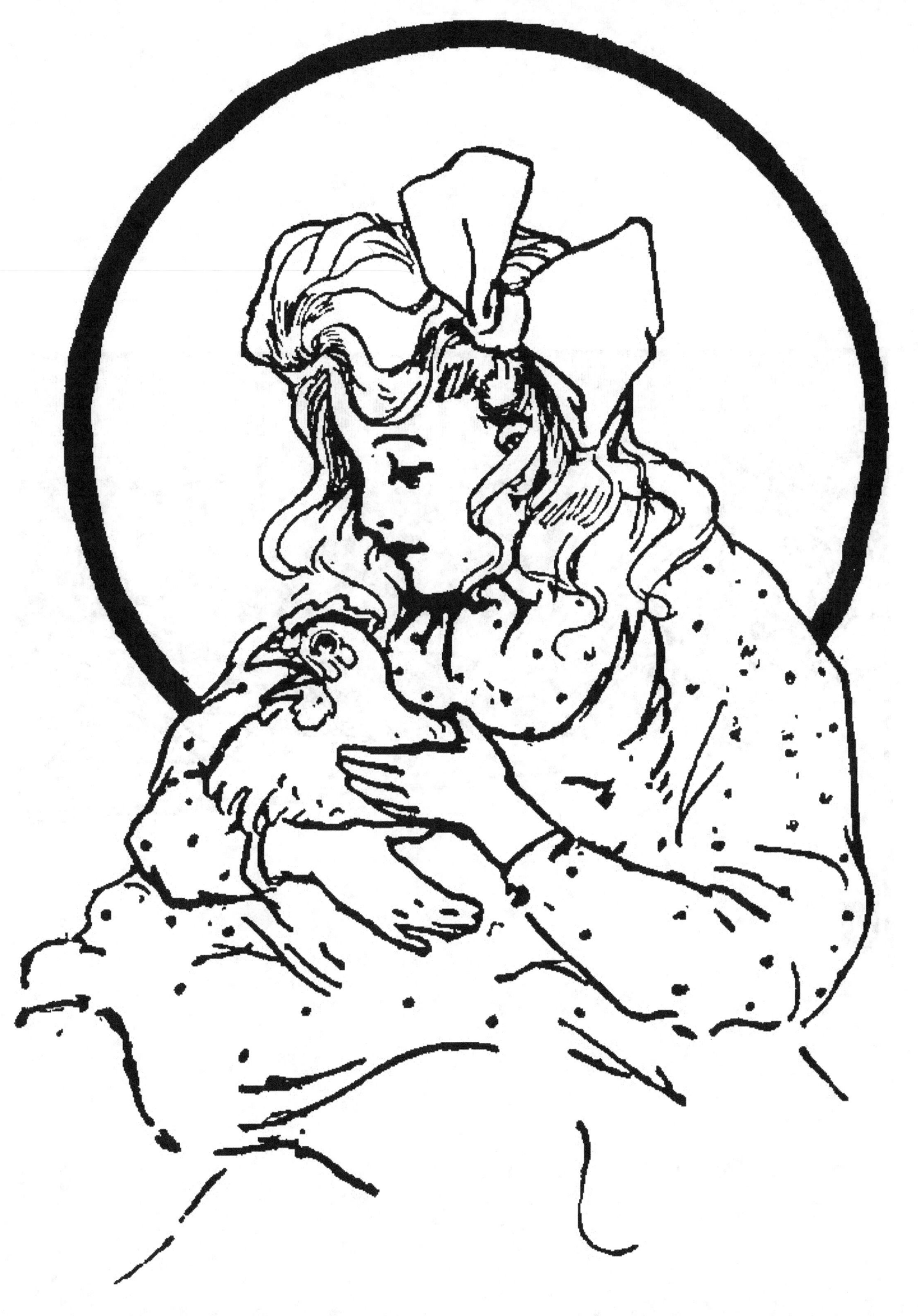

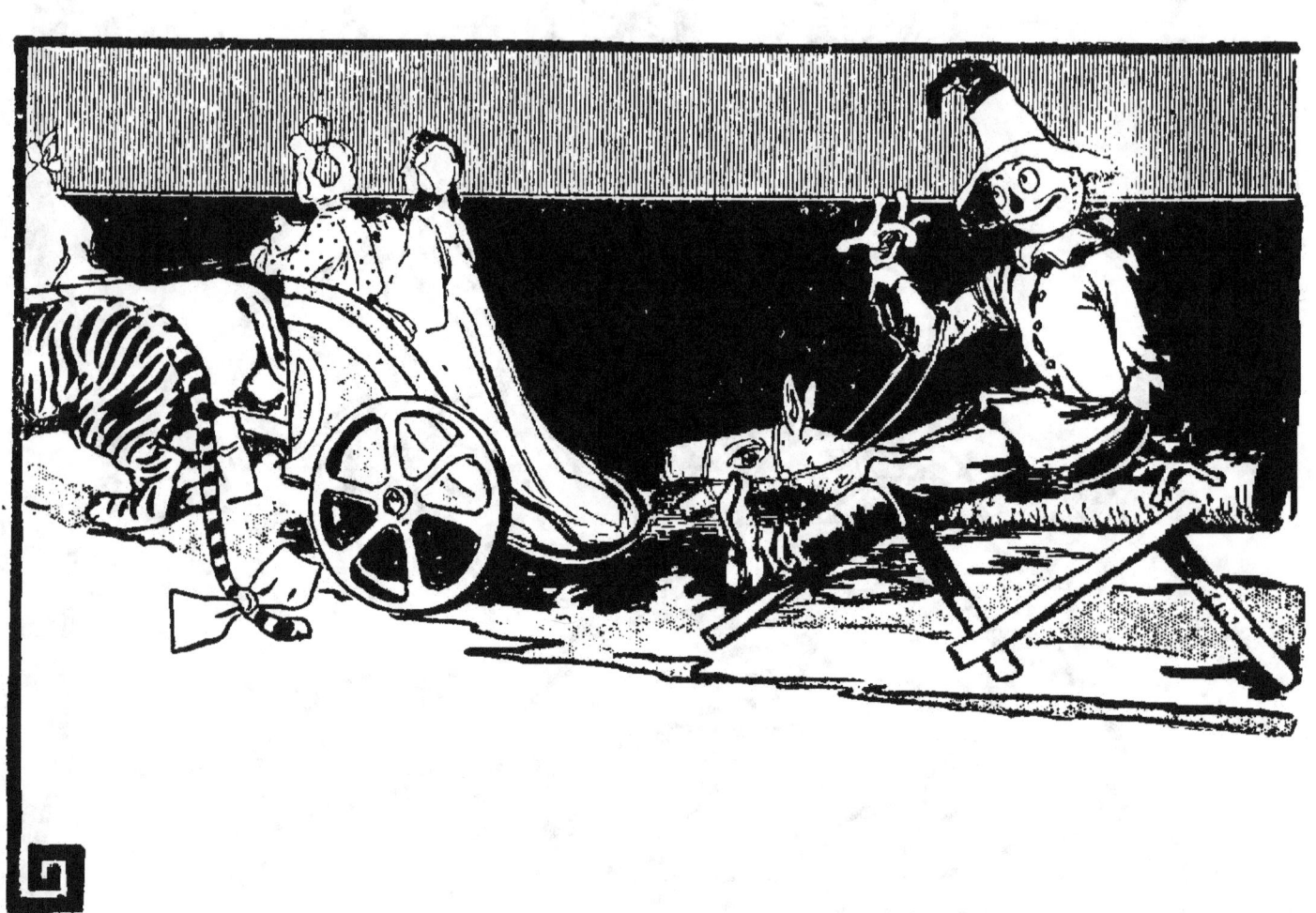

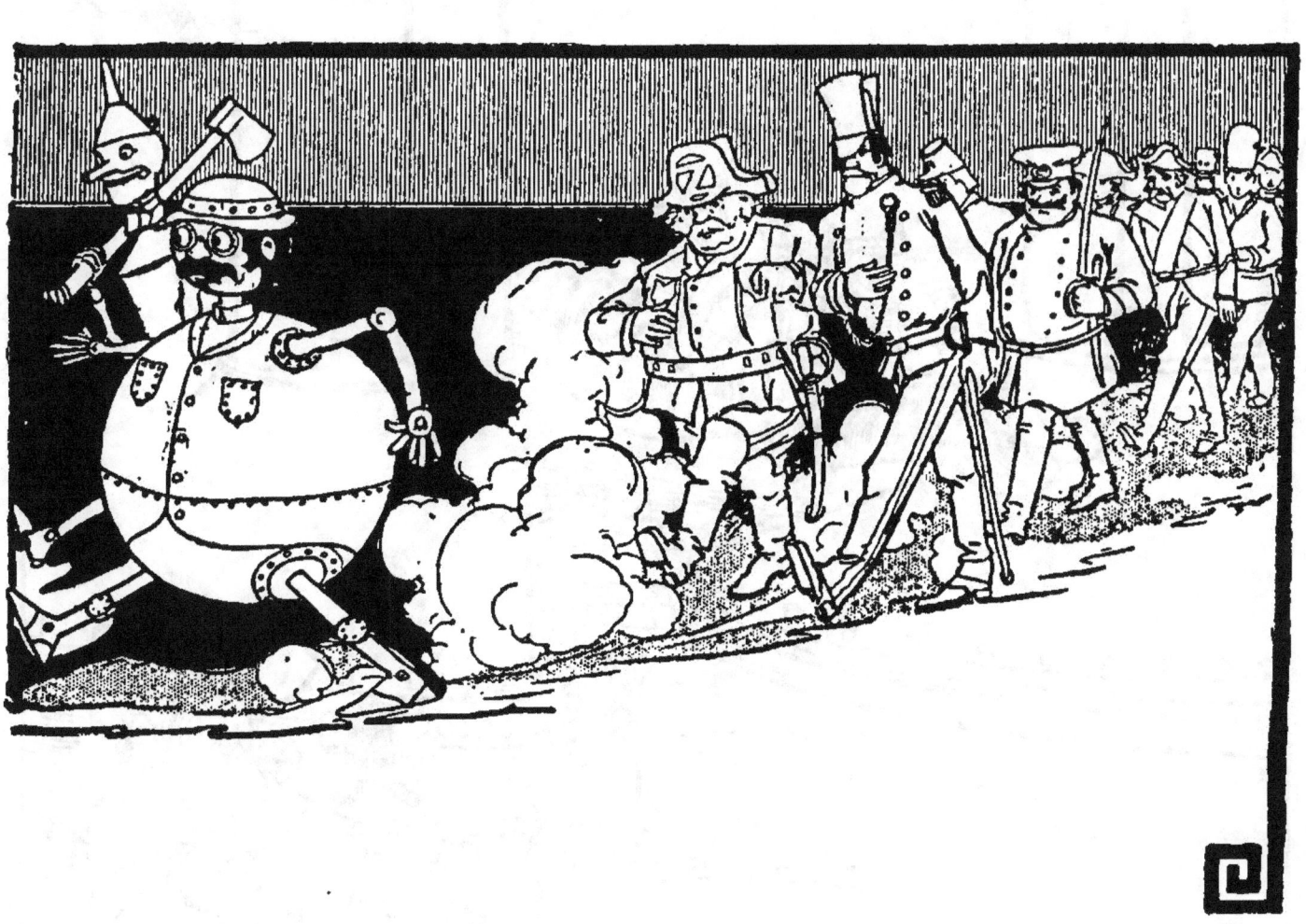

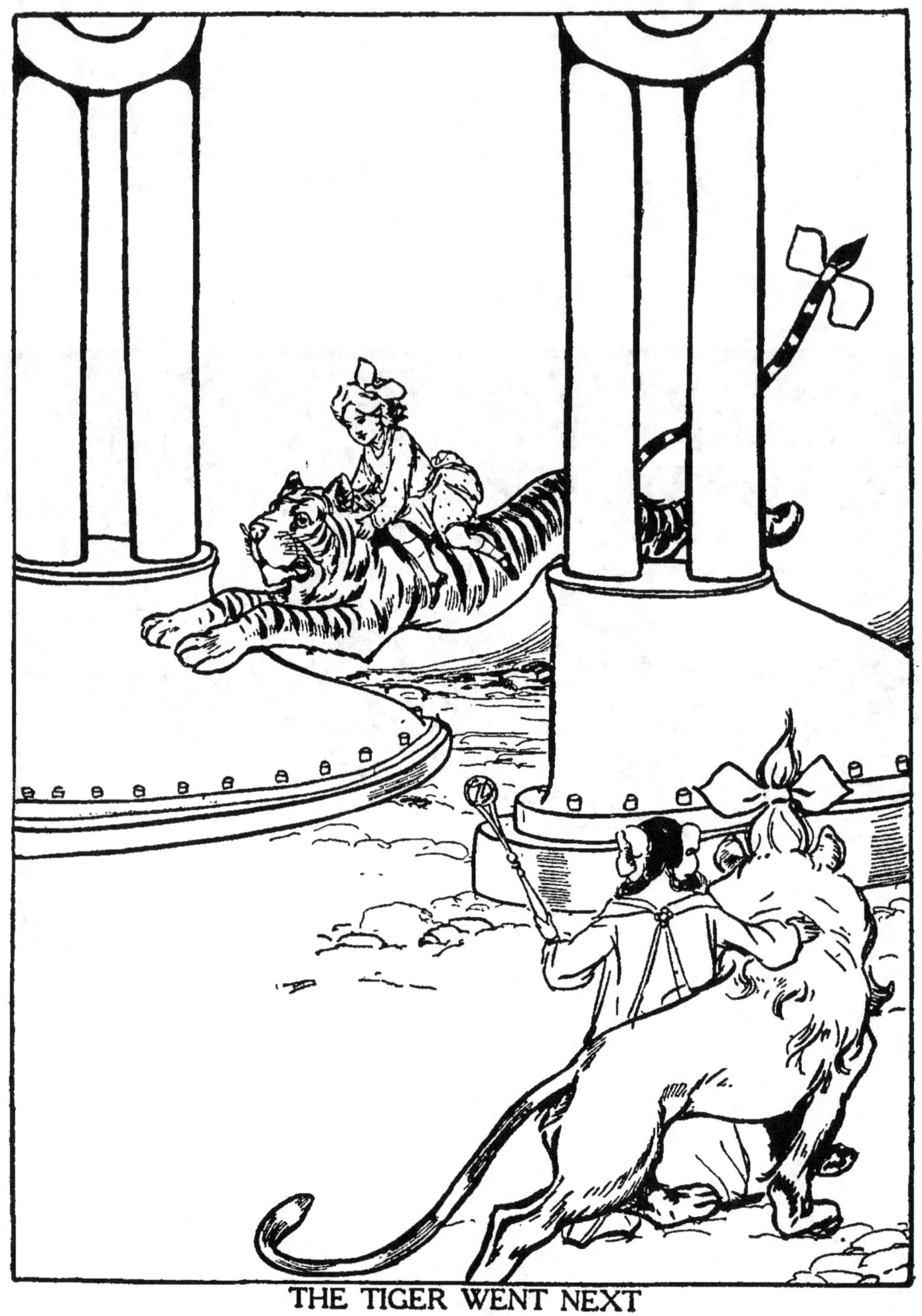

THE TIGER WENT NEXT

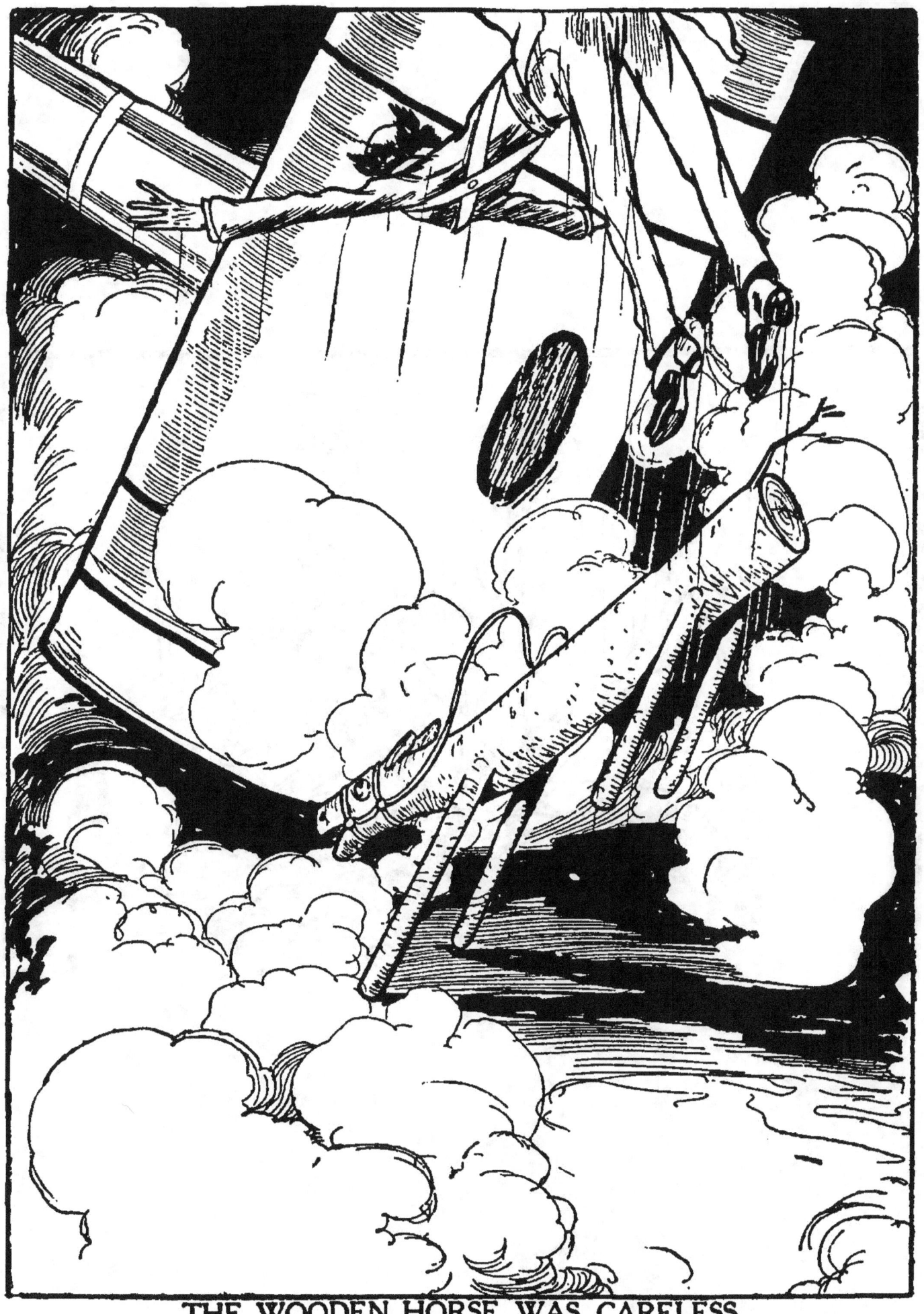

THE WOODEN HORSE WAS CARELESS

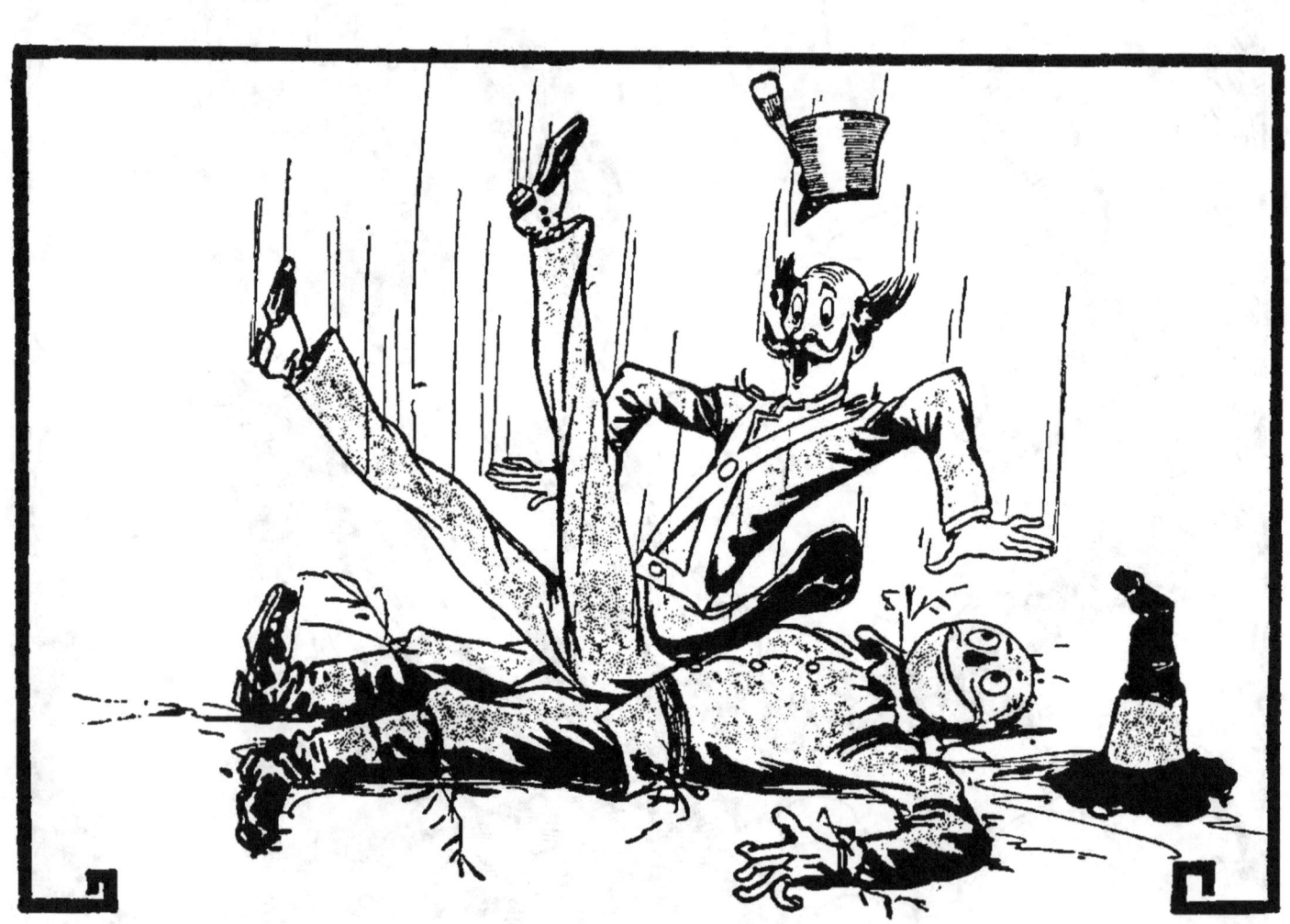

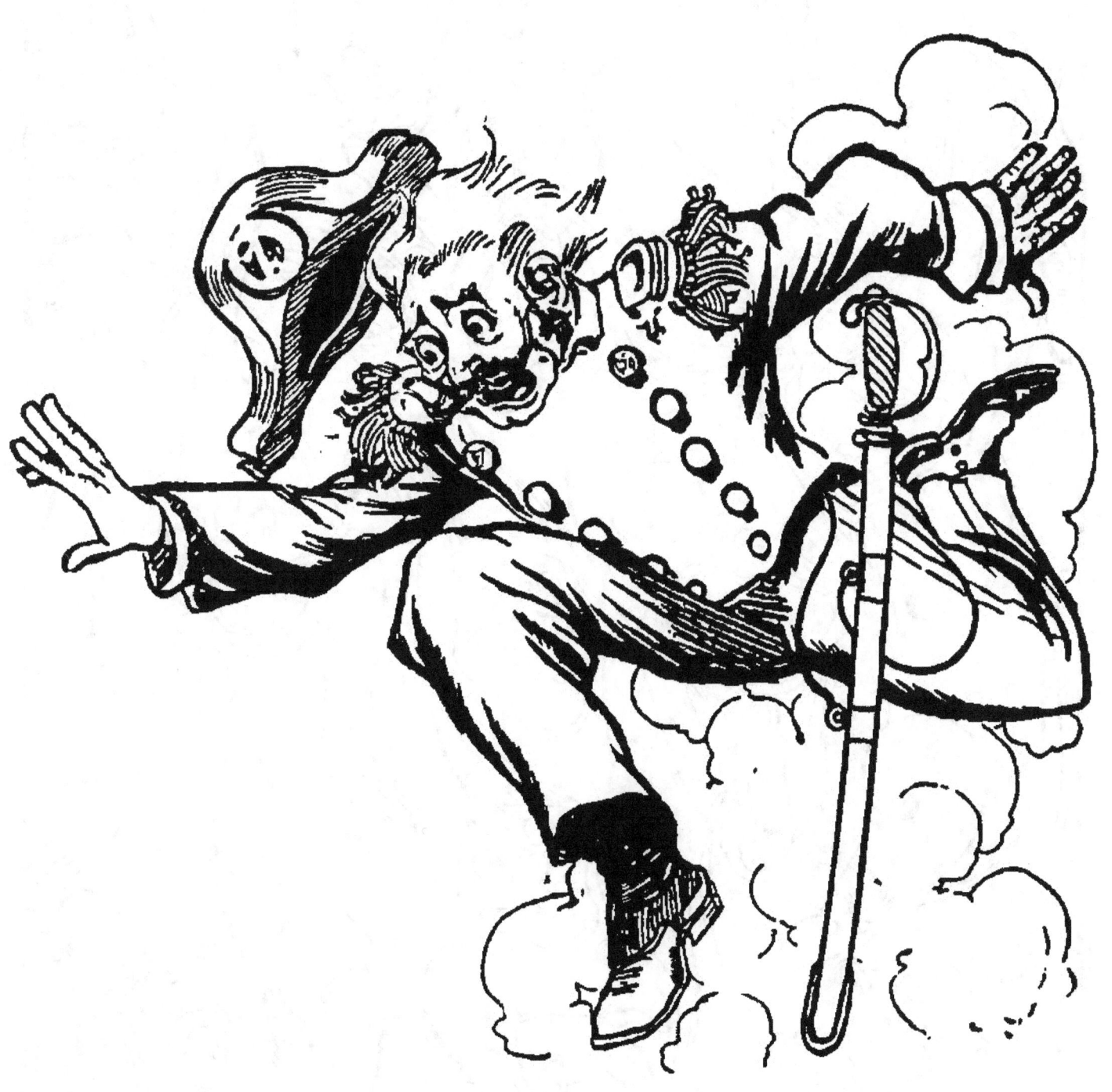

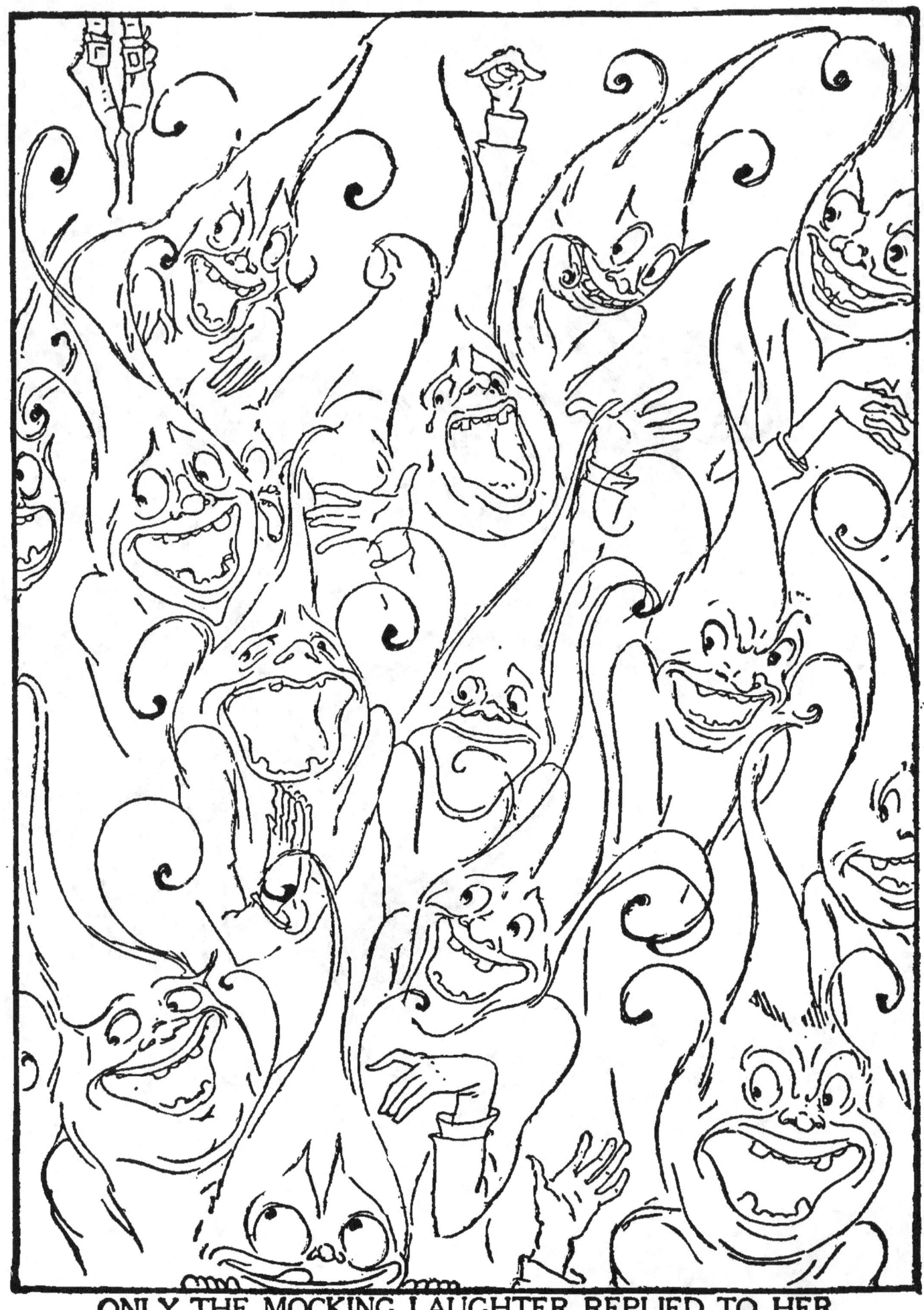

ONLY THE MOCKING LAUGHTER REPLIED TO HER

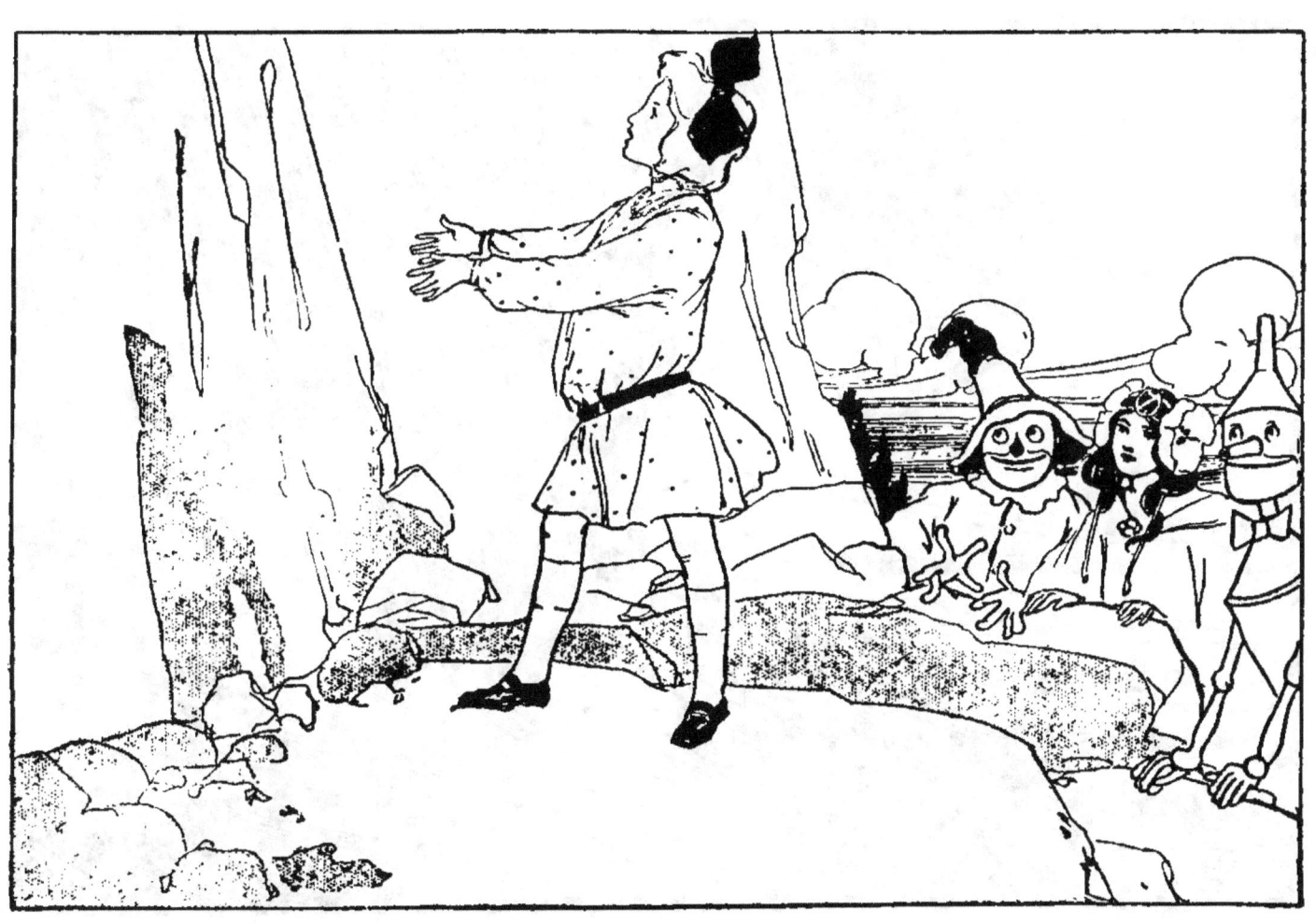

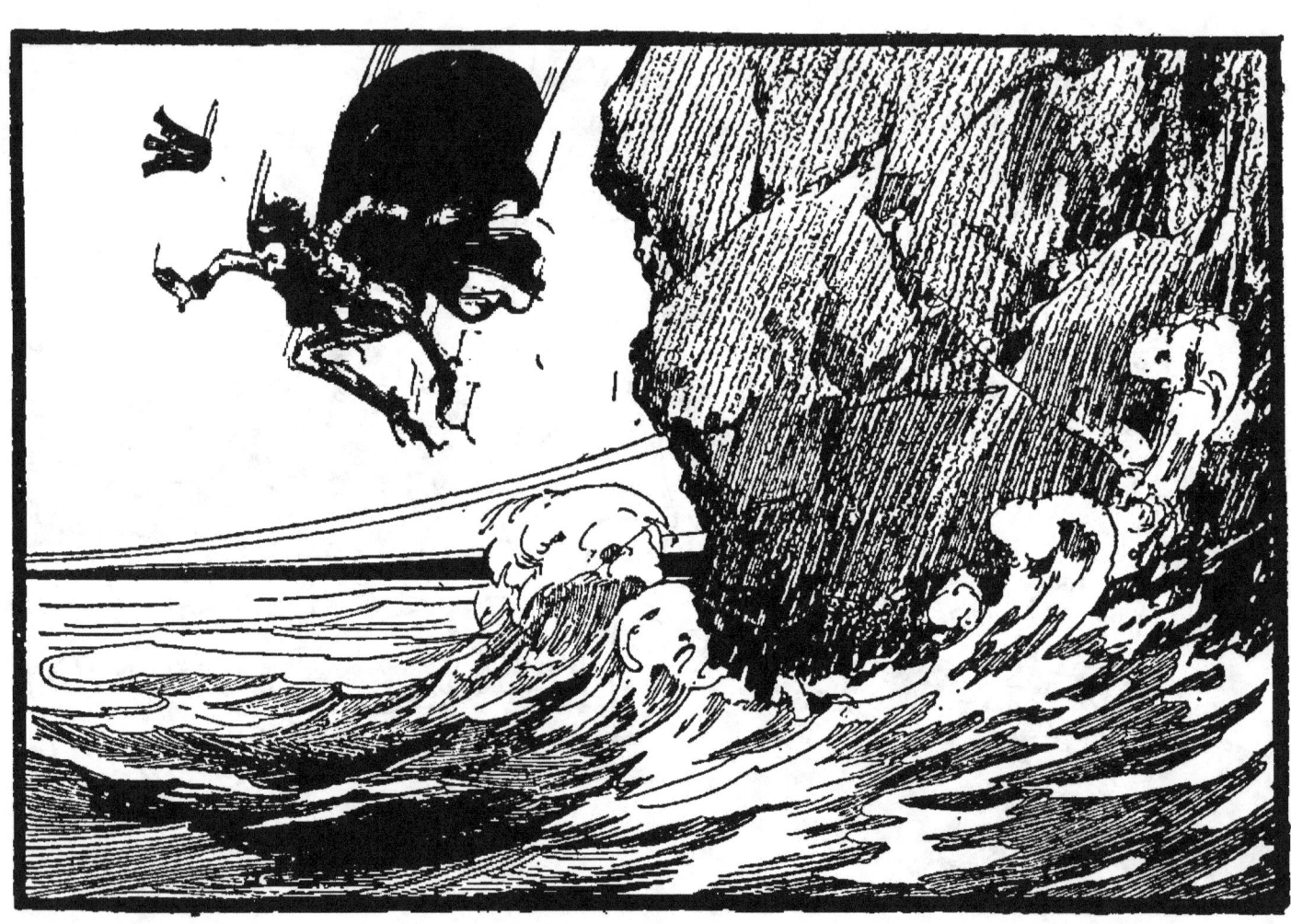

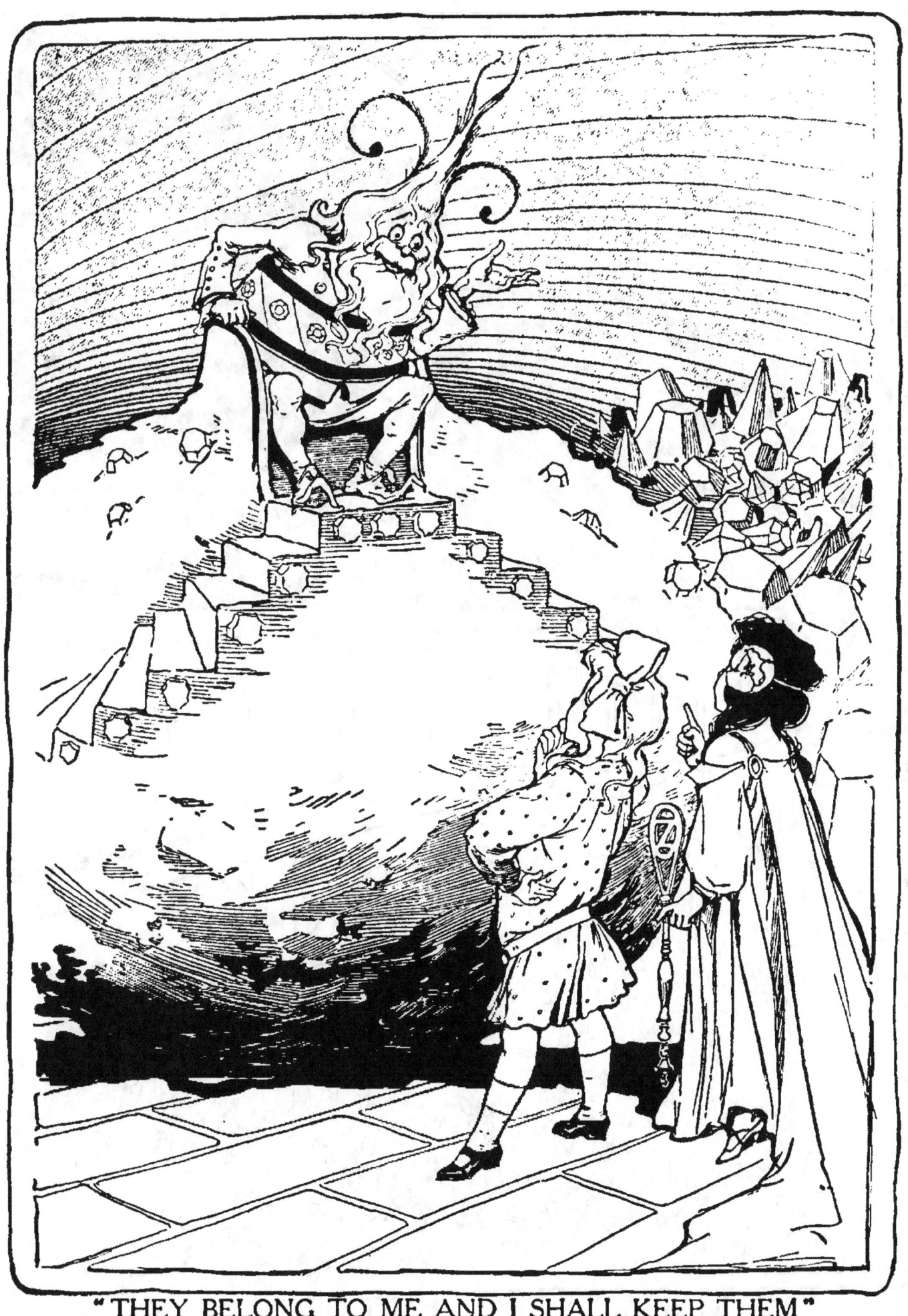

"THEY BELONG TO ME AND I SHALL KEEP THEM"

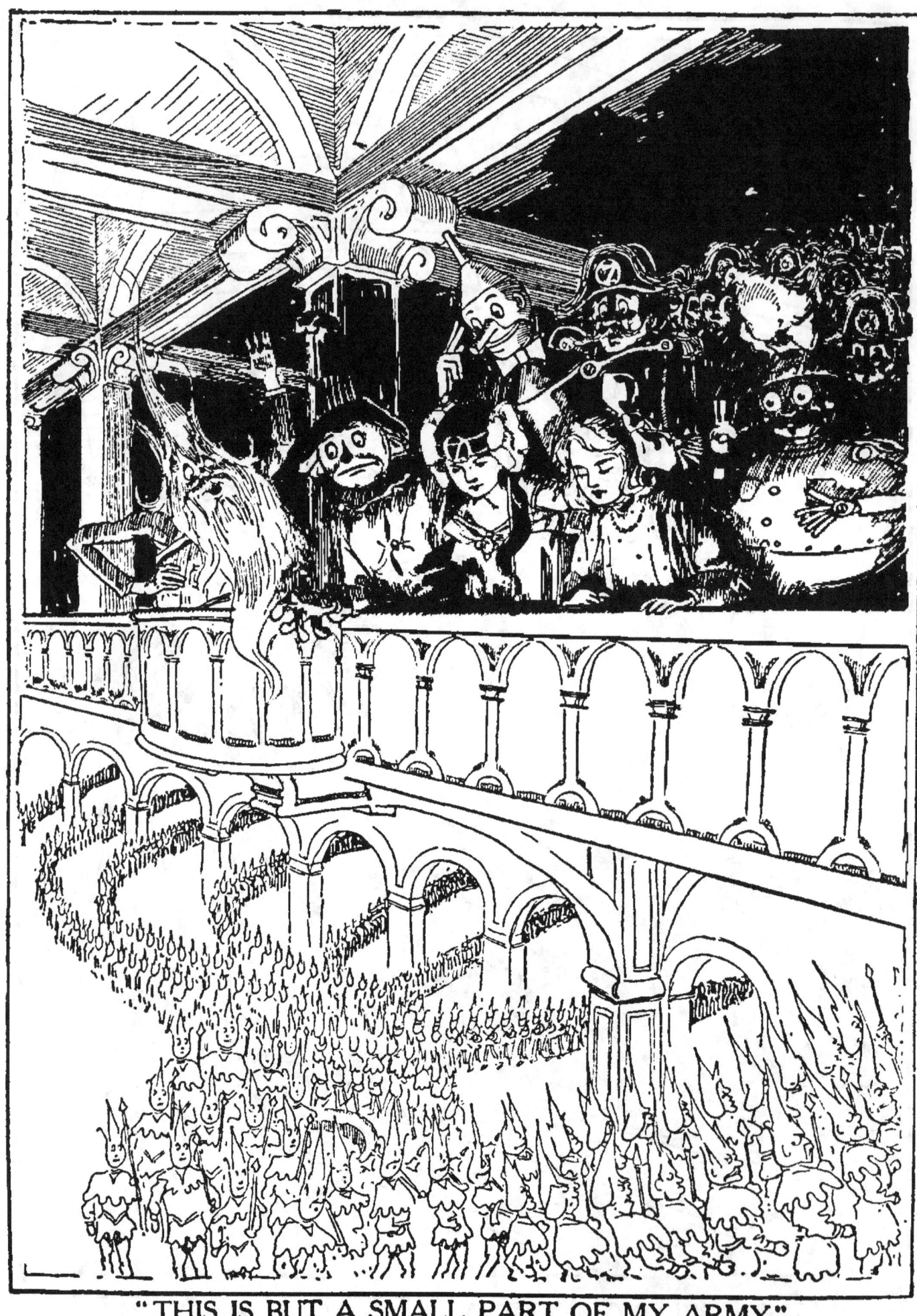

"THIS IS BUT A SMALL PART OF MY ARMY"

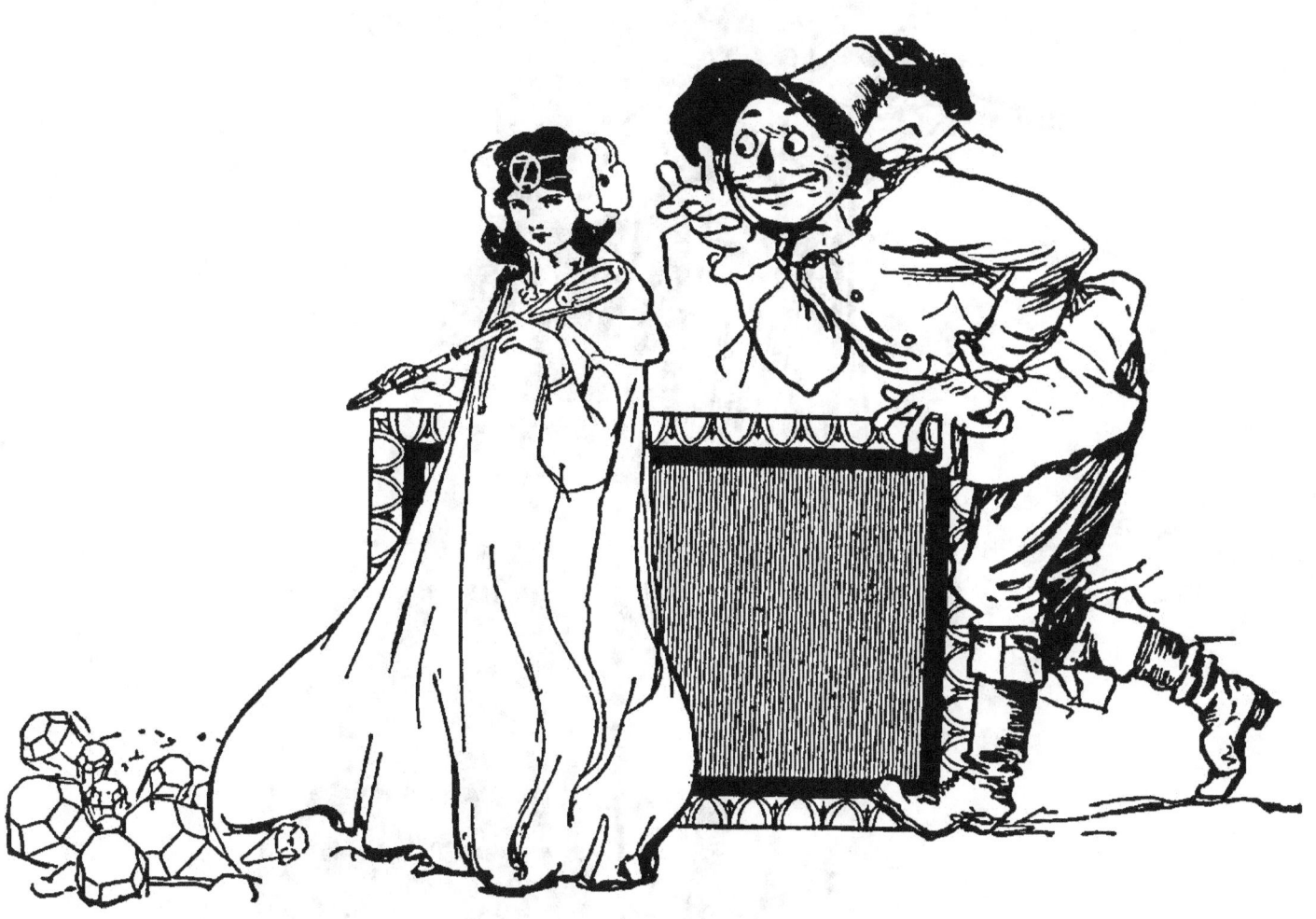

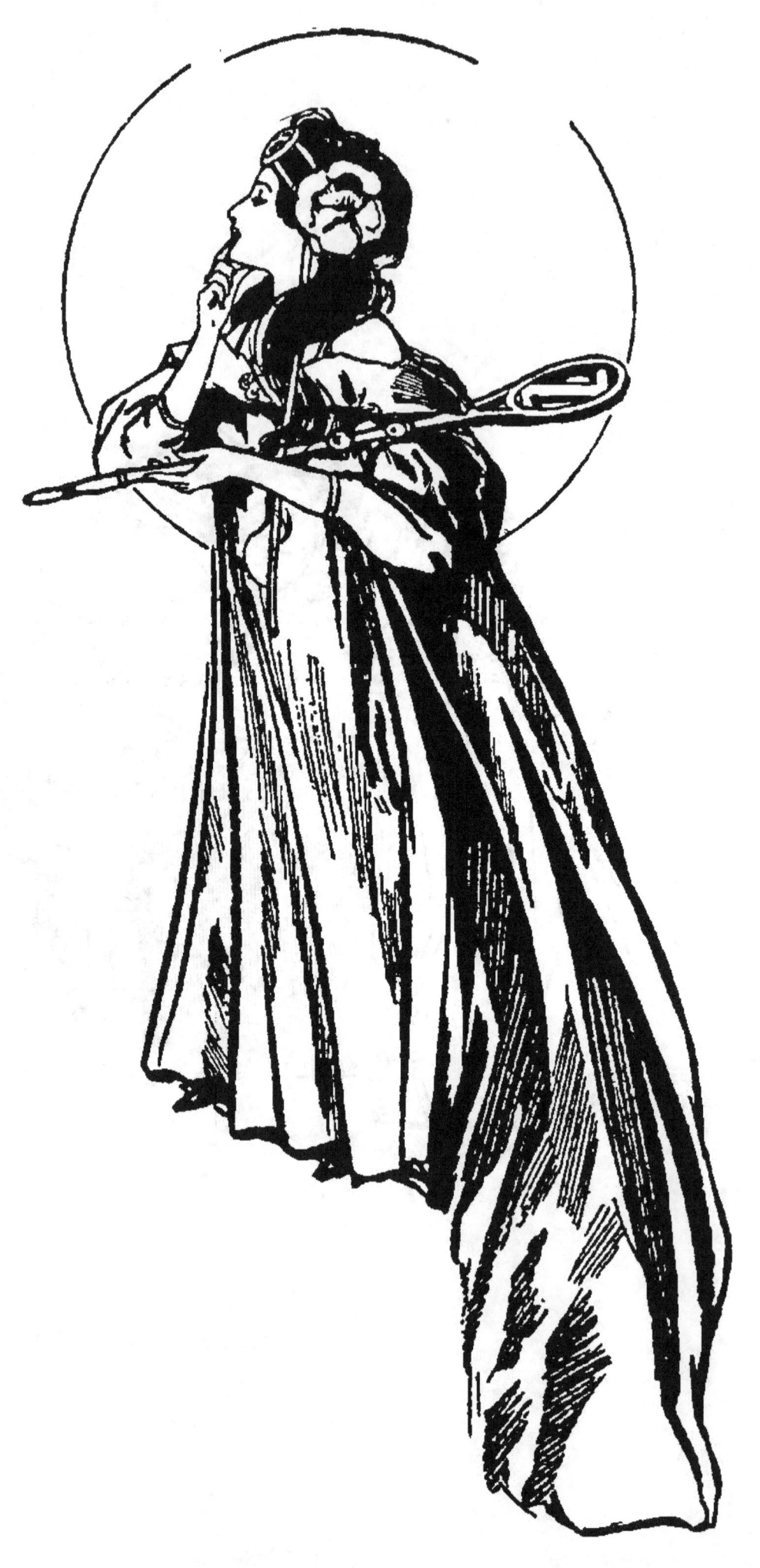

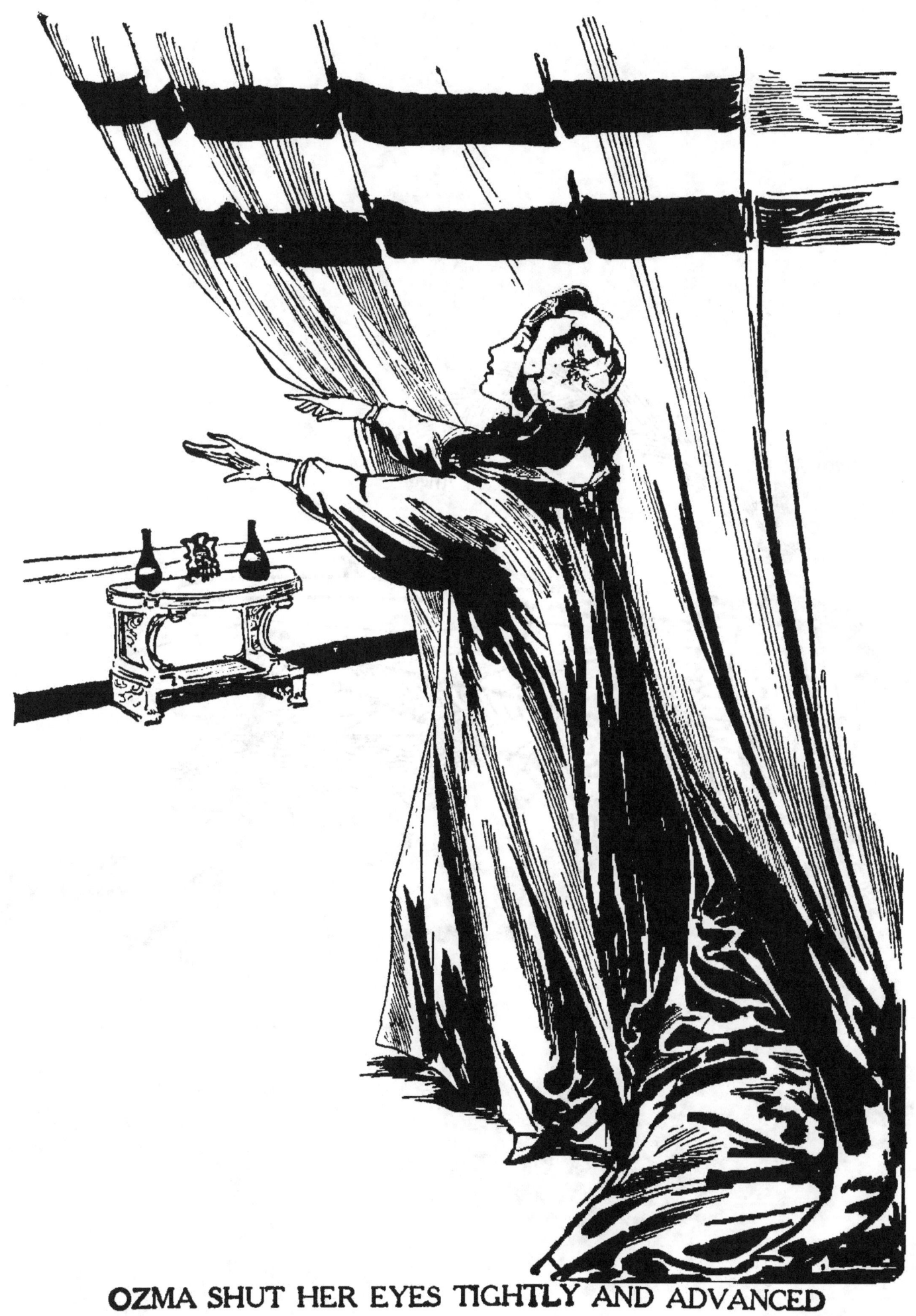

OZMA SHUT HER EYES TIGHTLY AND ADVANCED

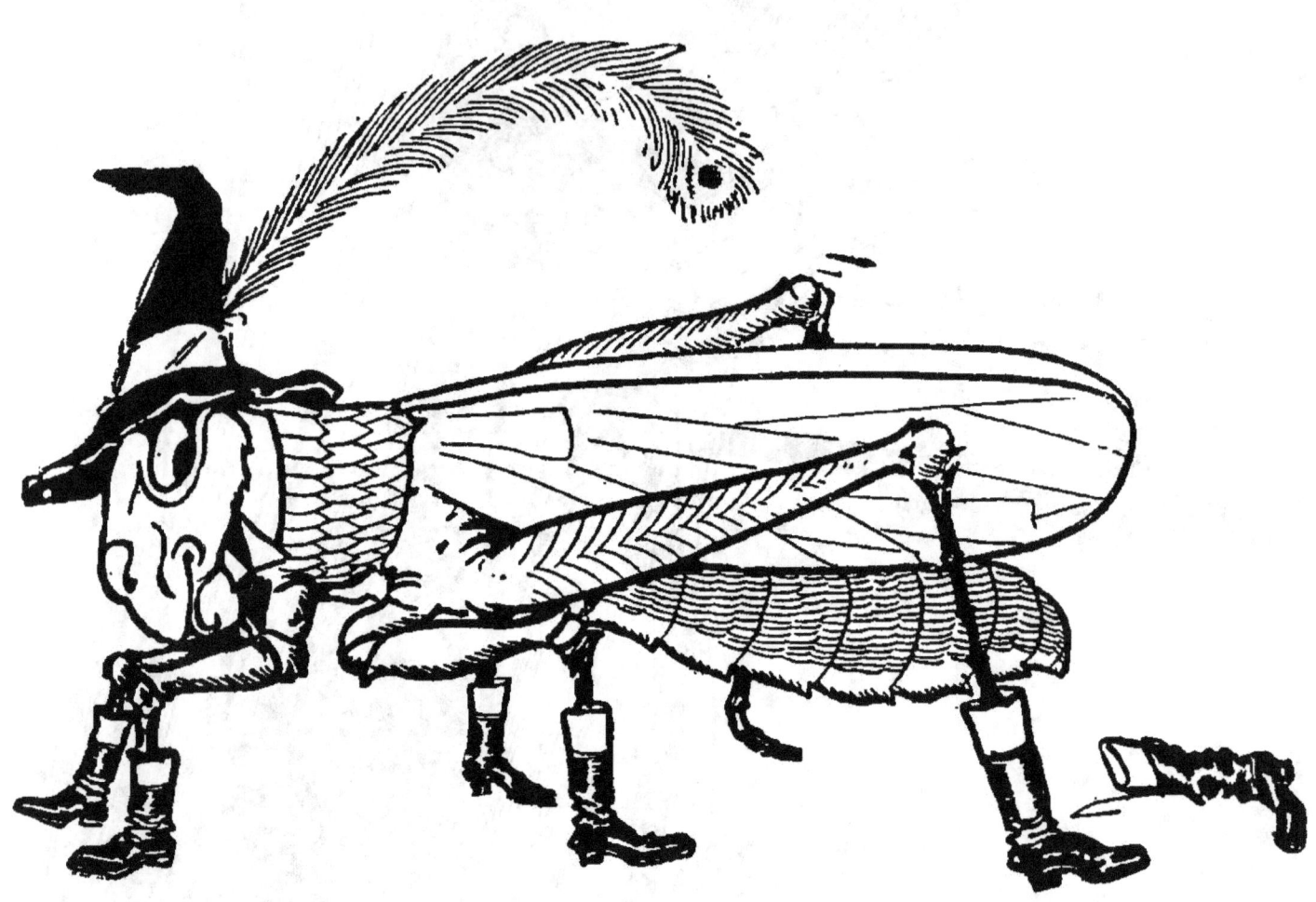

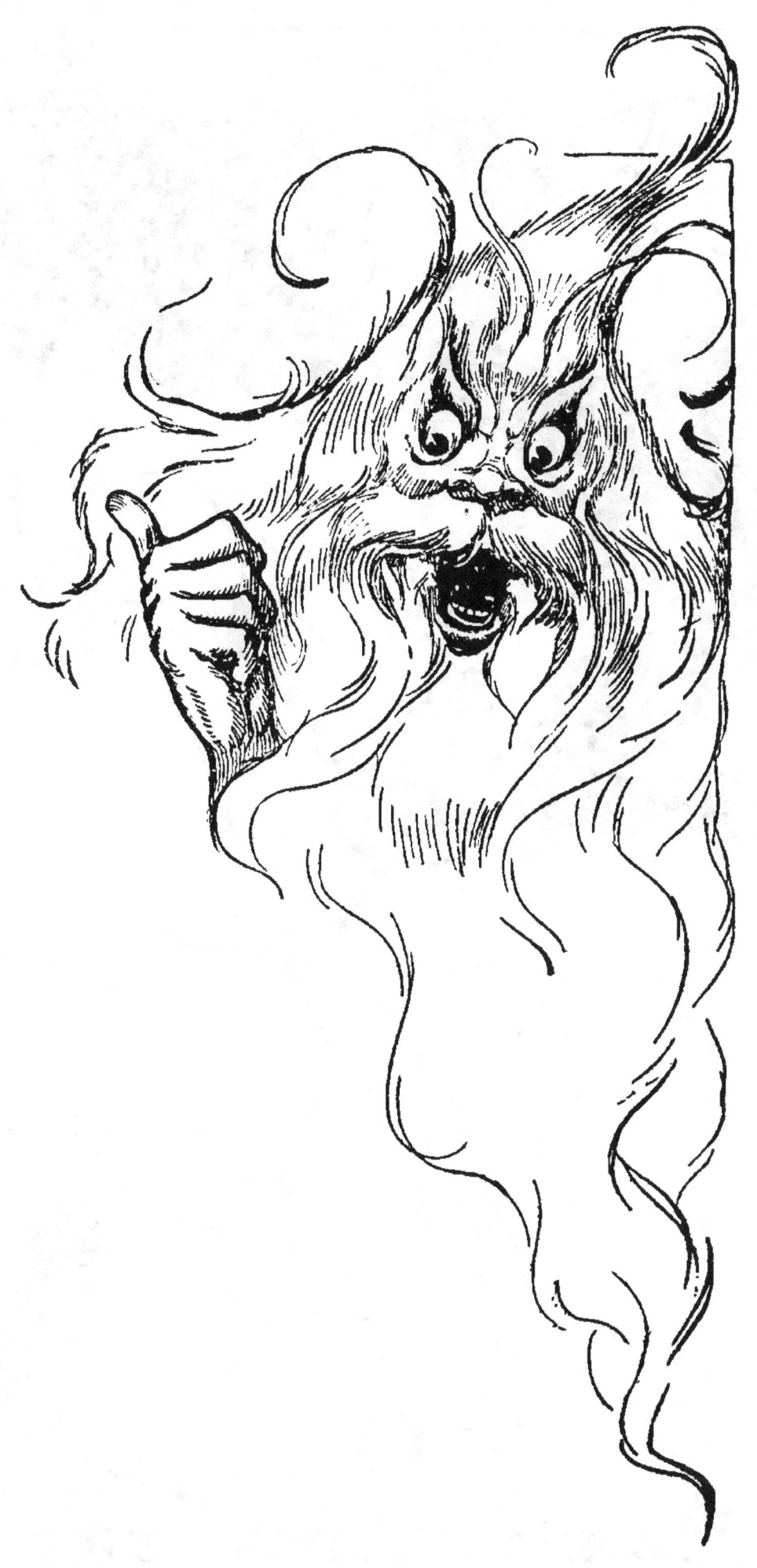

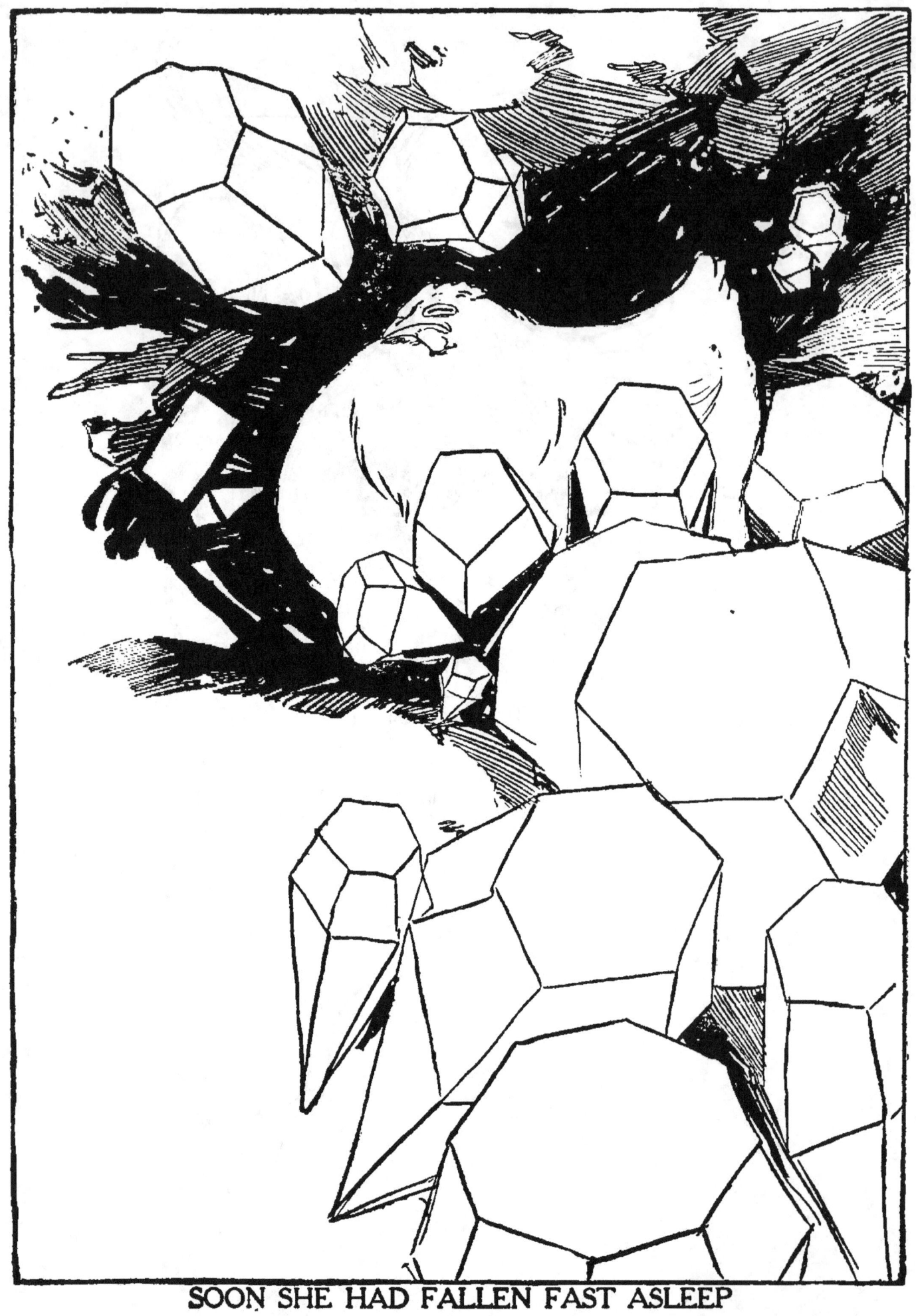

SOON SHE HAD FALLEN FAST ASLEEP

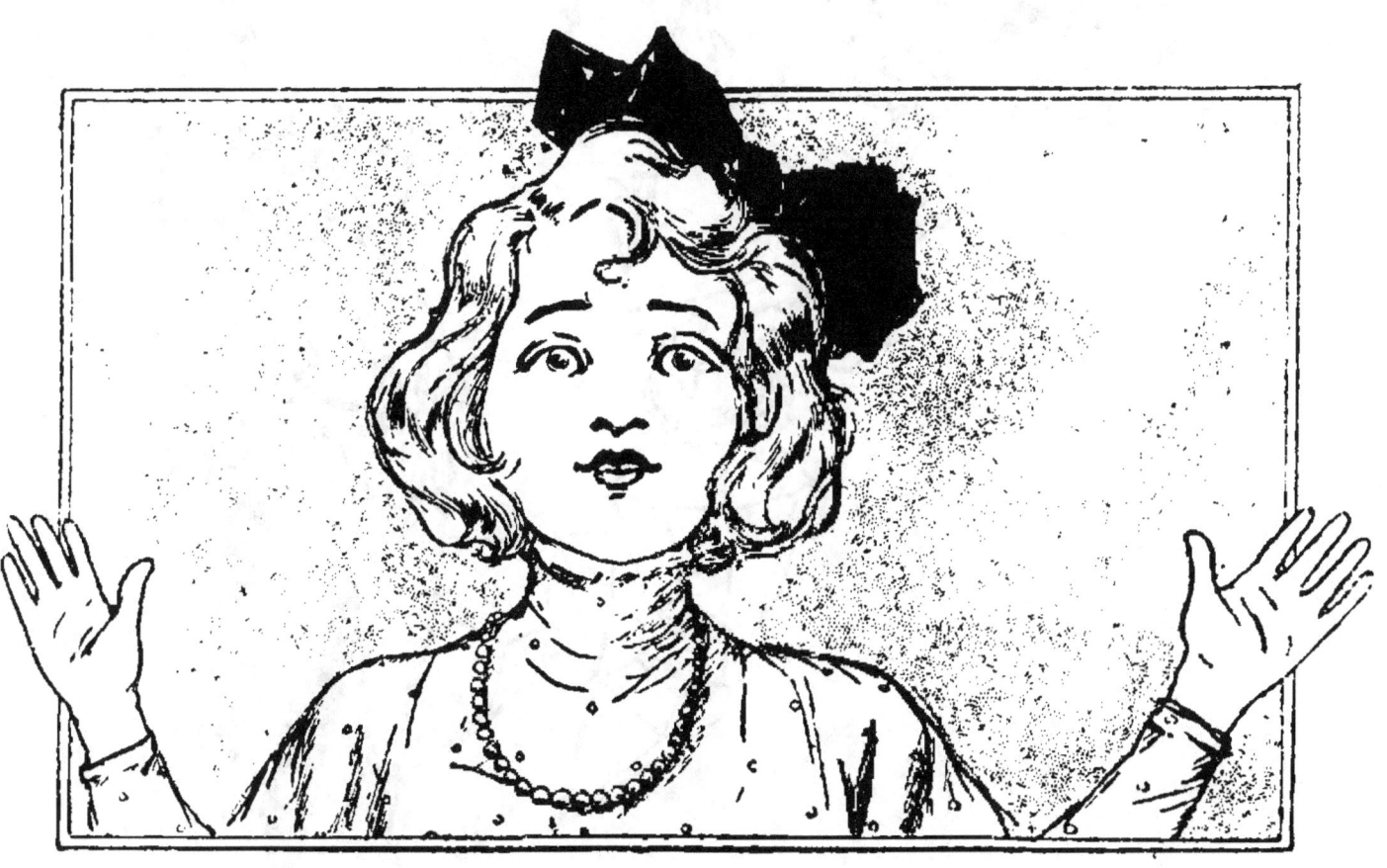

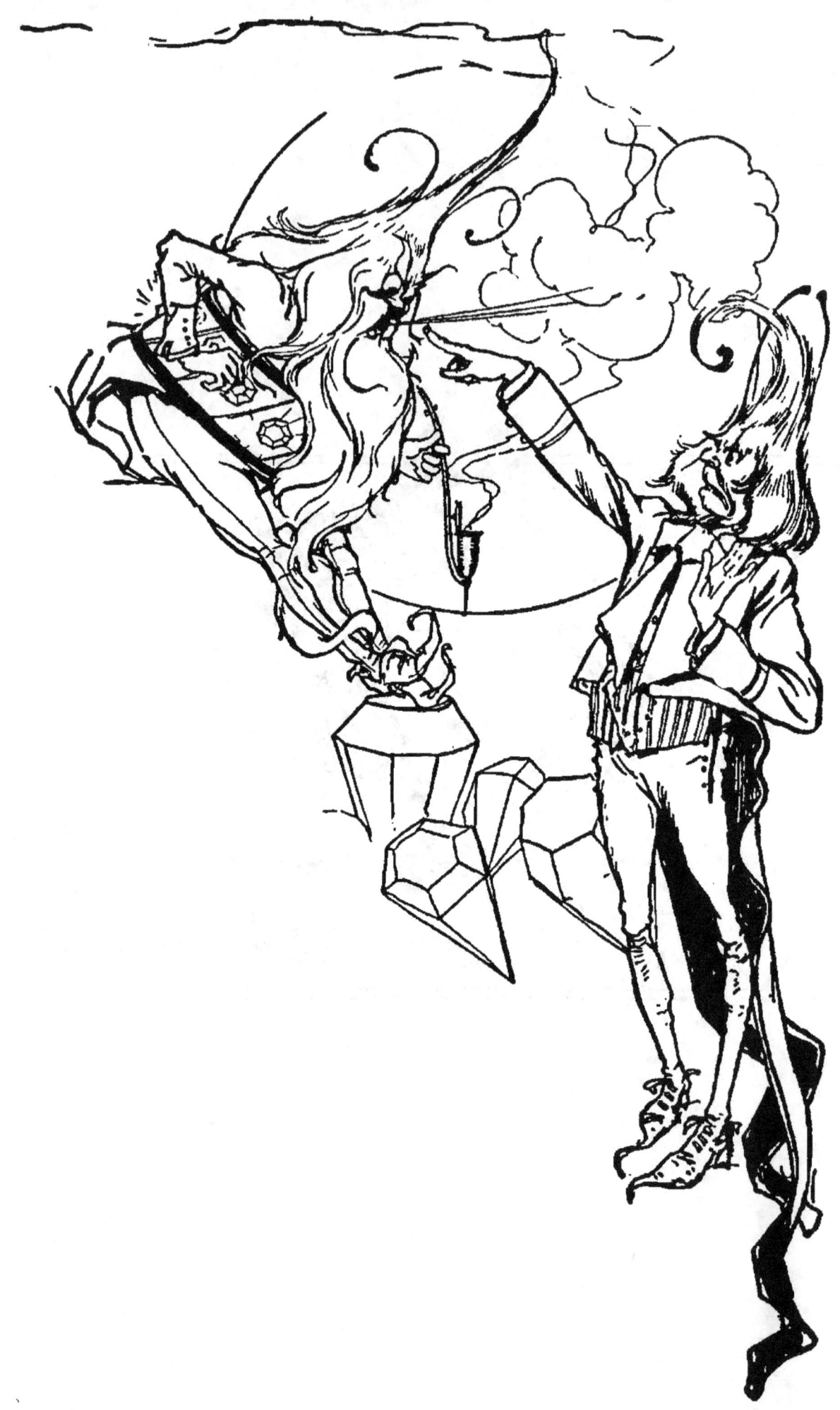

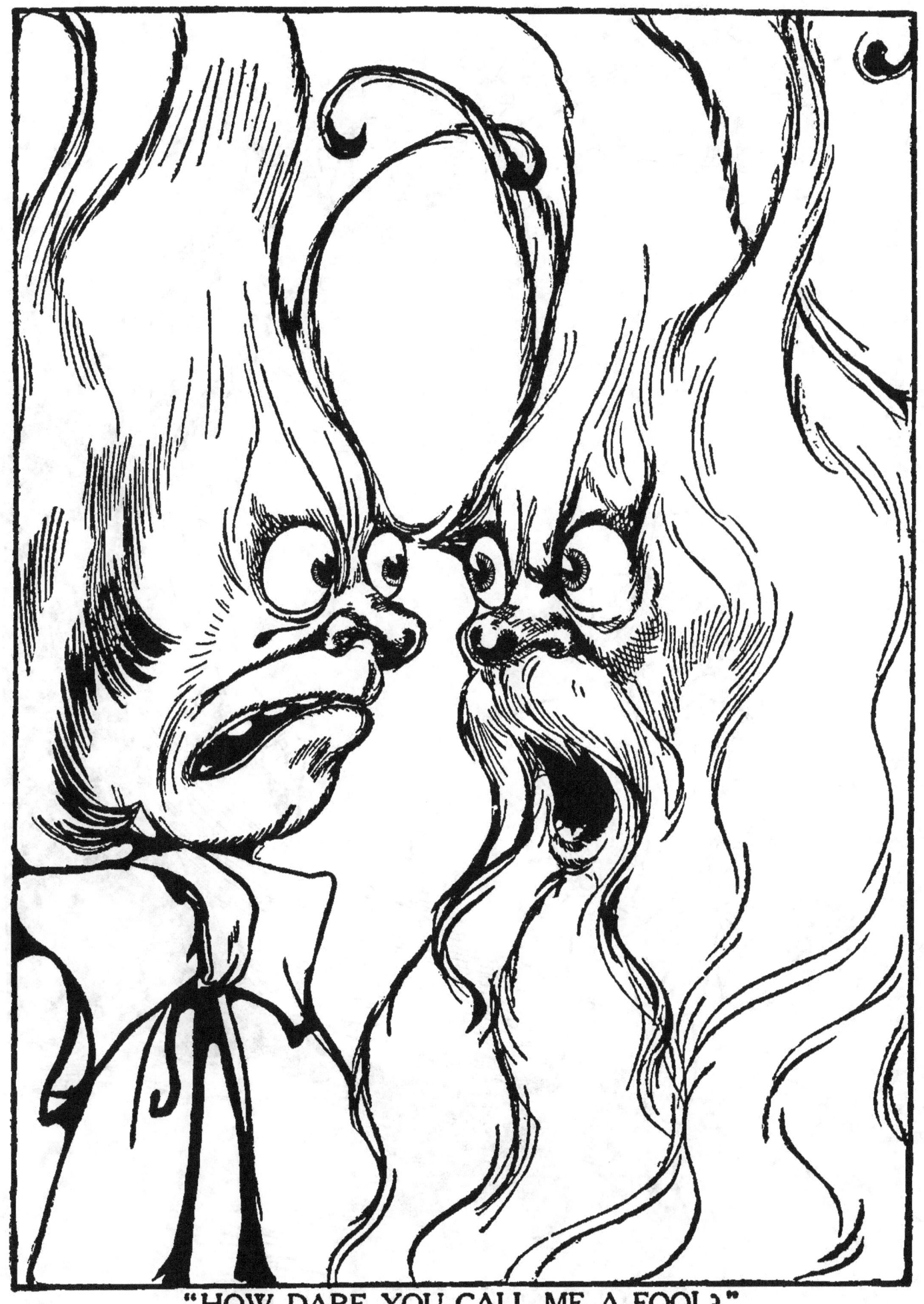

"HOW DARE YOU CALL ME A FOOL?"

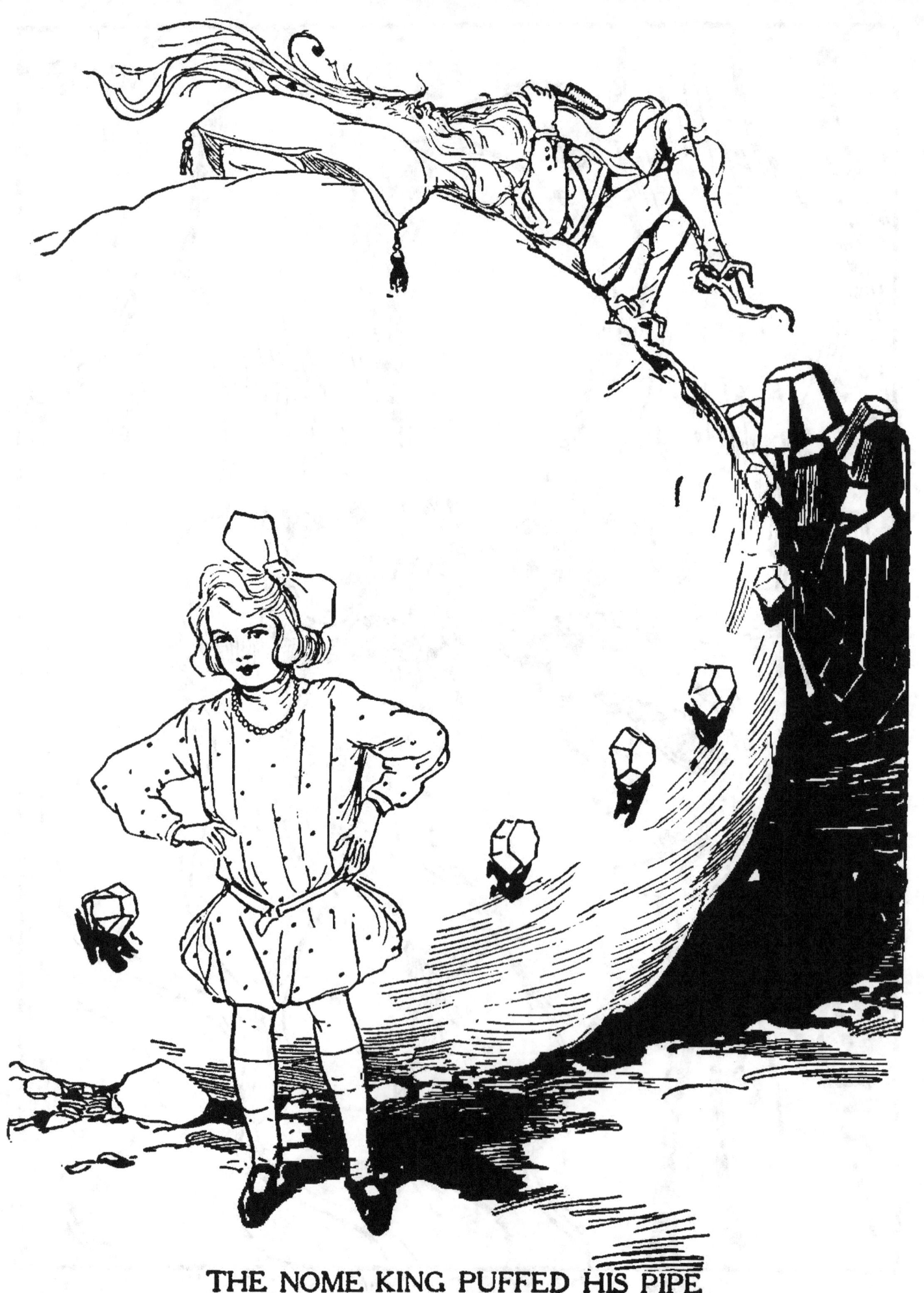

THE NOME KING PUFFED HIS PIPE

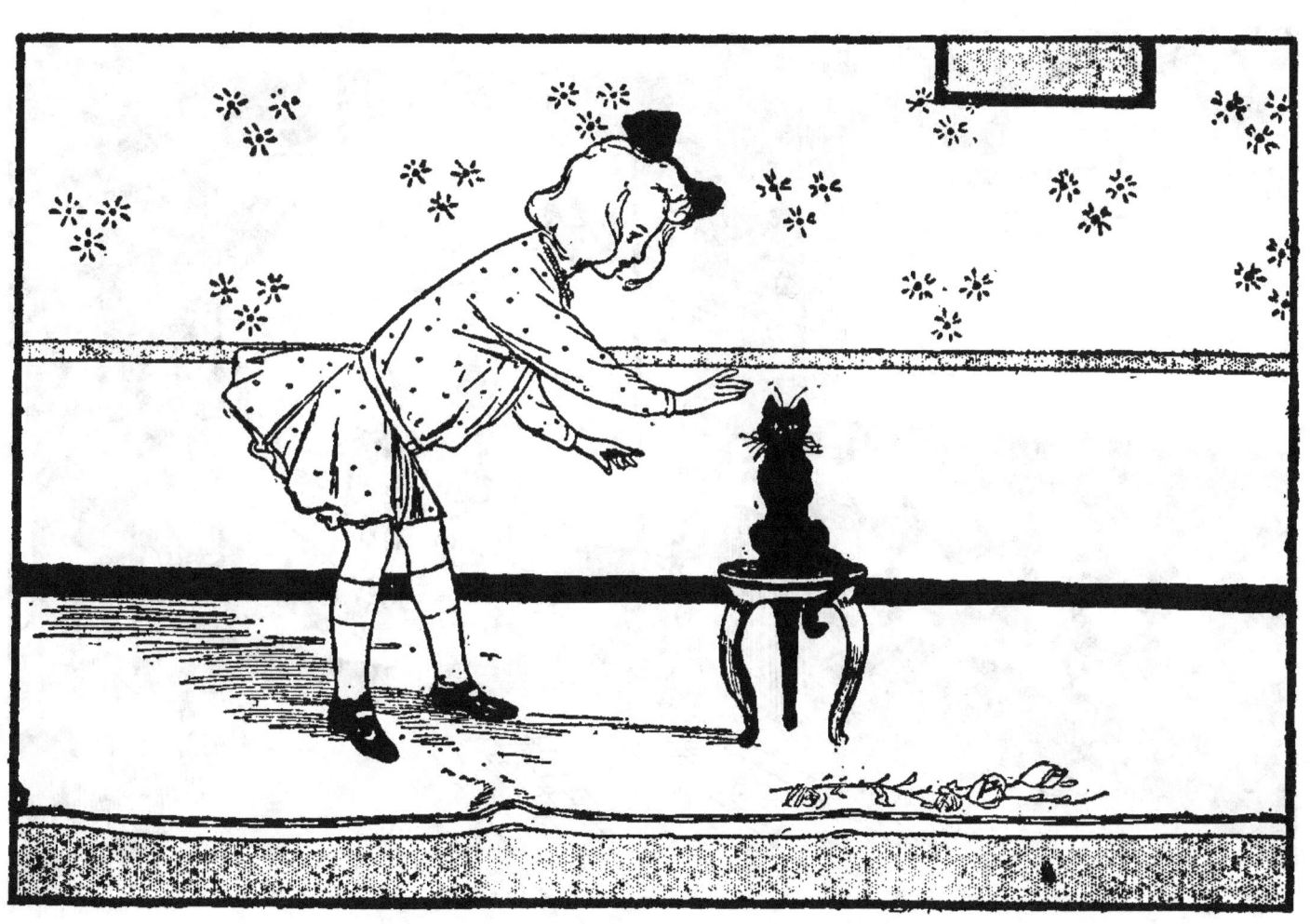

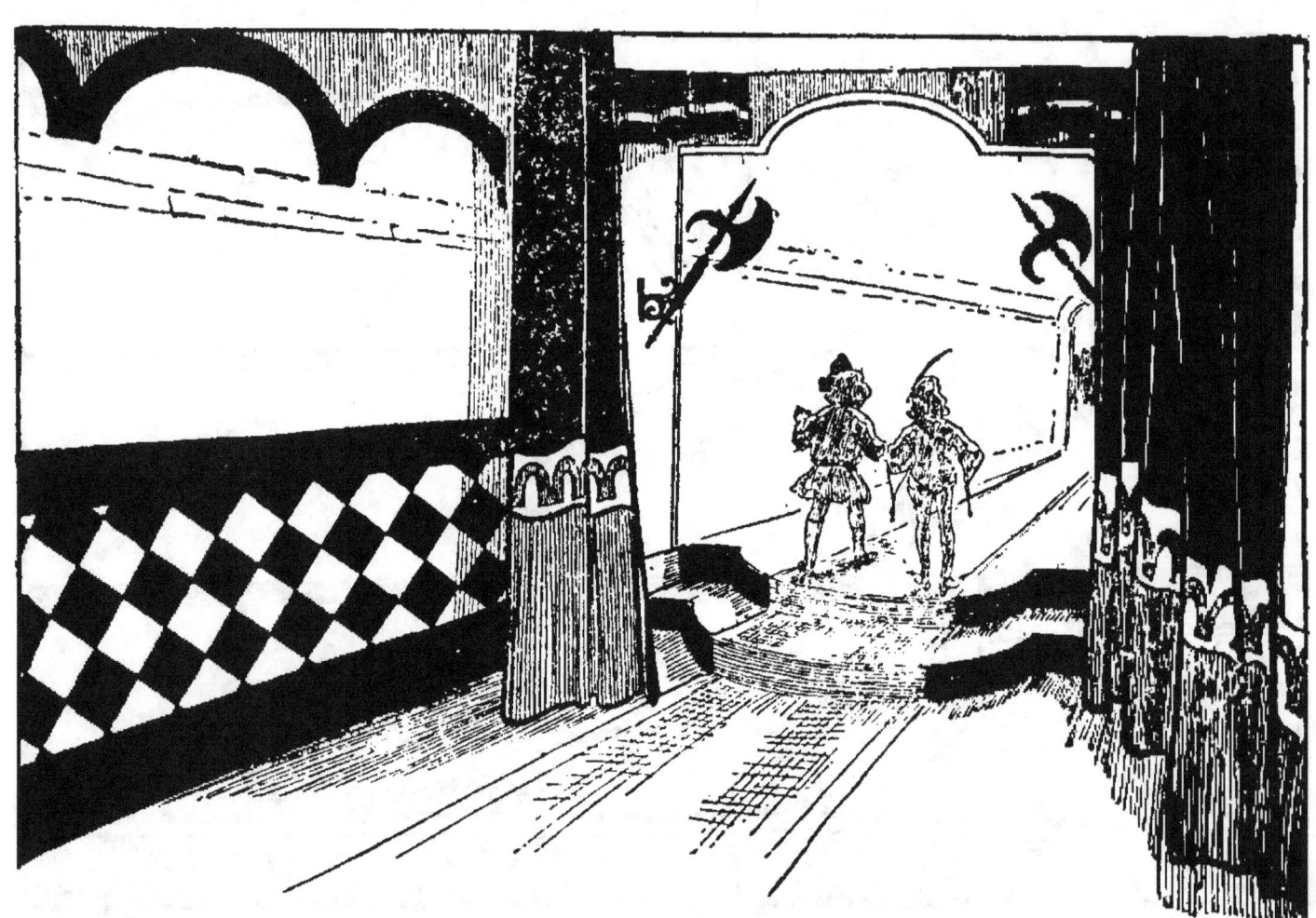

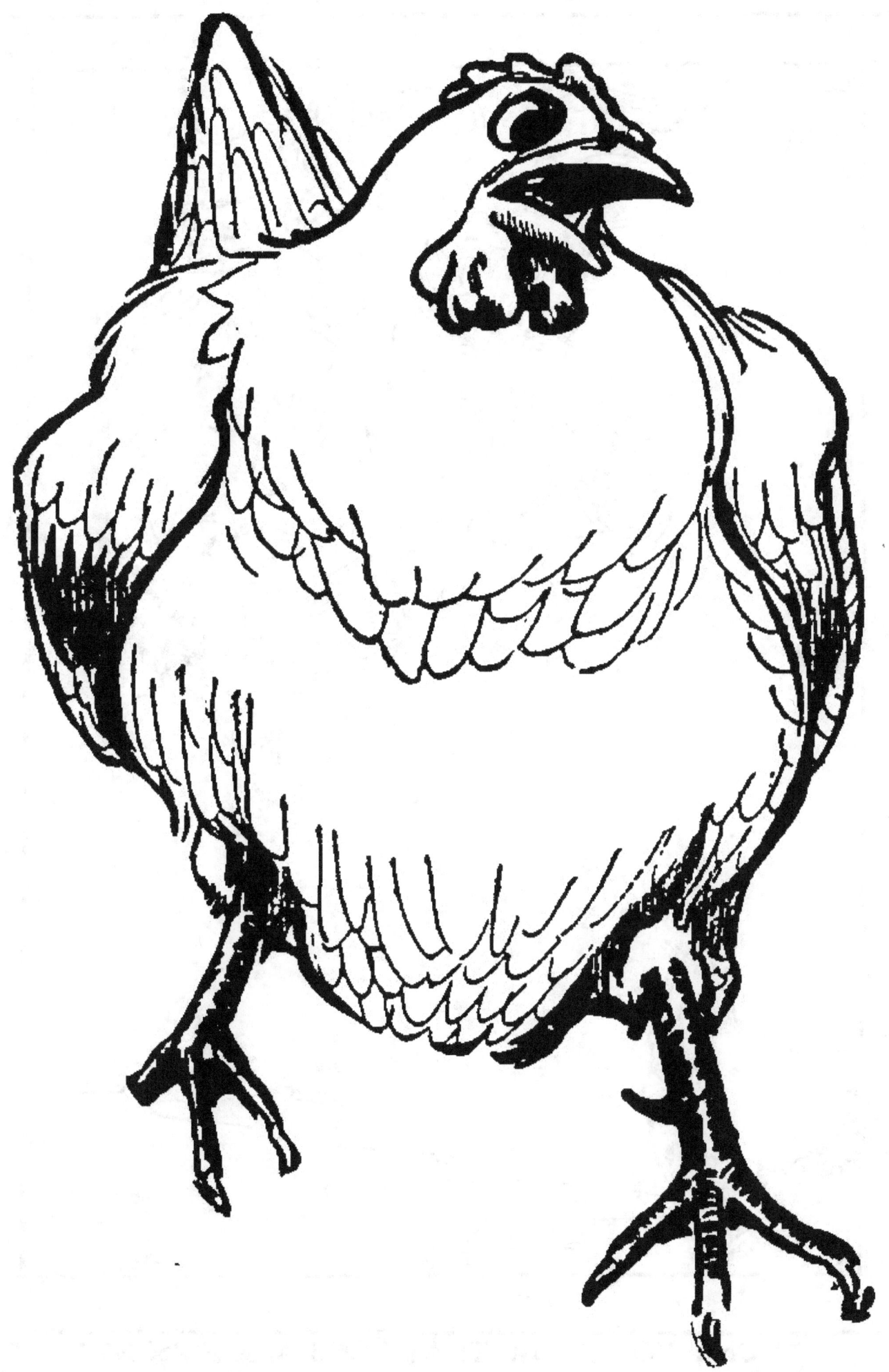

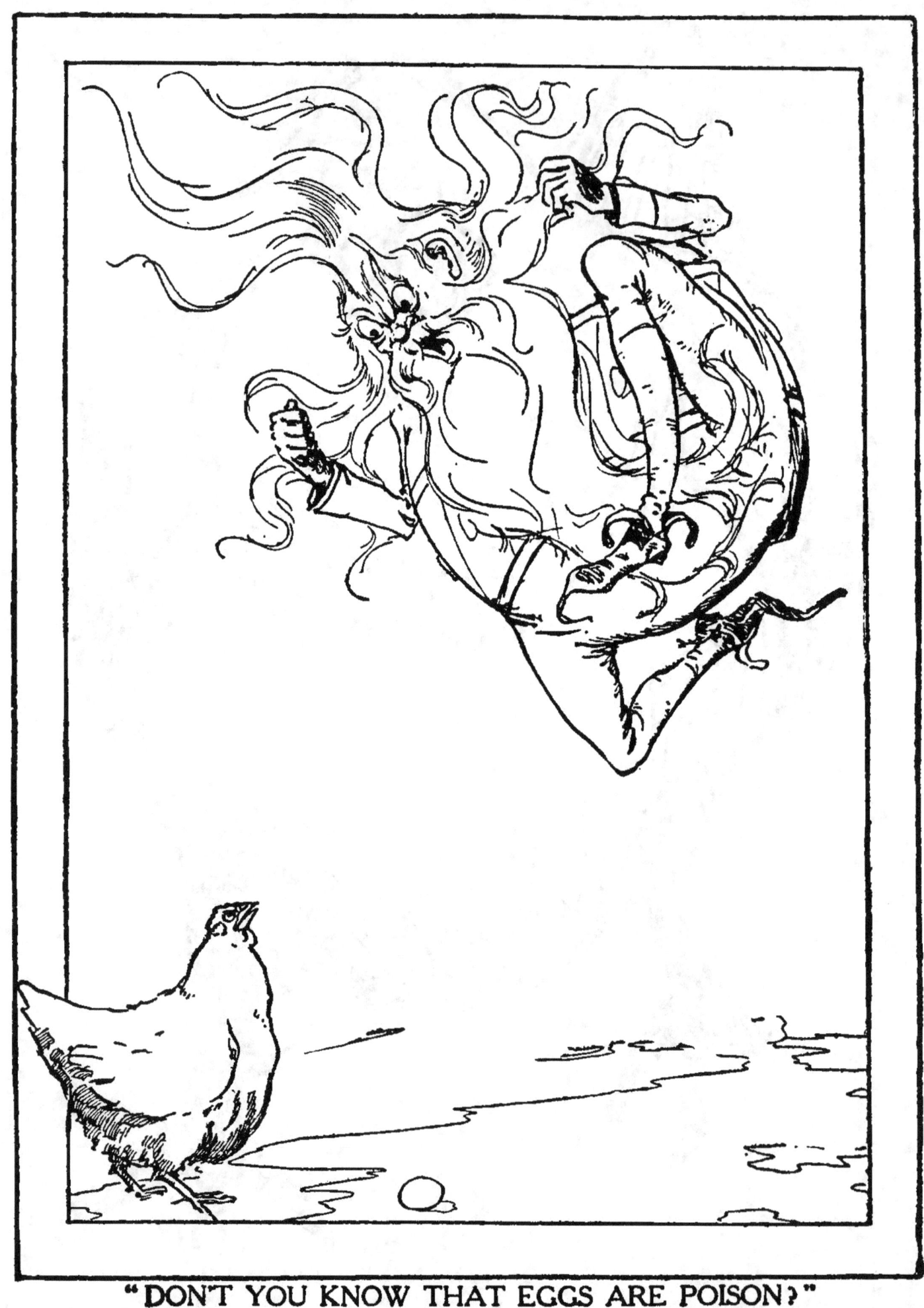

"DON'T YOU KNOW THAT EGGS ARE POISON?"

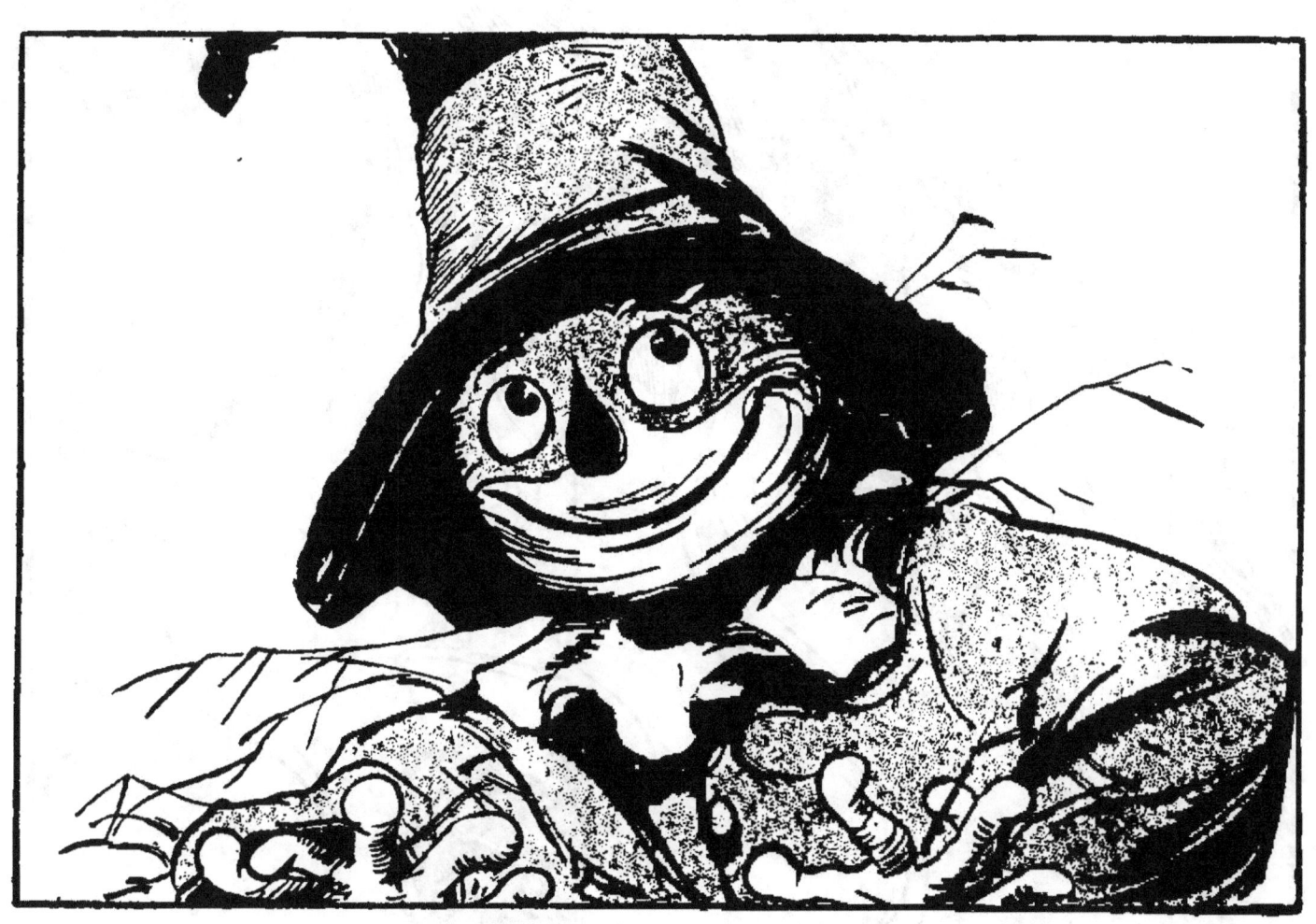

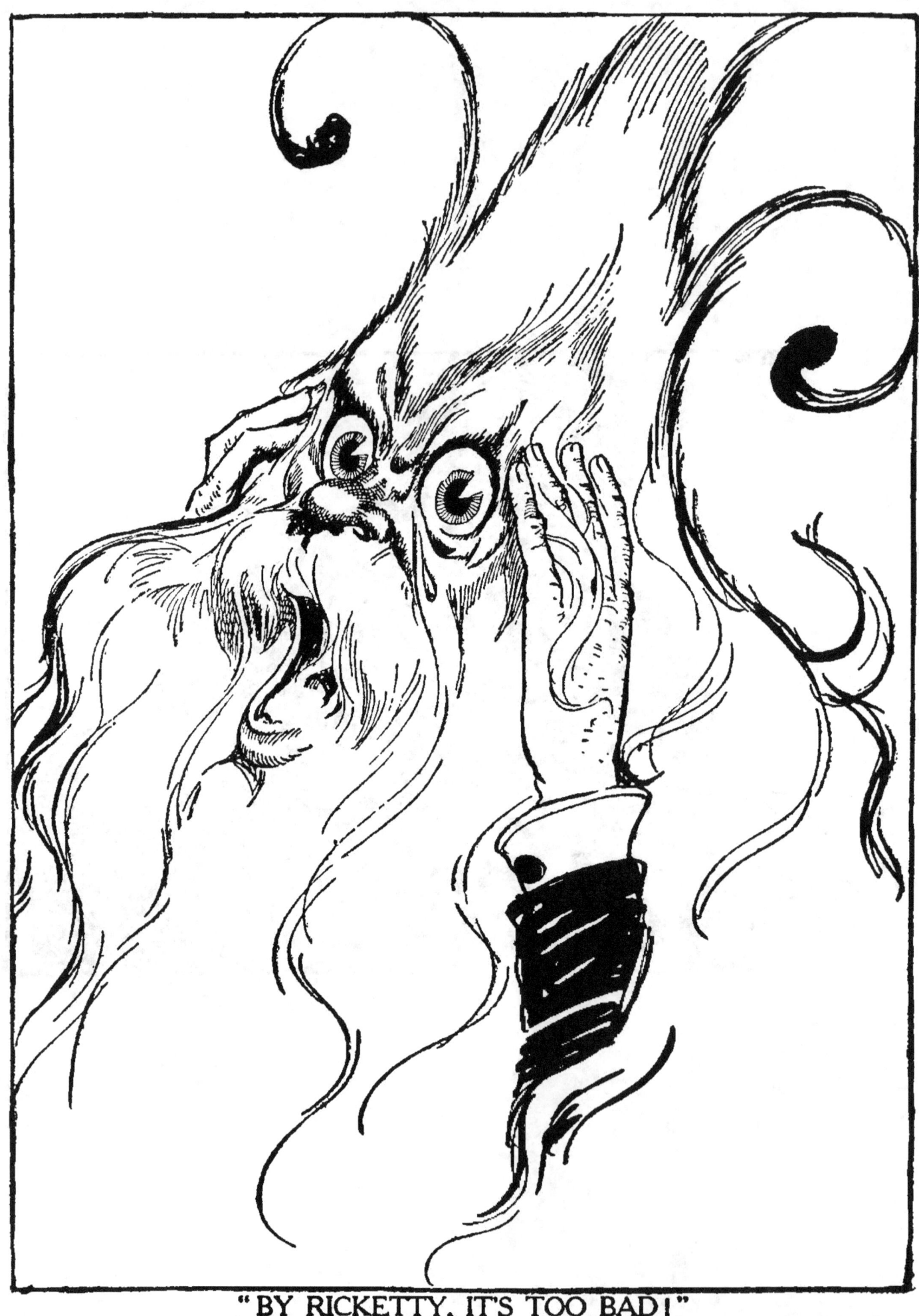

"BY RICKETTY. IT'S TOO BAD!"

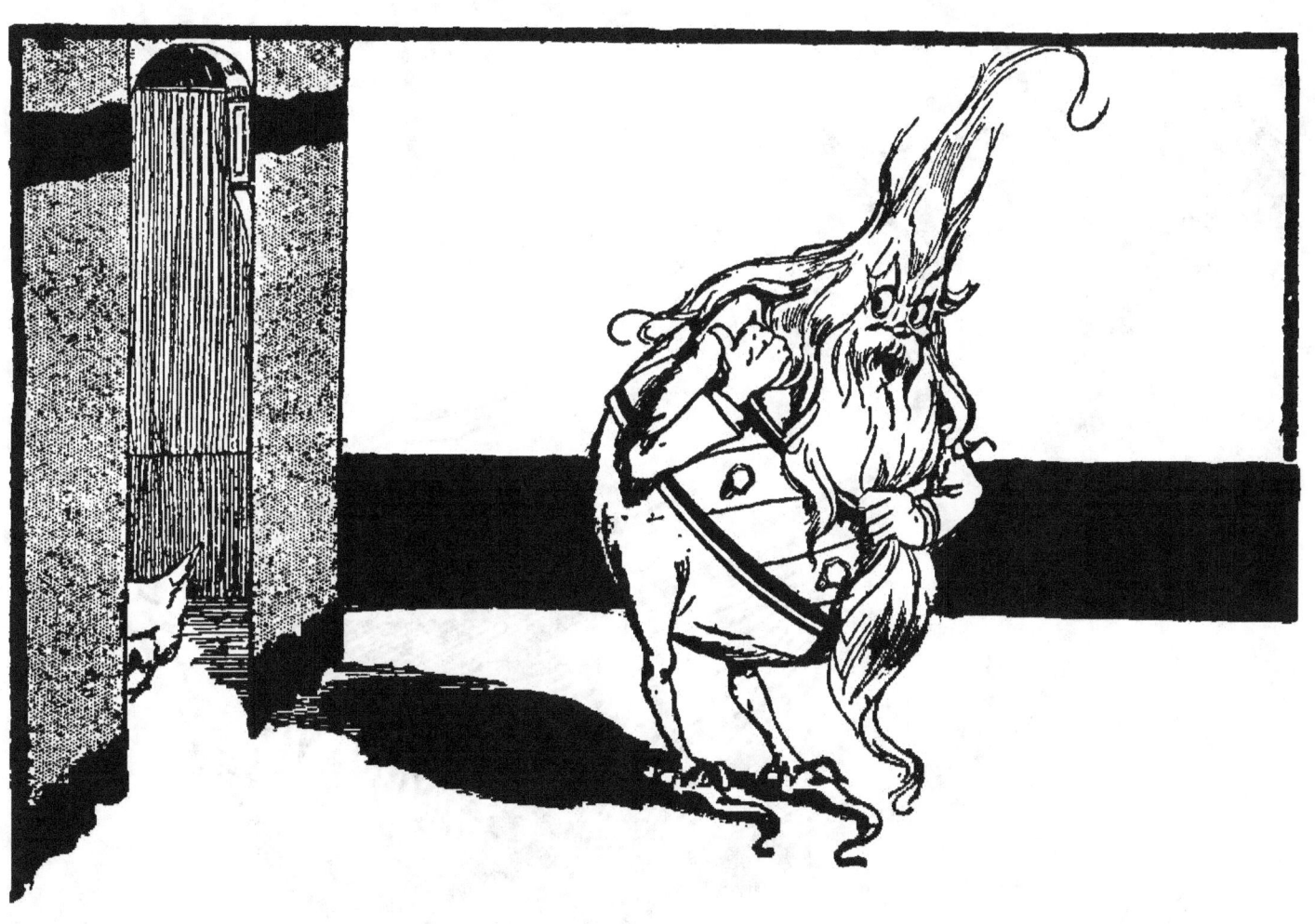

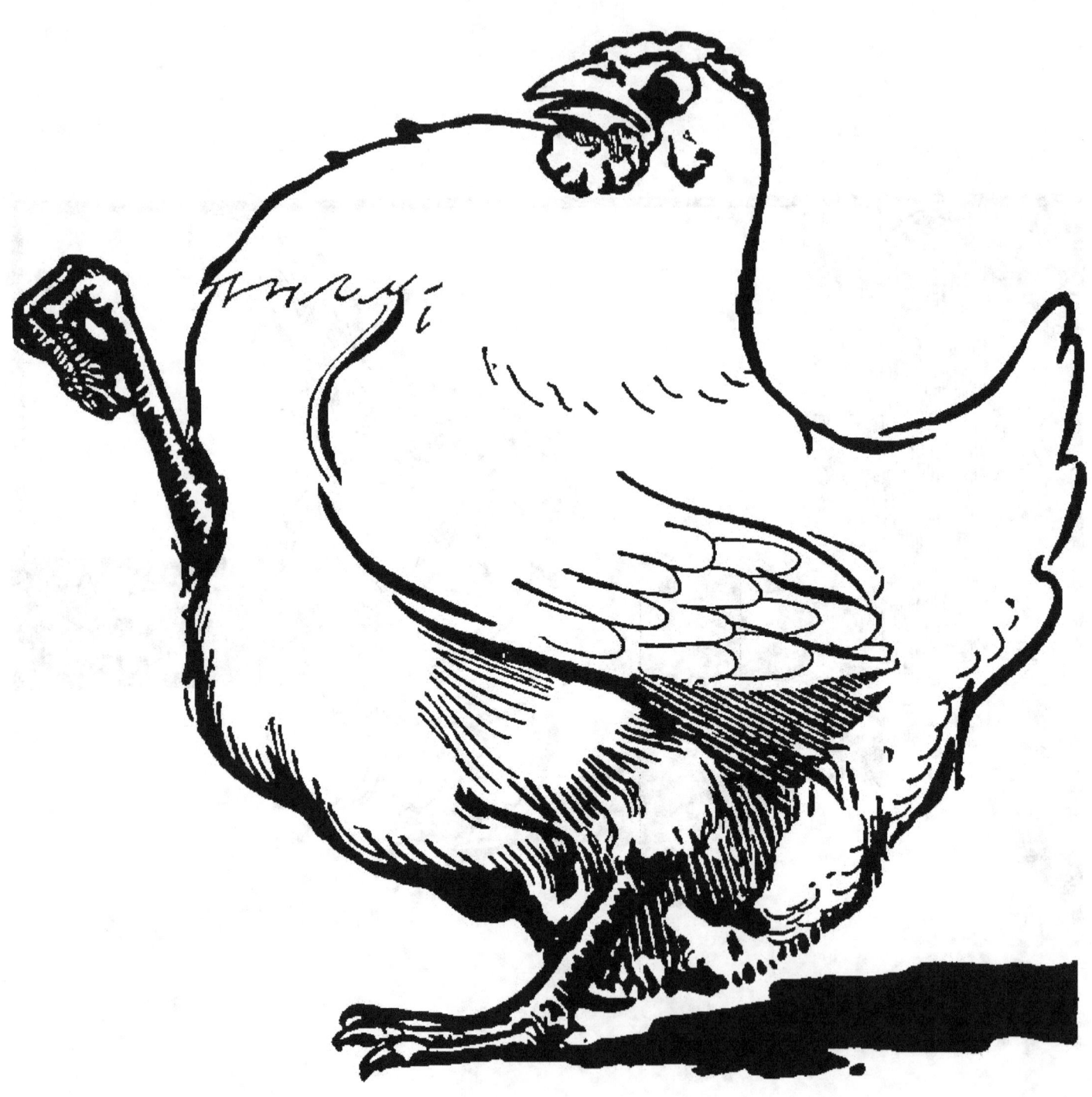

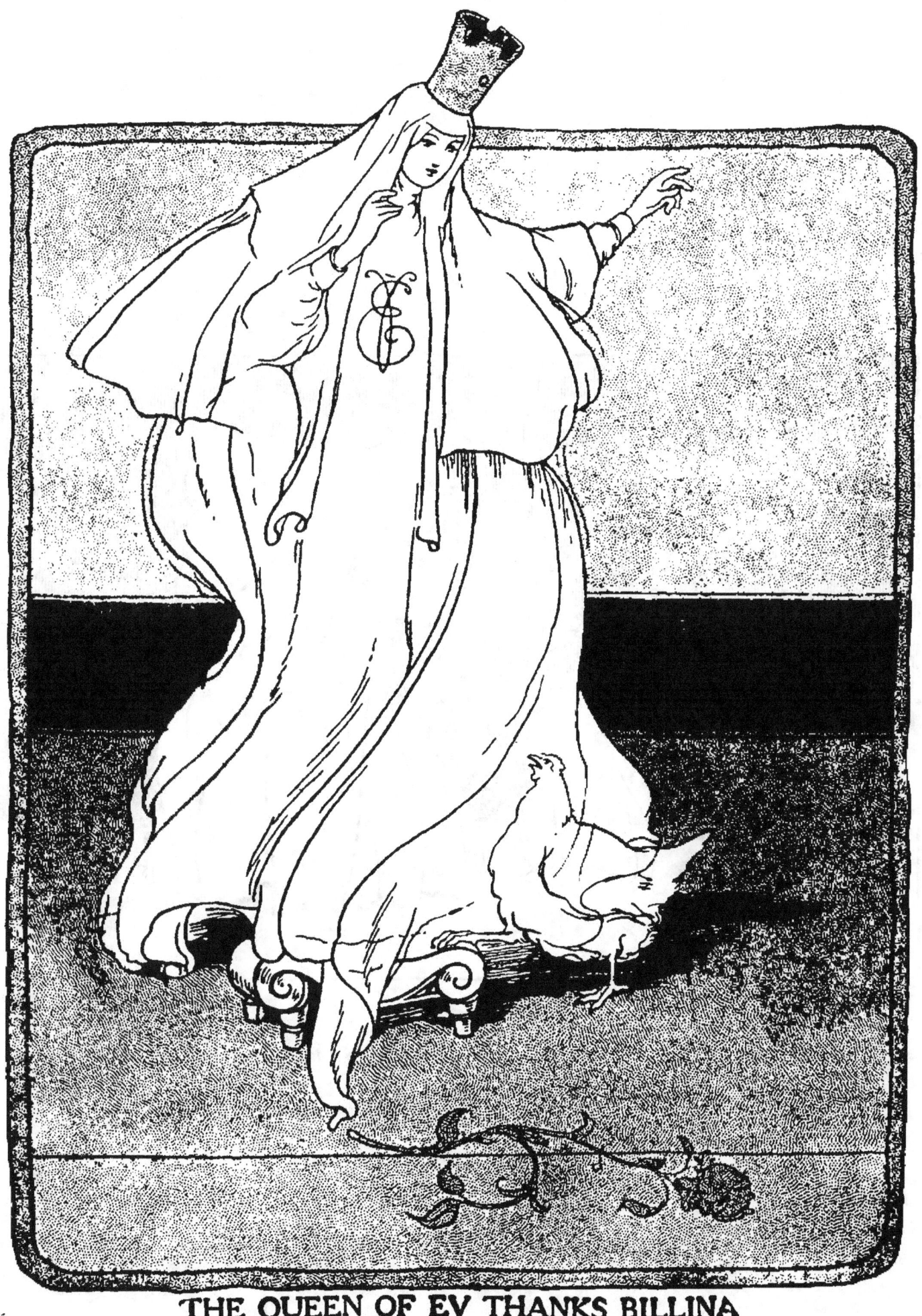

THE QUEEN OF EV THANKS BILLINA

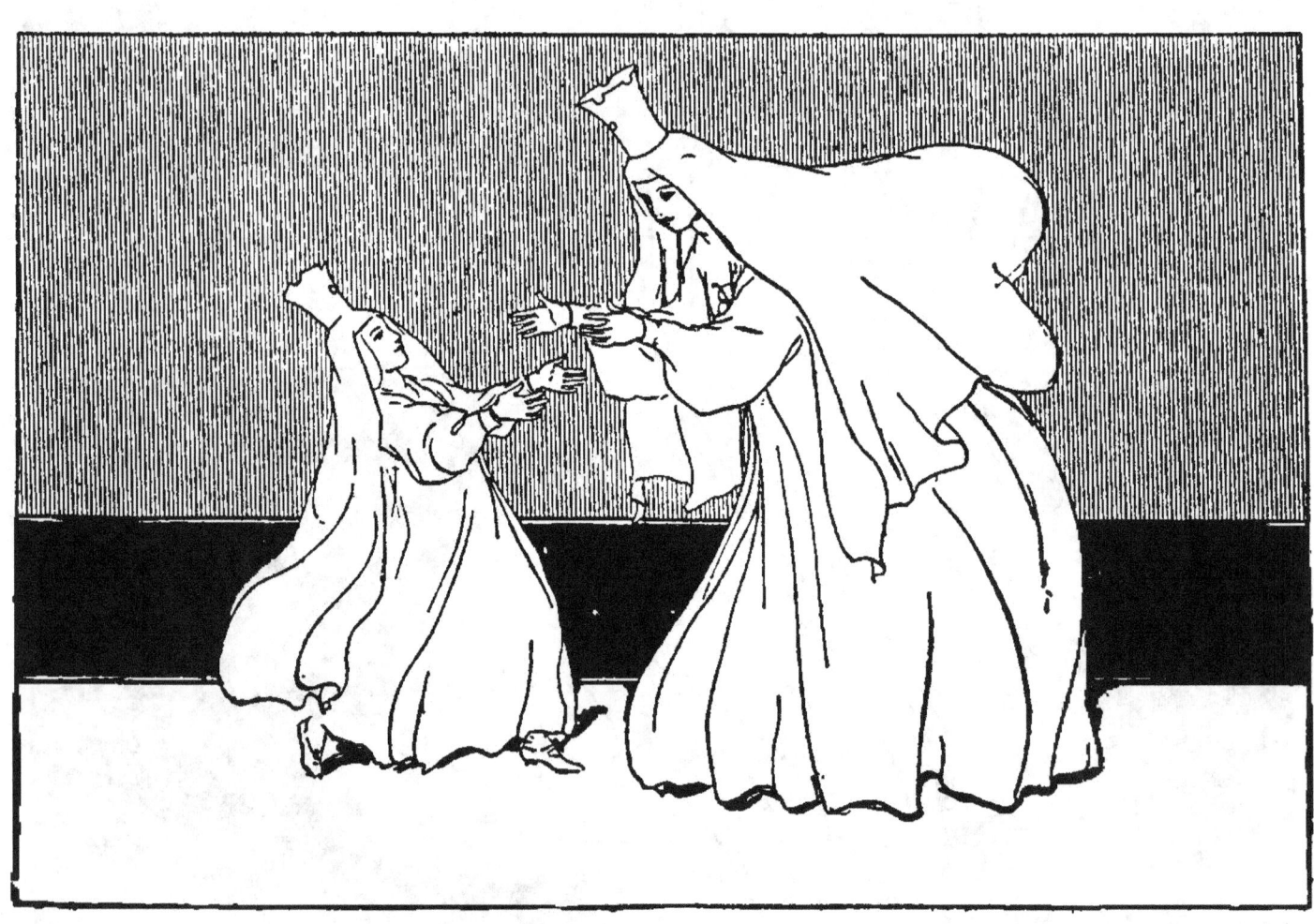

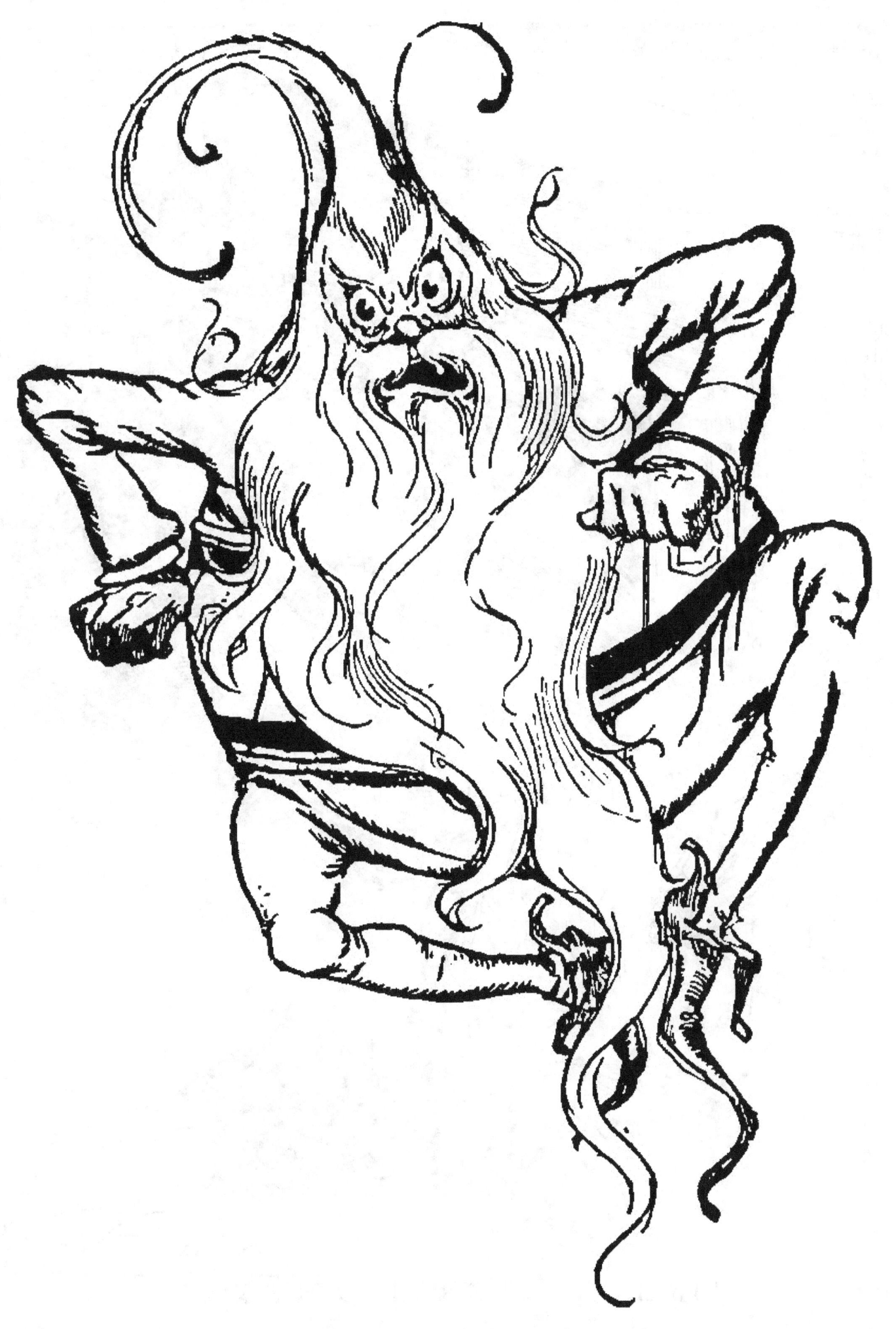

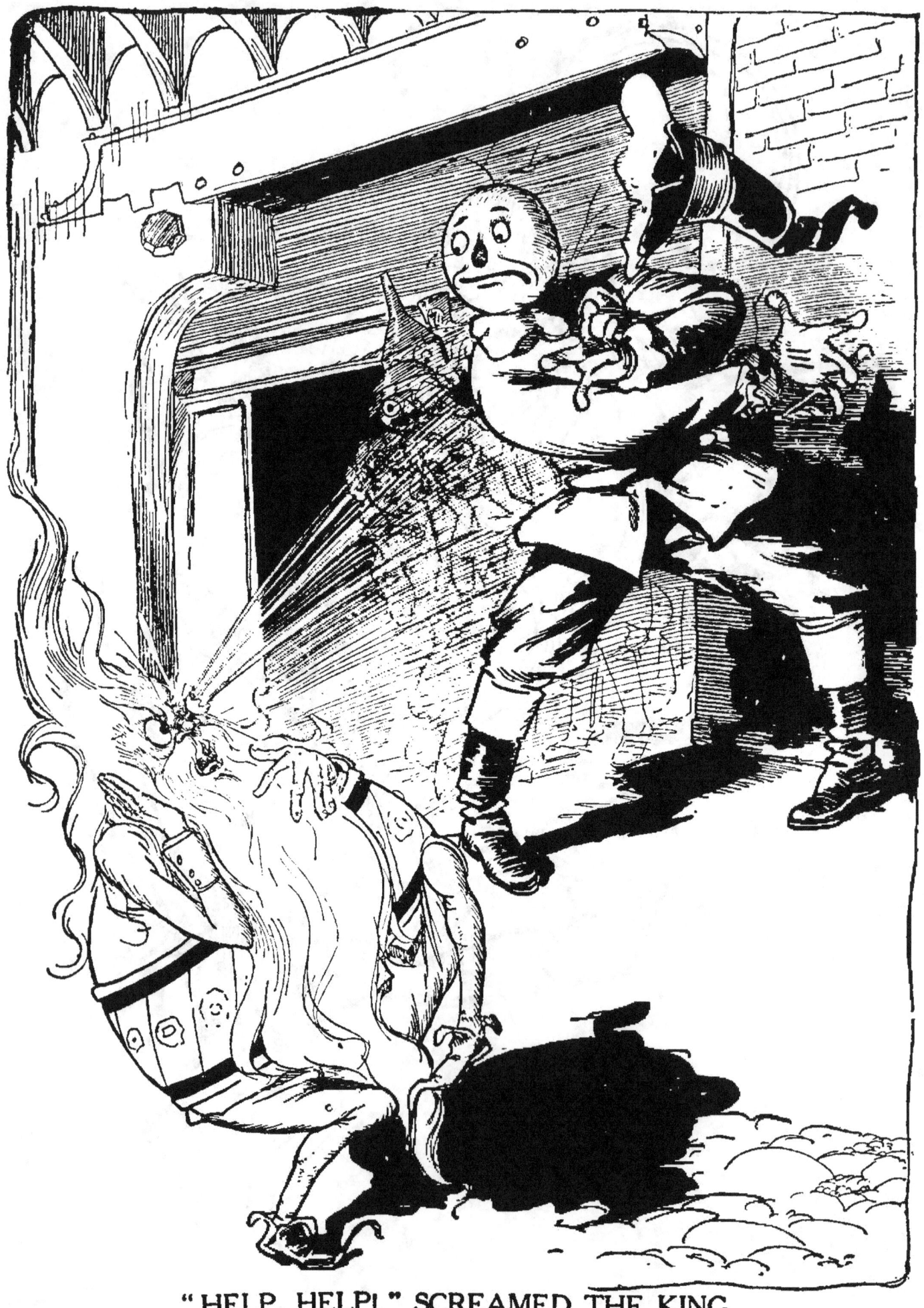

"HELP, HELP!" SCREAMED THE KING

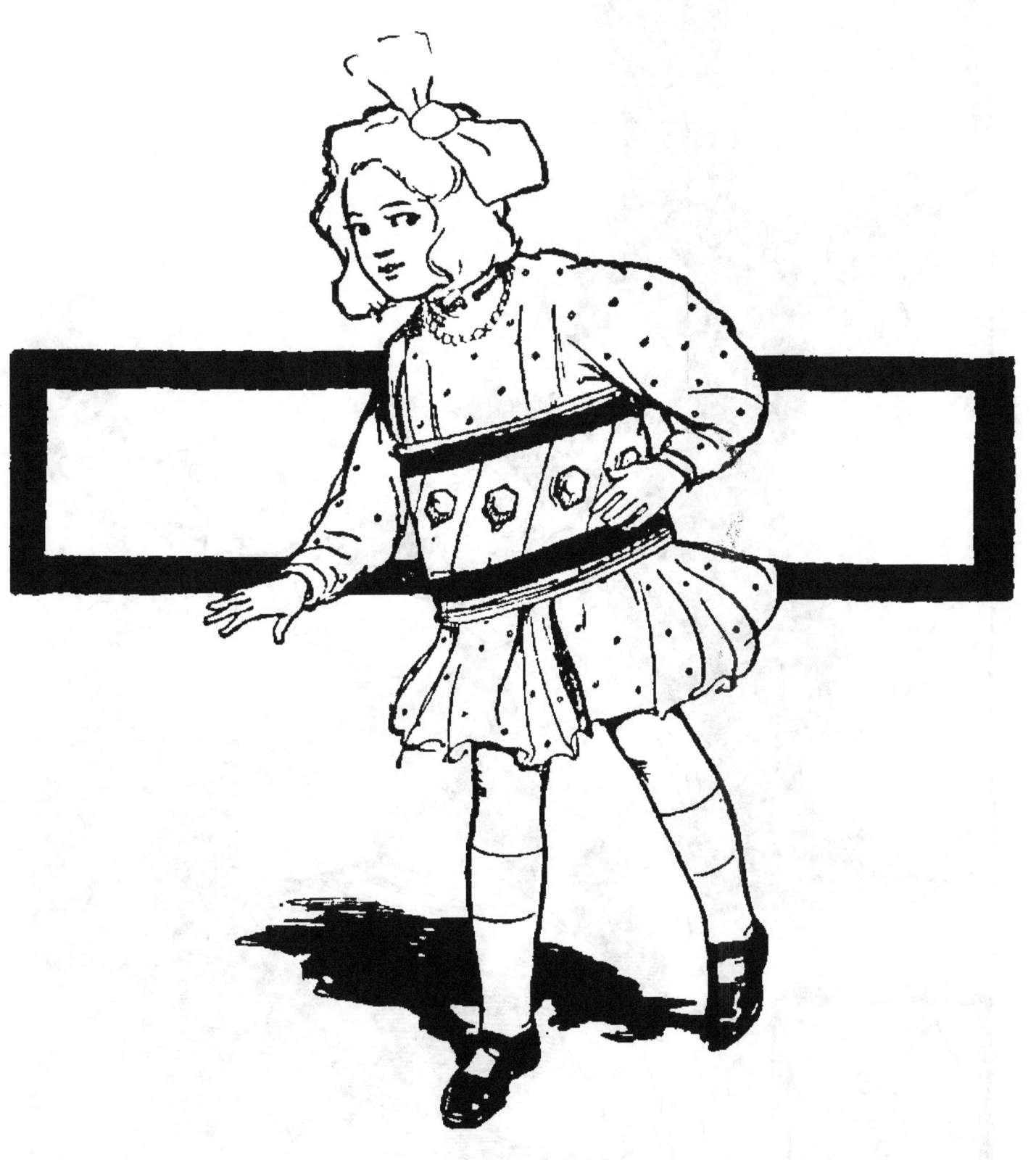

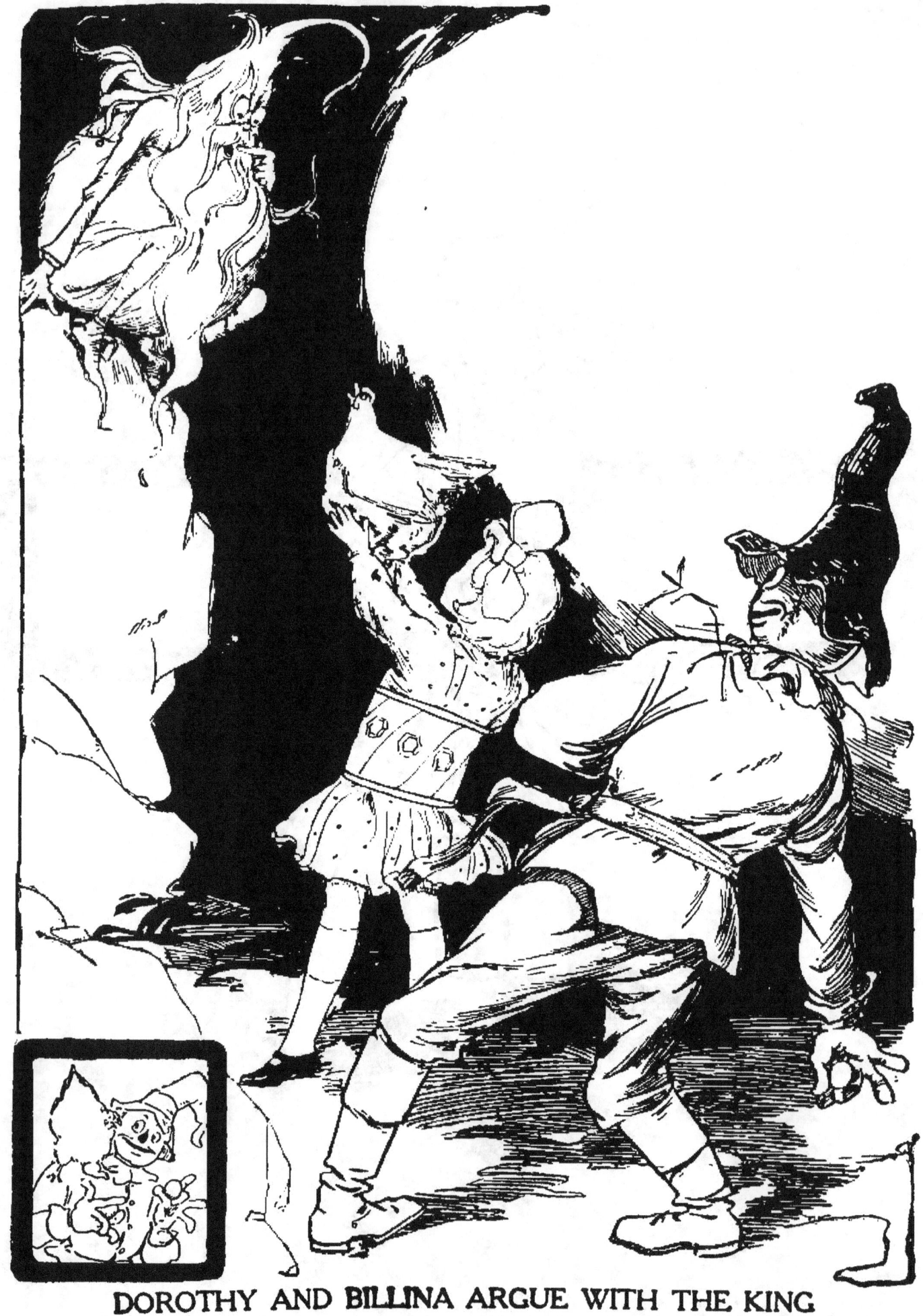

DOROTHY AND BILLINA ARGUE WITH THE KING

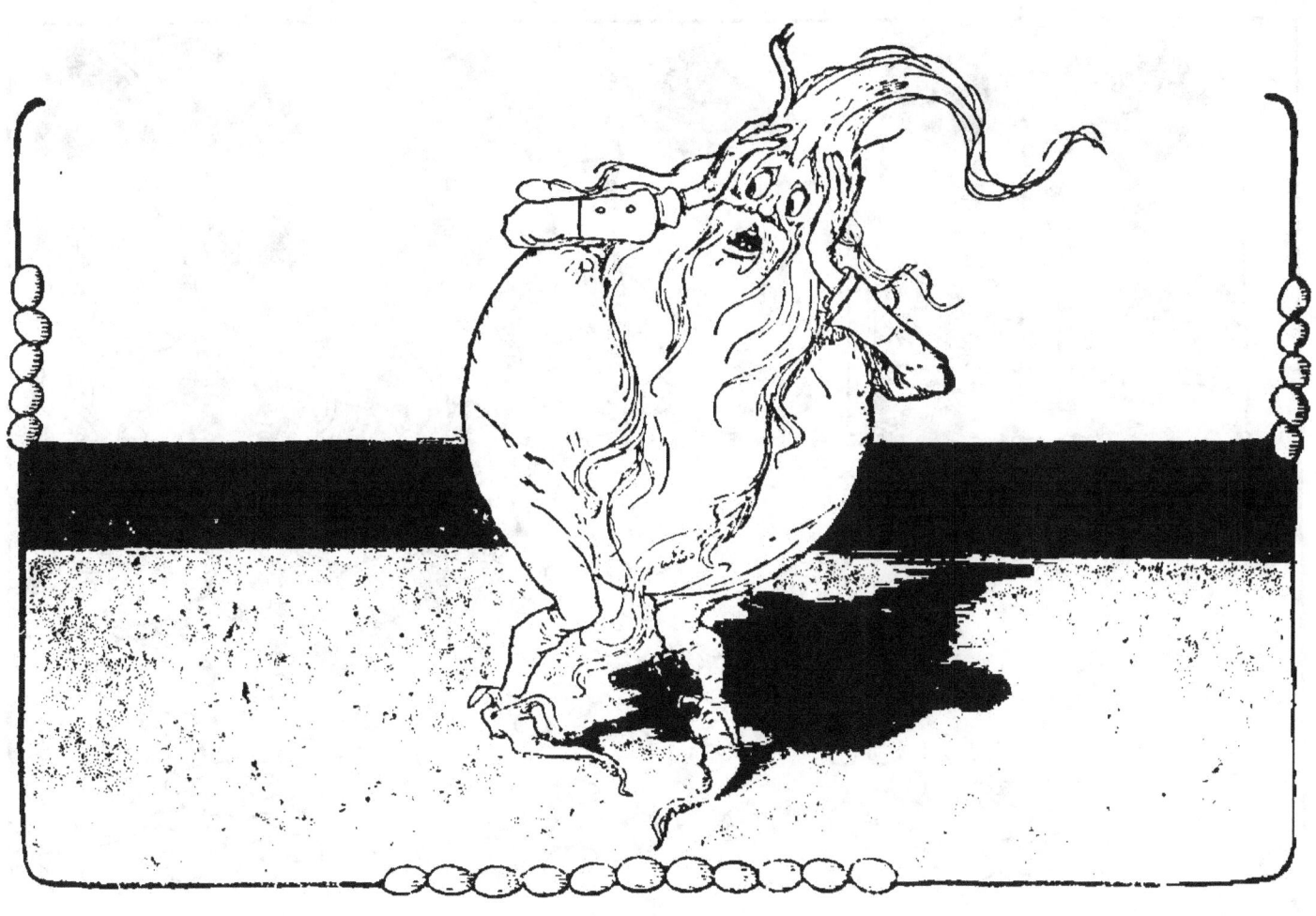

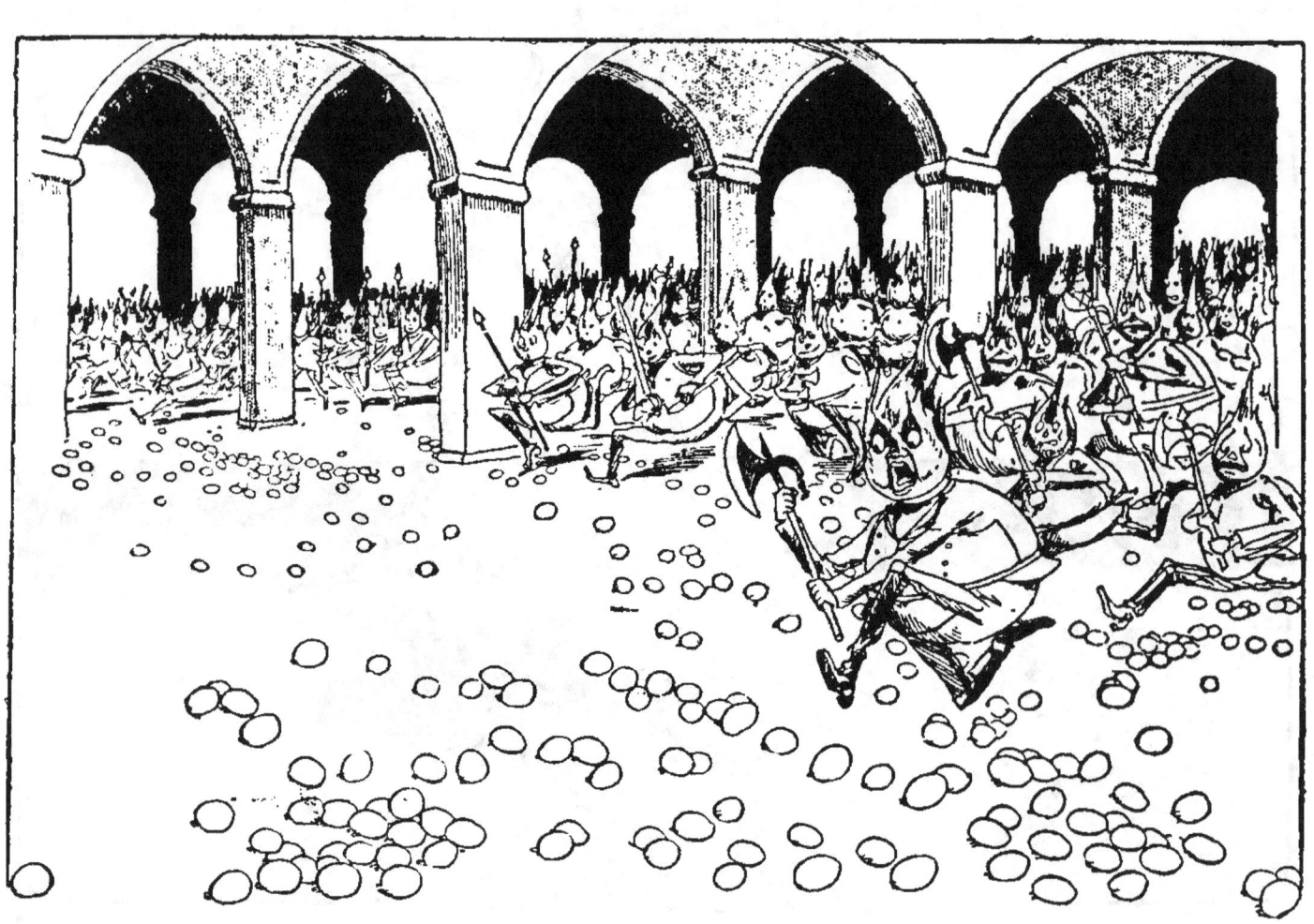

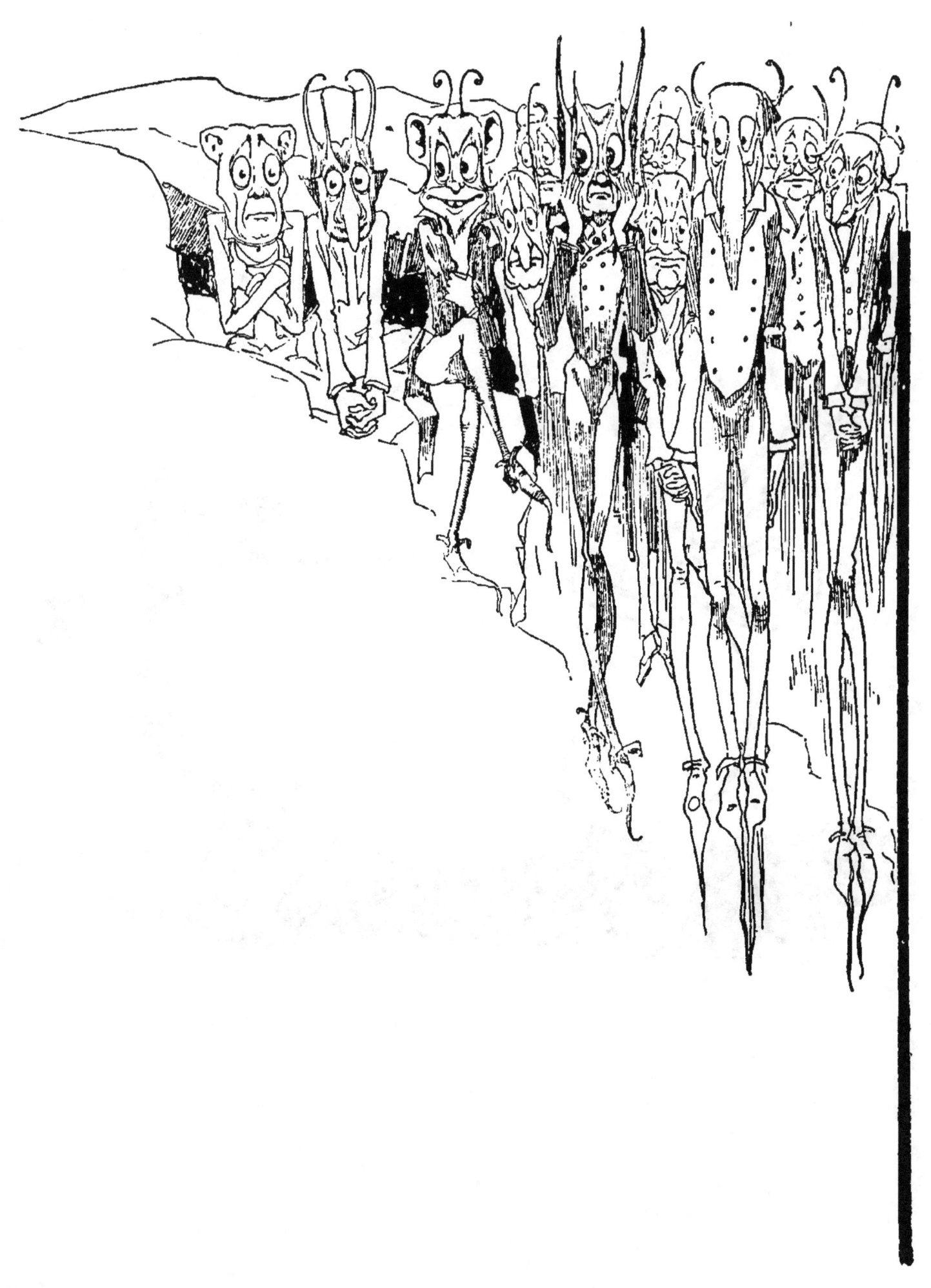

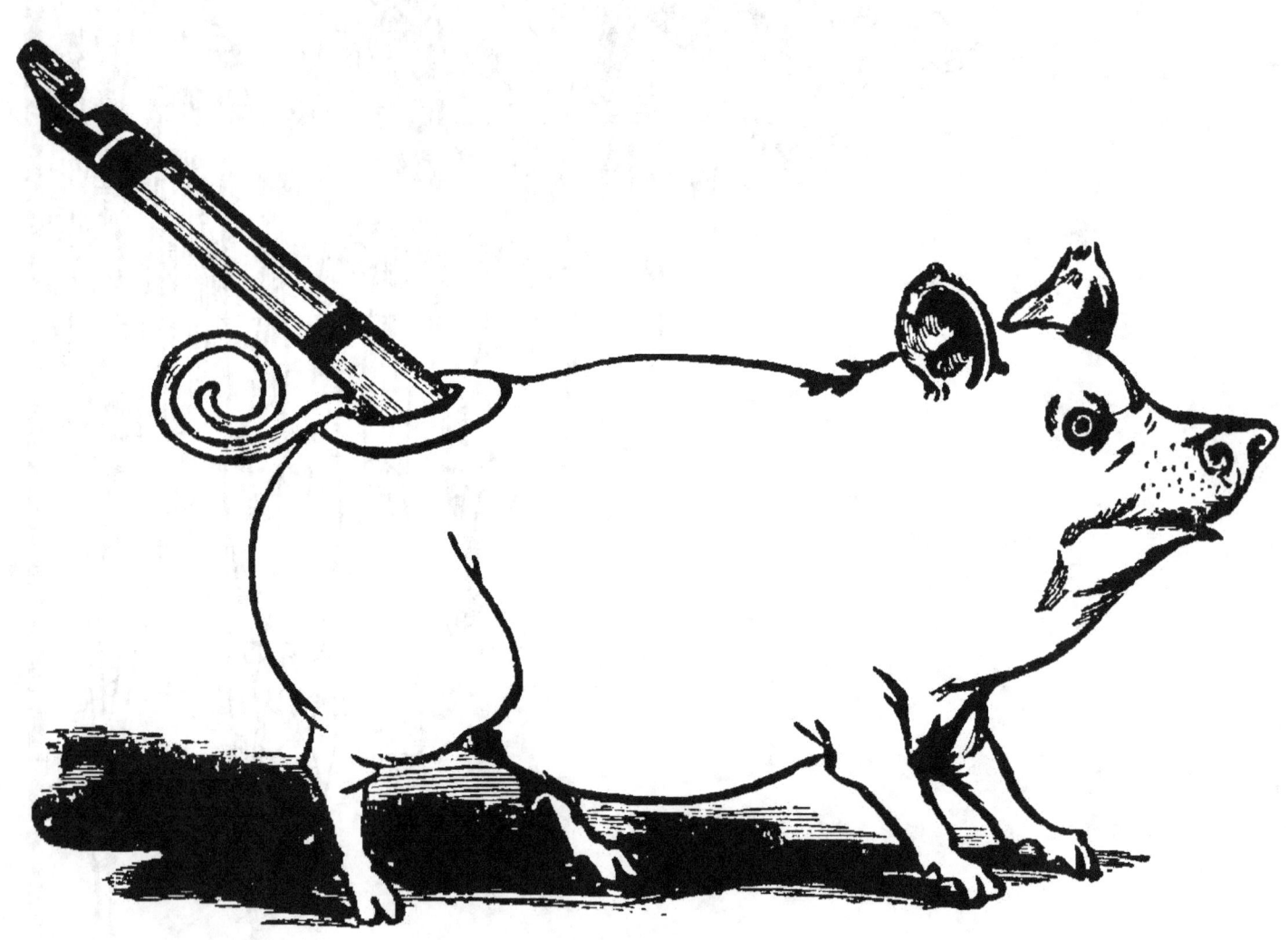

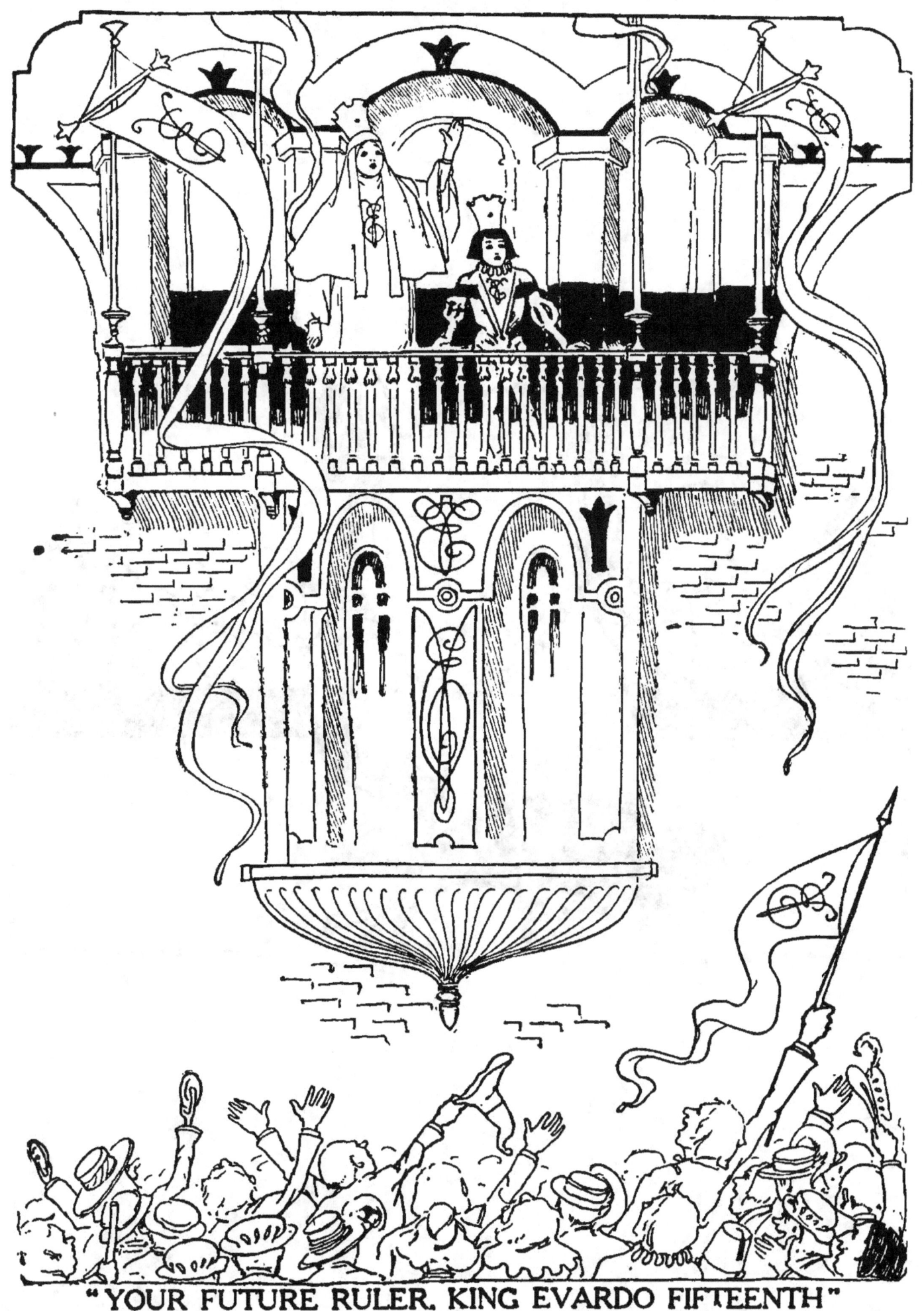

"YOUR FUTURE RULER. KING EVARDO FIFTEENTH"

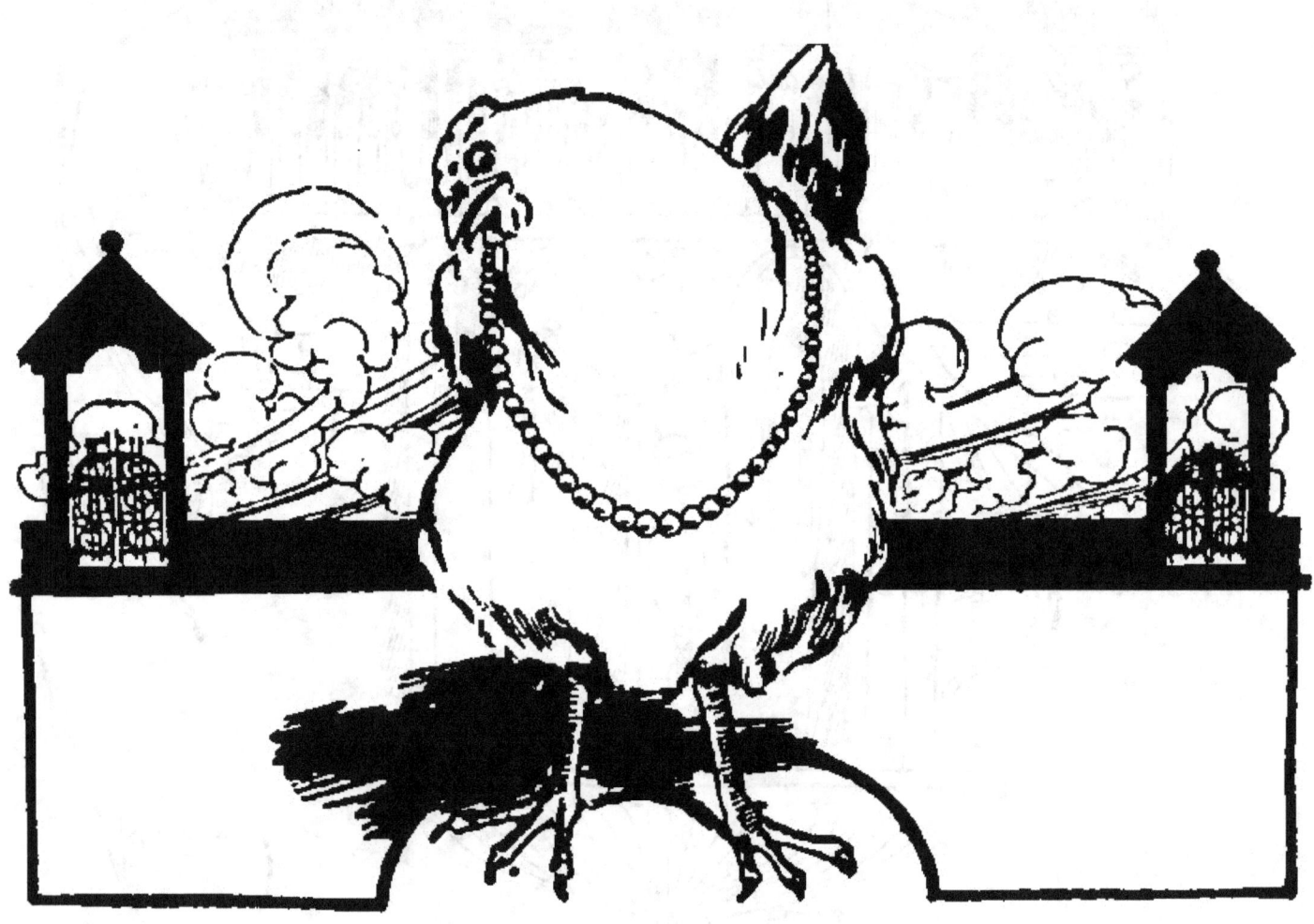

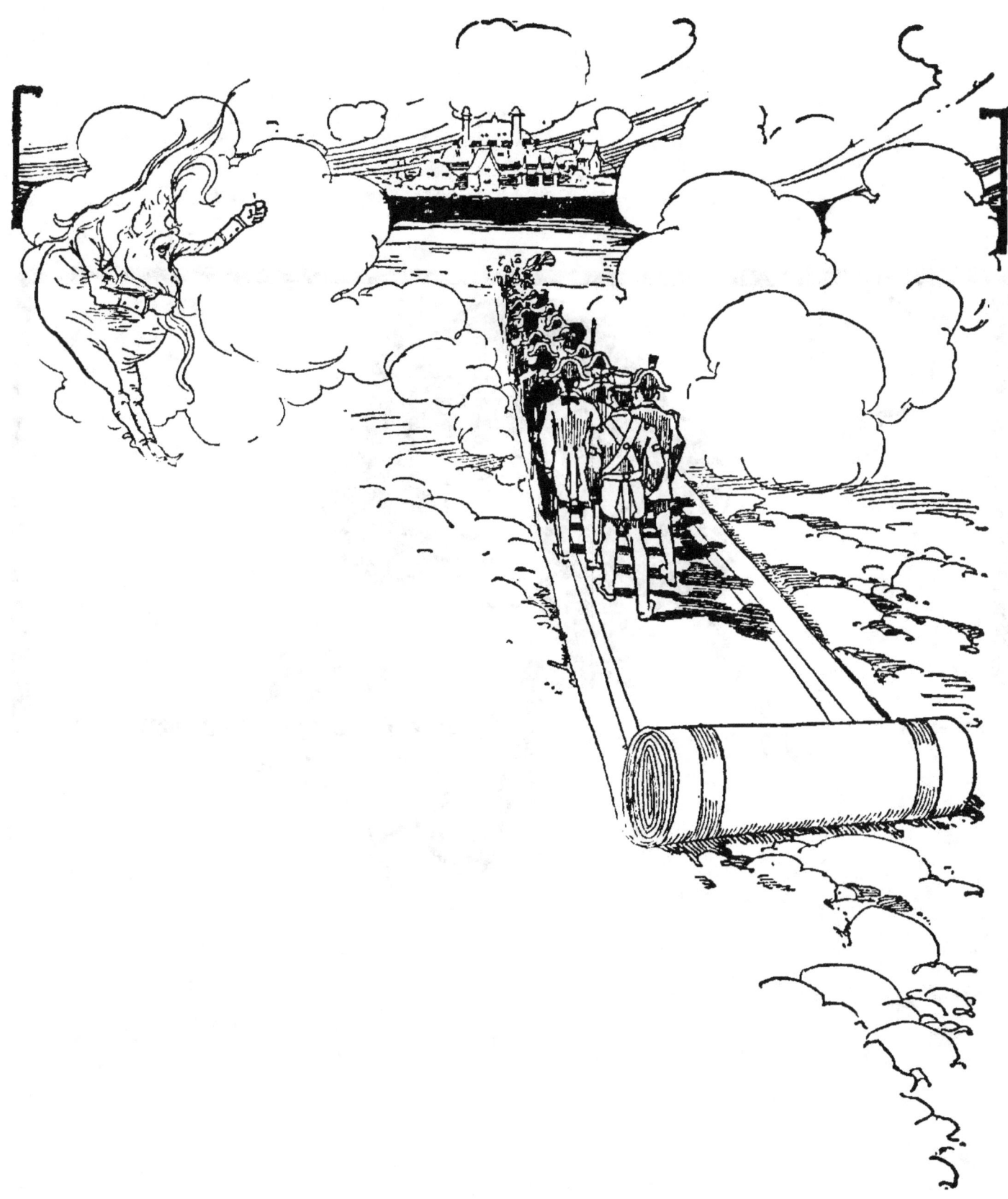

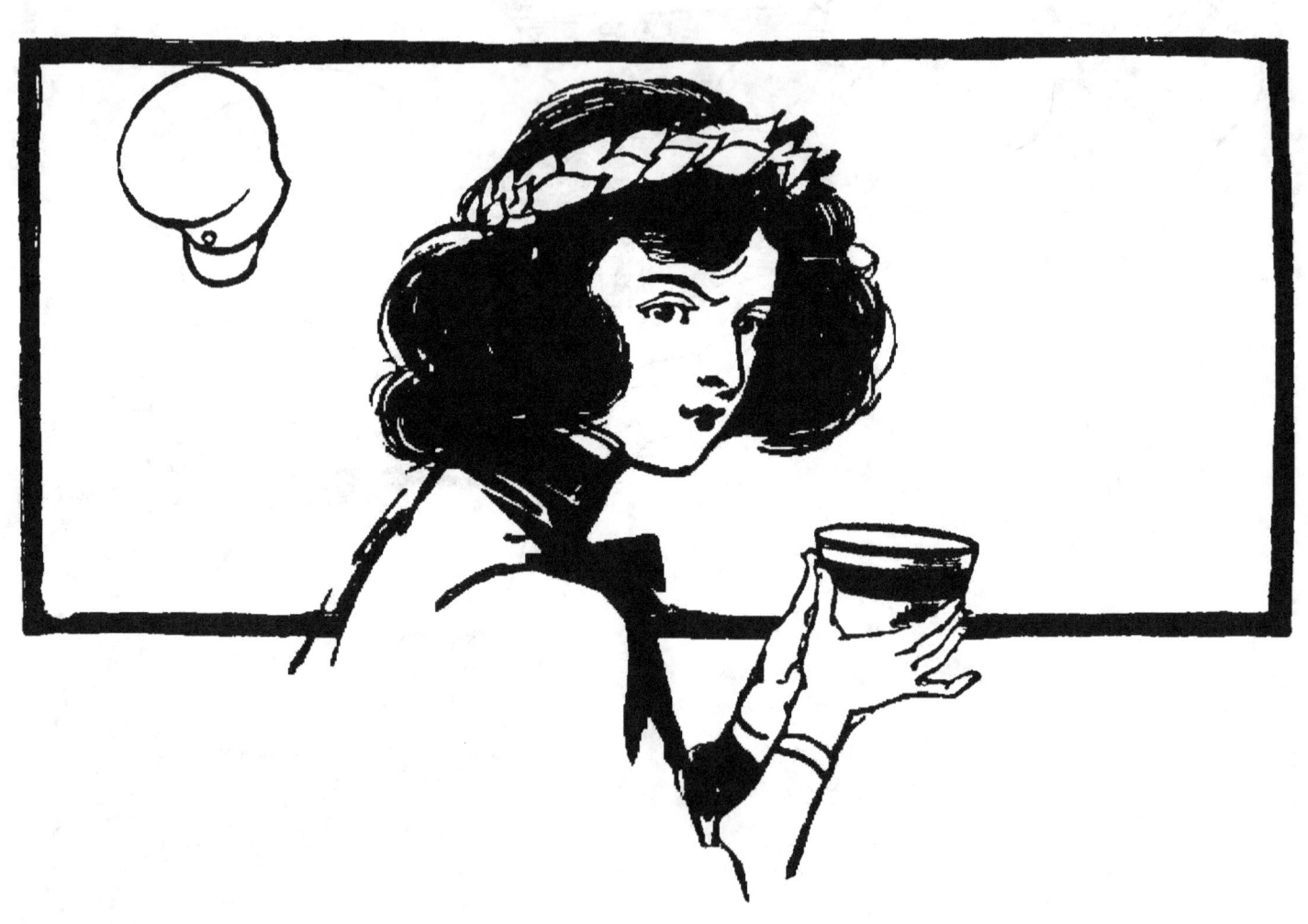

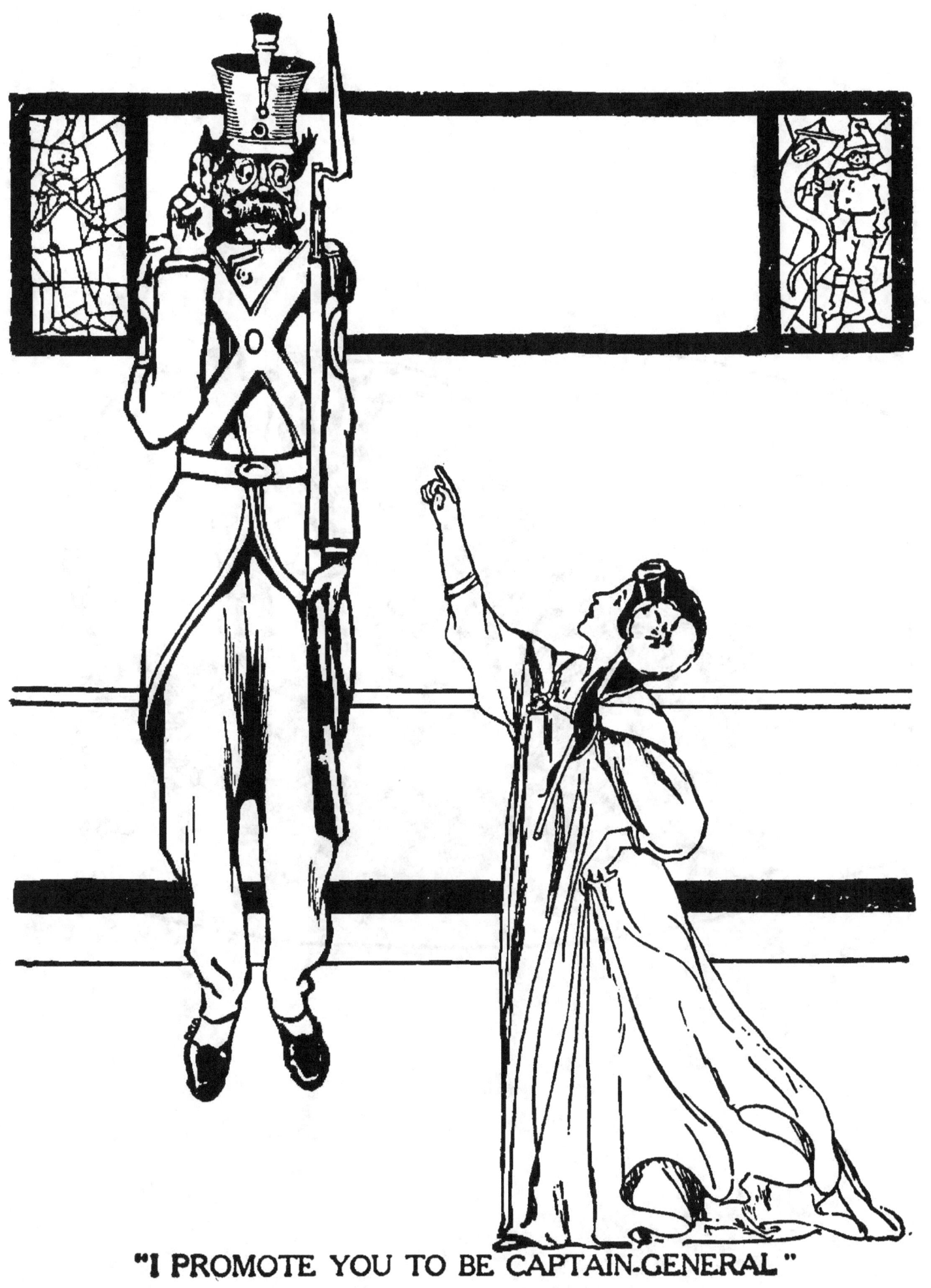

"I PROMOTE YOU TO BE CAPTAIN-GENERAL"

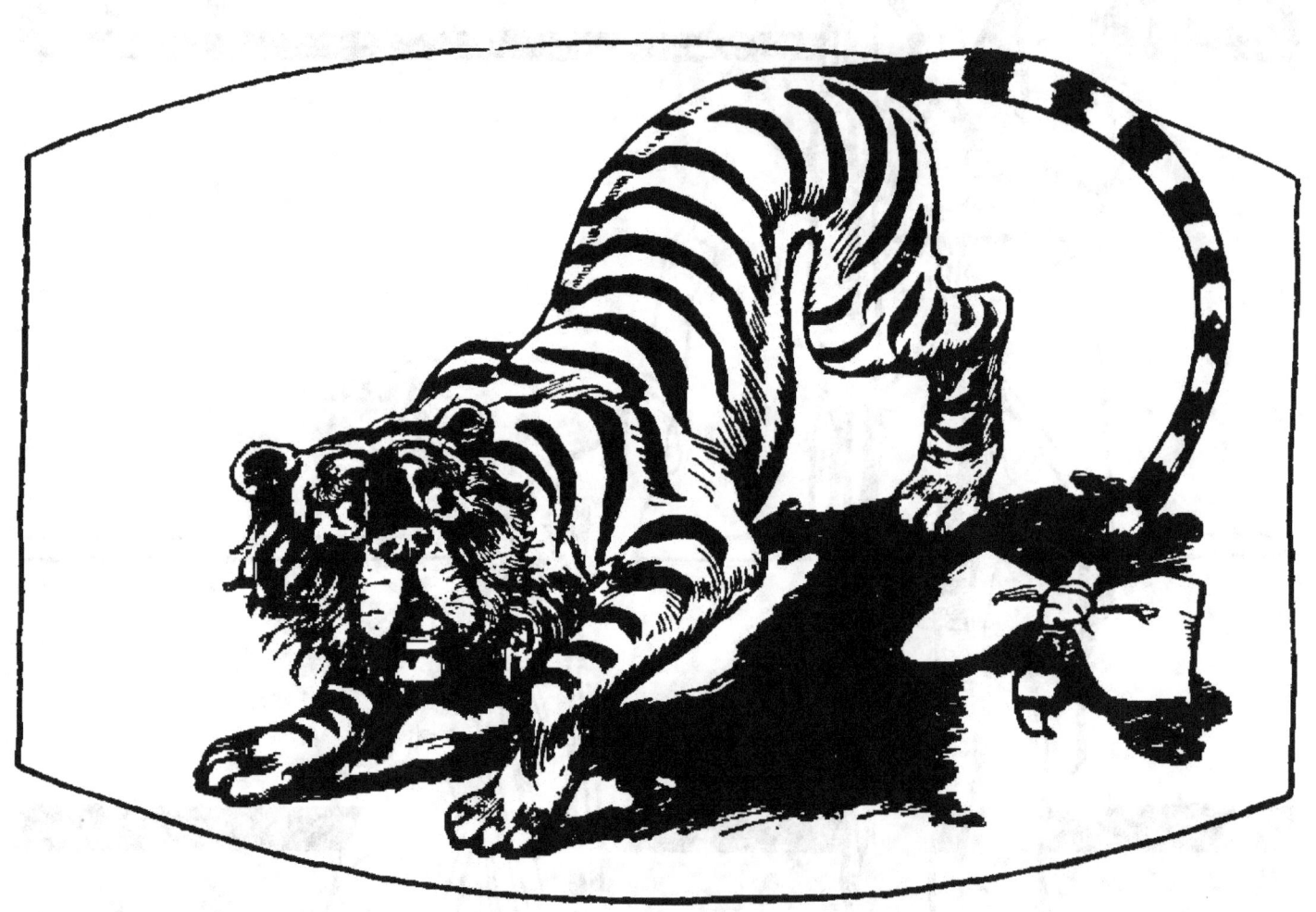

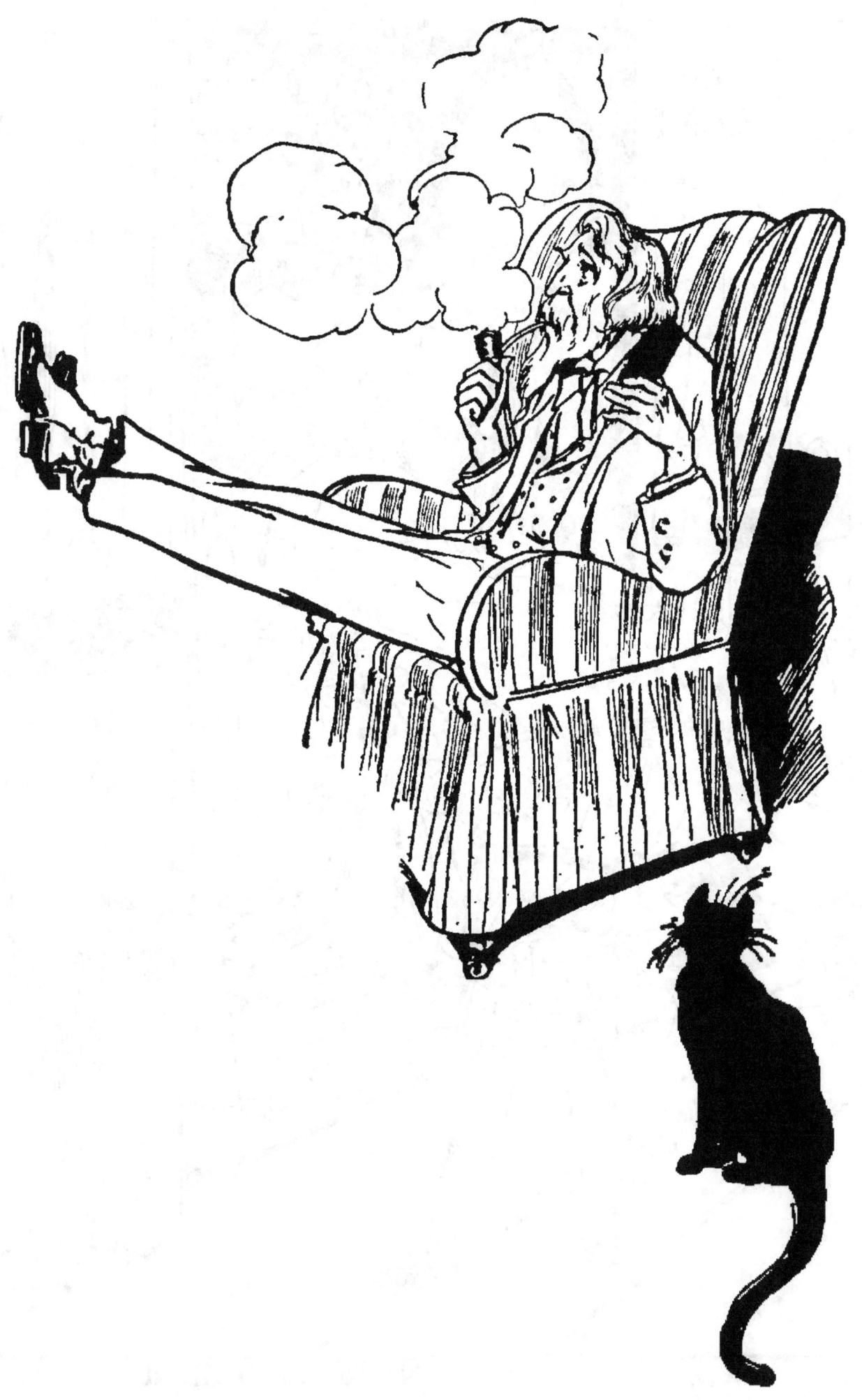

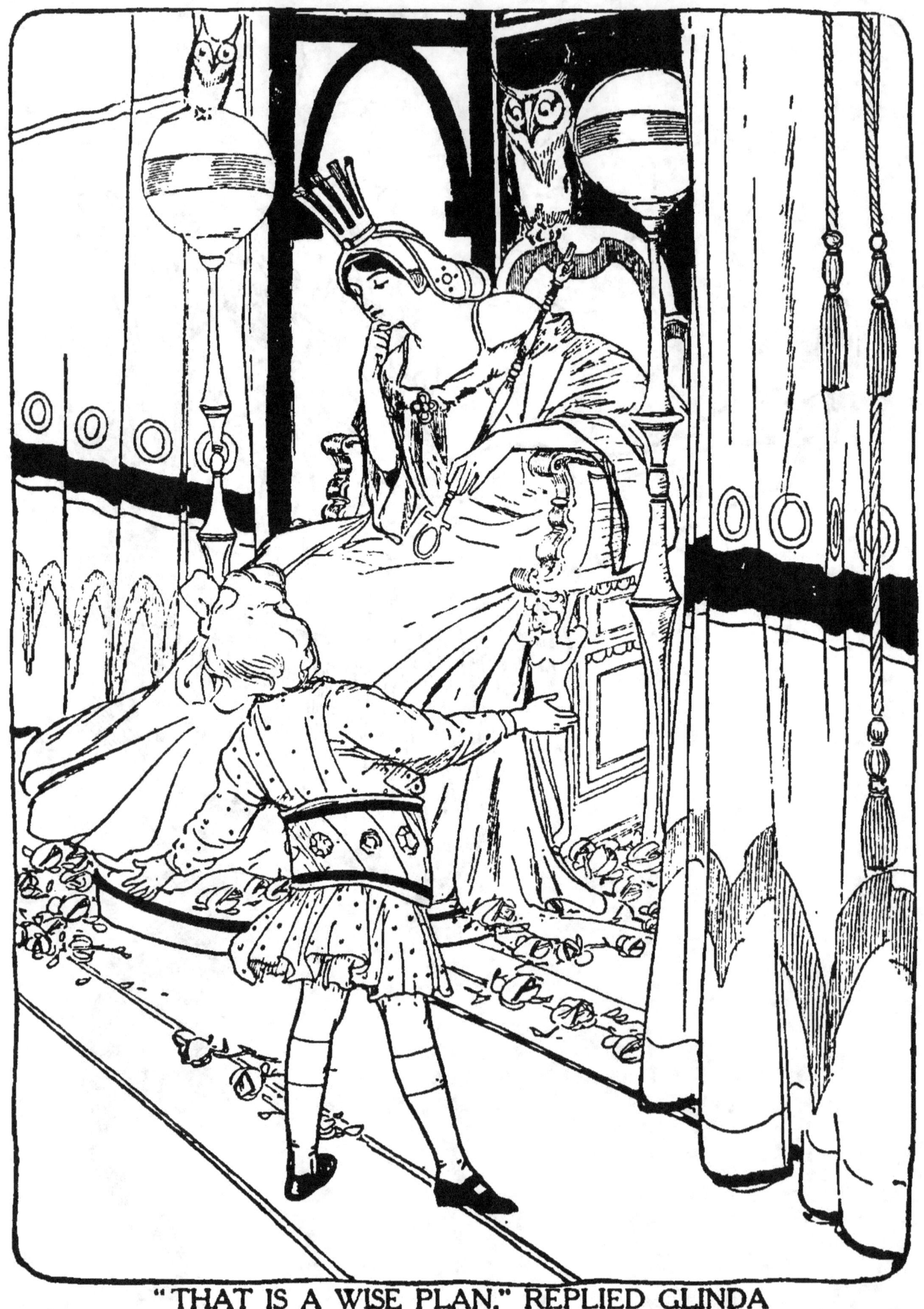

"THAT IS A WISE PLAN," REPLIED GLINDA

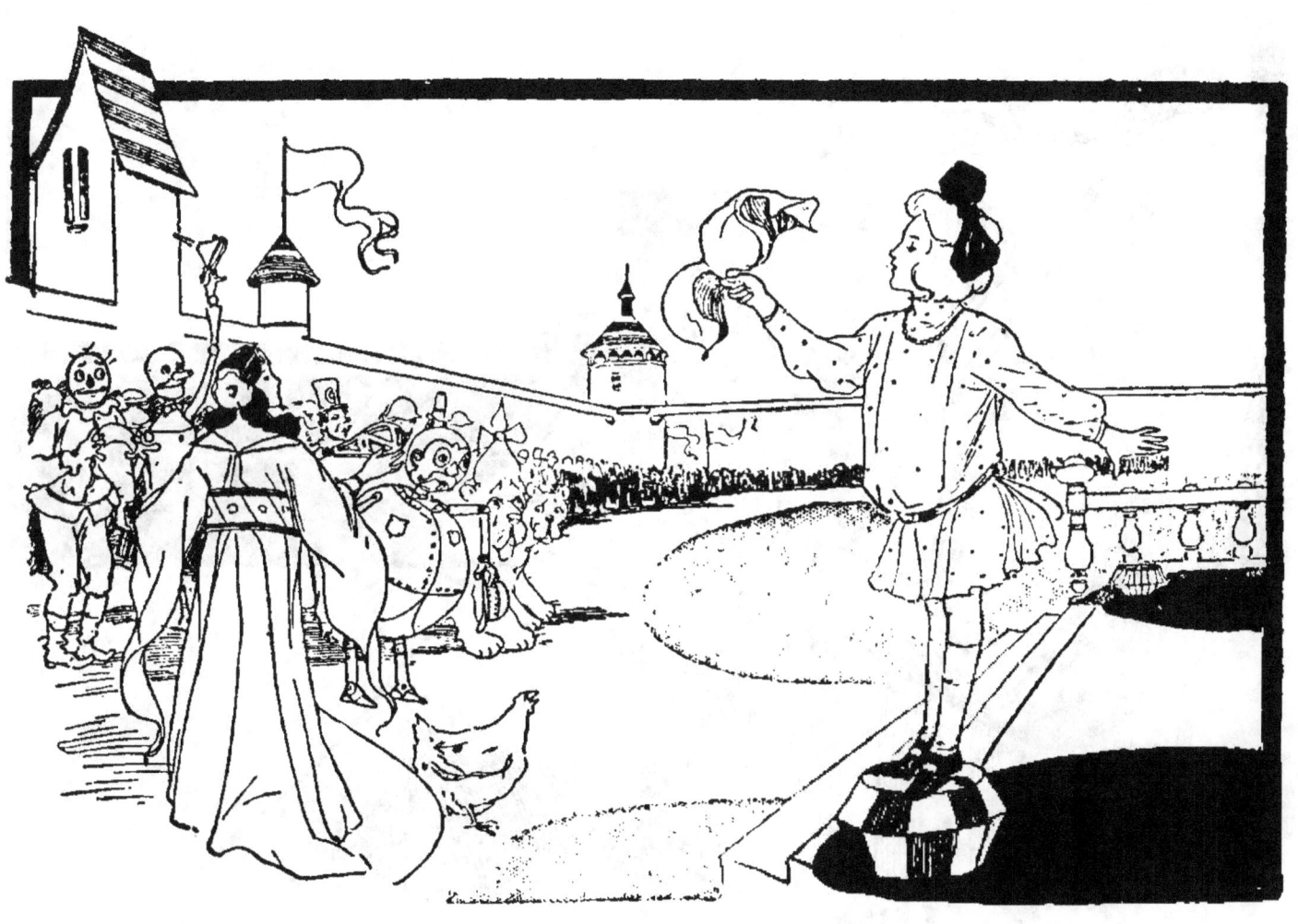

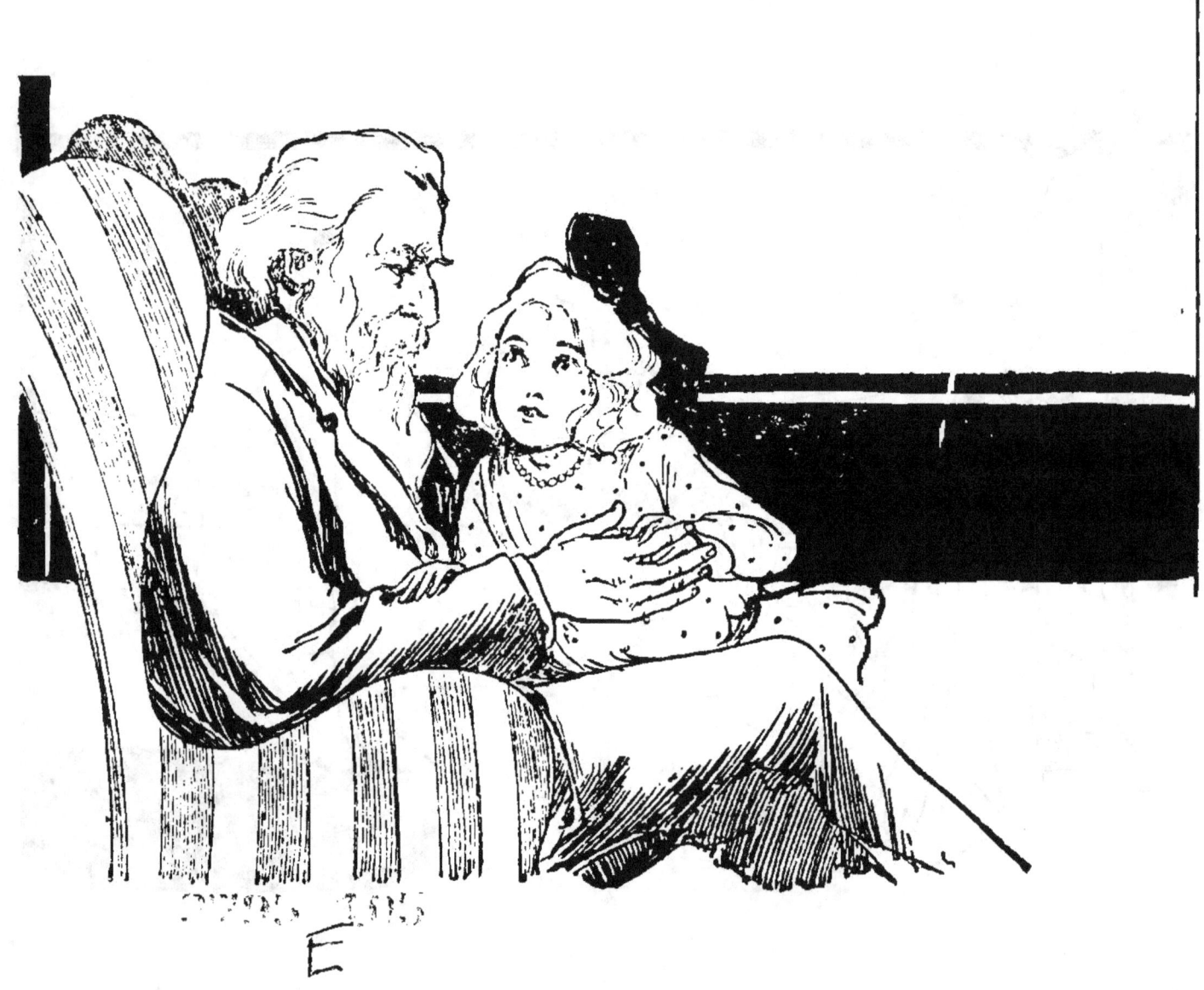